St Antony's Series
Series Standing Order ISBN 0–333–71109–2
(*outside North America only*)
You can receive future titles in this series as they are published by placing a standing order.
Please contact your bookseller or, in case of difficulty, write to us at the address below with
your name and address, the title of the series and the ISBN quoted above.
Customer Services Department, Macmillan Distribution Ltd, Houndmills, Basingstoke,
Hampshire RG21 6XS, England

Violent Politics

Strategies of Internal Conflict

Michael Addison

palgrave

in association with
St Antony's College, Oxford

First published 2002 by
PALGRAVE
Houndmills, Basingstoke, Hampshire RG21 6XS and
175 Fifth Avenue, New York, N.Y. 10010
Companies and representatives throughout the world.

PALGRAVE is the new global academic imprint of
St Martin's Press LLC Scholarly and Reference Division and
Palgrave Publishers Ltd (formerly Macmillan Press Ltd).

ISBN 0–333–73085–2

This book is printed on paper suitable for recycling and made from fully managed and sustained forest sources.

A catalogue record for this book is available from the British Library.

Library of Congress Cataloging-in-Publication Data

Addison, Michael, 1935–2000.
    Violent politics : strategies of internal conflict/Michael Addison.
        p. cm
    Includes bibliographical references and index.
    ISBN 0–333–73085–2
    1. Political violence. 2. Political violence – Ireland – History. 3. Political violence – Northern Ireland – History. 4. Terrorism. 5. Terrorism – Ireland – History 6. Terrorism – Northern Ireland – History. I. Title.

JC328.6 .A33 2002
322.4'2–dc21   2001054888

10 9 8 7 6 5 4 3 2 1
11 10 09 08 07 06 05 04 03 02

Typeset by EXPO Holdings, Malaysia

Printed and bound in Great Britain by
Antony Rowe Ltd. Chippenham, Wiltshire

Contents

List of Figures and Tables

Foreword by Bruce Hoffman*

The study of terrorism has long suffered from two separate but not unrelated weaknesses. One is the disjuncture between theory and empiricism that too often has divested otherwise erudite works of any policy relevance or practical application. The other is that most research on terrorism takes place in a vacuum: lacking the insight and perspicacity accessible only through first-hand observation of the political, social and cultural milieu in which terrorists – and the governments and security forces opposing them – operate. The result has been an academic discourse that at times seems completely divorced from reality and thus totally irrelevant to 'real-world' problems.

Violent Politics, however, is different. It was written by a soldier turned scholar who sought to make sense of what he had seen and done in confrontations such as Cyprus, Borneo and Northern Ireland. That the book's focus is on Northern Ireland – one of the perennially frustrating conflicts of recent times – makes it all the more valuable. Even though the literature on the latest iteration of the 'Troubles' is of course now vast, few treatments have addressed the subject with the same authoritative knowledge base of first-hand experience combined with scholarly rigour as *Violent Politics*. The reader, though, should be cautioned that this immeasurable strength is also the book's salient weakness. It is a work written with a distinct point of view – one forged by thirty years of military service commanding airborne sapper, commando, Gurkha and combat engineering units, but shaped and tempered by academic discourse and debate and most of all informed by an open, sceptical and enquiring mind. This unique combination of attributes and perspectives is precisely what makes *Violent Politics* both so interesting and important. Indeed, it stands as one of the few works on this subject to creditably bridge the chasm that has long separated theory from practice.

Mike Addison's interest in the challenges faced by governments in responding to terrorism and civil unrest began at a time when the

---

* Dr Bruce Hoffman is Vice President for External Affairs and Director of the RAND Corporation Washington, DC Office. He is also the author of *Inside Terrorism* and was previously Director, Centre for the Study of Terrorism and Political Violence, and, Chairman, Department of International Relations, University of St Andrews, Scotland.

British Empire had ceased to exist, but its military forces still remained enmeshed in the post-colonial ferment and upheaval afflicting some of its former possessions. He was commissioned in 1959 as a lieutenant in the Royal Engineers and a few years later found himself serving as a liaison officer with the United Nations peacekeeping contingent deployed to Cyprus. Conditions on that divided island in 1964 exemplified the challenges of military operations in an ambiguous, highly fluid and potentially explosive environment. Nicosia, for example, was not some neatly defined battlefield where opposing armies clashed and the enemy was clearly identified, engaged and defeated, but a densely populated urban area within which the terrorist effectively concealed him or herself, indistinguishable from the surrounding populace, until they emerged from hiding to strike only to disappear once again. An officer had therefore to be flexible and clever, not least perceptive and decisive. Restraint and uncomfortably restrictive rules of engagement were paradoxically the essential elements required to keep the peace and maintain order in hopes of rebuilding intercommunal confidence and encouraging negotiation. Delicacy and tact, in sum, counted for more than force and firepower.

Borneo was another formative experience in Mike's thinking about the role of the military in internal conflict. Although his time spent with the Gurkha Rifles in the jungles along the Indonesian border could not have been more different from that with the UN in Cyprus, the overriding imperative of restraint in the use of force was still the same. Rather than having to separate two warring communities, the confrontation in Borneo involved the defeat of a rebellion fomented by Jakarta in tandem with the removal of cross-border staging bases established by the Indonesian Army. Here, the challenge was to apply pressure in a manner calculated to compel the Indonesians both to withdraw and desist from aiding the rebels, whilst still preventing a further escalation of hostilities. The operation's success underscored the importance of innovation, adaptation and fresh thinking in the conduct of military operations in politically sensitive and complex situations.

By the time Mike arrived in Northern Ireland in 1973, he had therefore amassed a diversity of experience and wealth of knowledge that was a great asset to understanding the deteriorating security situation in that beleaguered province. The violence had reached its peak the year before with the Provisional Irish Republican Army (PIRA) unleashing a massive bombing campaign. Car bombs, containing anywhere from a few pounds of explosives to over a thousand pounds, had become a melancholy fixture of daily life. Incendiary devices were planted in shops and department stores and letter bombs were dispatched via the post. Snipers shot soldiers, mortars bombarded police stations, military barracks and civilian airports, and delayed-action explosive devices and booby traps taxed the ingenuity of the security forces. As commander of a parachute squadron in Belfast, Mike was again confronted with the challenge of exercising restraint whilst simultaneously maintaining law and order in a hostile urban environment populated by gunmen and innocent civilians alike. The daily balancing act performed by the security forces under such conditions made a deep and lasting impression on him that is reflected in *Violent Politics*.

Mike returned to Northern Ireland on a second tour of duty in 1976. As commander of the Royal Engineers detachment in the province, his responsibilities now included rural as well as urban areas and thus provided him with a broader appreciation of the other aspects of military operations in so deeply polarized a society. He spent considerable time in rural South Armagh – which the soldiers called 'bandit country' because of especially heavy PIRA activity and cross-border infiltration of men and weapons – and was instrumental in improving the design and construction of the fortified observation posts that proved so critical an asset to army operations there. It was then that Mike decided to apply for the Defence Fellowship which subsequently brought him to St Antony's College, Oxford, in 1978. Thus *Violent Politics* initially took shape as an M Litt thesis – supervised by perhaps the world's preeminent authority on modern warfare, Professor Sir Michael Howard – and submitted to the Faculty of Social Studies in 1983.

Having been awarded his degree that same year, Mike moved on to several other military assignments before retiring from the army in 1989, having attained the rank of brigadier. He went on to an equally successful second career as hospital director, but continued to think about how he might go about revising and updating his thesis for publication as a book. In 1996 Mike put his plan into action. He resigned his hospital post and was invited back to St Antony's, now as a Senior Associate Member, where he commenced the necessary revisions. Mike spent three years re-researching, rewriting, and updating the thesis. Meanwhile, he and his wife returned to their native Scotland. Mike completed work on the new manuscript in 1999 and submitted it for publication. He was still awaiting word on its fate when, in September 2000, Mike died suddenly and tragically, following a brief illness.

Violent Politics thus is a fitting testament to a person who was a man of thought as well as action. Mike Addison had an unusual capacity for reflection and assessment, which he sought to harness in order to understand his own experiences as a soldier within the wider context of politics and violence – and the zone between war and peace with which he was so familiar, violent politics. To many with whom Mike served and studied, he was also a mentor. Those fortunate enough to have been under his command, remember Mike, according to one obituarist, as 'very much a soldier's soldier, leading from the front, tough, firm and fair'. Others, who were fellow postgraduate students with Mike at Oxford, were equally lucky to have been able to benefit and learn from his prescience and perspective as colleagues in Professor Howard's weekly strategic studies seminar, *circa* 1978 through 1981. Indeed, to one callow doctoral candidate, just then embarking on the study of terrorism, Mike's influence and guidance was invaluable in helping him to understand the dynamics of this complex phenomenon and the challenges inherent in effectively countering it. The publication of *Violent Politics* now provides others with that same opportunity and is therefore warmly recommended as essential reading for anyone interested in understanding the challenges of responding to internal conflict.

BRUCE HOFFMAN

Foreword by Simon Winchester*

I first arrived in Northern Ireland as a reporter late in 1969, and like most newcomers I was bewildered, puzzled and utterly mesmerised by what I found. Three different but interlinked aspects of what I saw, heard and experienced particularly fascinated both me and the small number of like-minded participants whom I respected most as colleagues.

Perhaps, outwardly, it was the sheer unfamiliarity of just about everything that was most fascinating of all – the traffic policemen wearing revolvers as standard issue; the classified ads in the Belfast papers saying almost innocently 'Catholics need not Apply'; the fact that the very name of the province – Northern Ireland, the North of Ireland, The Six Counties, Ulster – was always up for argument; the existence of farmer–thugs with billy clubs who turned out to be special police constables, and who were quite cheerful about being photographed beating harmless students – particularly if they happened to be Catholics – on the peace march that always seemed to be criss-crossing the province in those early days.

The depth of mutual loathing that seemed to be shared by the divided communities was another reason for our wide-eyed amazement – with the crude and ugly corrugated iron curtain walls that were built to keep them apart, and then the young British soldiers wearing steel helmets and unrolling coils of barbed wire who were deployed among the ruins and burned-out cars to stand between the people and try to keep the peace. That these British troops were seen from the very beginning, by some who had the essential long historical perspective, to have been lured there as part of a trap, not as agents of some benevolent altruism, and that they themselves were inevitably to become enemies and not peacekeepers at all, was something that few in those early, heady days ever guessed.

And yet it was this ever-present need to be firmly on one's historical guard, and to have the radar of the long-term historical perspective ever

---

* Simon Winchester was Northern Ireland Correspondent for The Guardian from 1969 until 1972 and the author of In Holy Terror (Faber, 1974). He is now a writer and lives in Massachusetts.

switched on, that provided the third, and perhaps the most intellectually satisfying reason for fascination. The strangeness, the depth of the hatred – these were obvious, in a way. The historical view: that had to be listened to, to be absorbed osmotically, to be rigorously and dispassionately learned – that was a subject for real and studied fascination.

The situation had always been complicated and nasty, of course – and as any Irishmen of whatever stripe or inclination would tell you if ever you ventured into a Belfast bar, it all went a long, long way back. But just how long – well, that depended on your background, your education, *which foot you dug with*, your willingness to maintain an open mind. The conventional view was that the most symbolically powerful date of all was 12 July 1690, the moment when the Catholic King James II was defeated in battle by the Protestant William of Orange in the water meadow in the valley of the River Boyne – with the celebrations held annually by Protestants in honour of all those long-dead but never-to-be-forgotten warriors invariably the trigger for violence of ever-increasing viciousness. This conventional view, in other words, was that the Irish problem was three hundred years old, give or take a handful of decades.

Yet older men in darker bars, men whose wisdom and sense of history tended to increase in direct proportion to their consumption of Bushmills and Guinness, would tell you otherwise, and suggest quite credibly that it all went back a great deal longer than that: to the westward flight of French Huguenots in the wake of the collapse of the Edict of Nantes five years before the Boyne; to the repressive might of Oliver Cromwell in 1651; to Queen Elizabeth's settlement of loyal Scotsmen in the counties of Armagh, Derry and Down in 1607; and even to King Henry II's invasion of Ireland in 1169, when he was sent there by Pope Adrian IV on a mission to keep the Irish – to keep Shakespeare's 'rough, rug-headed kerns' – in strict compliance with the laws of Catholic Rome.

It was truly important, if one wanted to make any sense in writing articles about the place, to try to listen to those who told of such things. I was first told of this last date, 1169, during one long late night conversation some time during the autumn of my first visit. The discussion, which had a significance that I only vaguely realised at the time, took place in a most appropriate venue, the oak-panelled snug of The Crown Bar – the bar into which James Mason had staggered out of the Belfast winter cold and the gunfire in that most evocative of films of earlier troubles, *Odd Man Out.*

I remember saying to my new friend, a wise old gent from Queen's University, that it struck me then that the troubles – how bland and yet how *Irish* a euphemism, for so pervasive a tragedy! – that were just then getting under way once again in Ireland were enjoying, if that was the word, an anniversary – since if you believed this particular interpretation of history (and he did indeed make a very reasonably case for it) then they had their logical origin precisely eight hundred years before. King Henry had come across the Irish Sea in 1169; and the *Guardian* had sent me across those same waters in 1969. There was trouble then; there were *Troubles* now.

Ah yes, replied my informant, and wasn't the anniversary a historical form with which Ireland was peculiarly obsessed? Quite so, I replied, but looking to the future – unfamiliar territory for the classic Irishman, it seemed somewhat patronisingly to me then, if less so now – didn't it thus seem most unlikely that my generation, or at least *this* generation could manage to throw up any people or ideas who would or could bring so ancient and time-worn a dispute to a satisfactory conclusion?

Was there truly any possibility that what was about to begin – an unrolling of vicious and violent events that might well go on to be fortuitous for my own burgeoning newspaper career, but which would prove unutterably wretched for the Irish and for many British who were about to be swept up in its tides – could in fact *ever* be ended? Fully eight centuries worth of bitterness and hatred had by now been deeply and indelibly chiselled onto the landscape of the Irish mind: surely, I said to my friend, they would prove almost impossible to erase.

And, dismayingly, he agreed. To underscore his concurrence he slid a slim and grubby volume from his raincoat pocket, and thumbed through it until he came to the page on which was printed what I later learned was one of the more egregiously depressing – but most famously prescient – of Winston Churchill's thoughts on the same subject.

Churchill, neither a great friend nor great admirer of the Irish, yet a man with an undoubted and unrivalled historical perspective, was addressing Parliament in 1922, speaking on the vexed matter of the Irish Home Rule Bill. He was reviewing recent history, and thus placing Ireland in a more global context when he famously said:

Then came the Great War. Every institution, almost, in the world was strained. Great Empires have been overturned. The whole map of Europe has been changed. The position of countries has been violently altered. The modes of thought of men, the whole outlook on affairs, the grouping of parties, all have encountered violent and tremendous changes in the deluge of the world.

But as the deluge subsides and the waters fall short, we see the dreary steeples of Fermanagh and Tyrone emerging once again. The integrity of their quarrel is one of the few institutions that has been unaltered in the cataclysm which has swept the world.

And the uttering of that homiletic was, in essence, my introduction to the province – my introduction to thirty months that I then spent writing about, travelling through, and falling under the spell of, Ireland. History taught me pessimism and reality; it stripped me free of any jingoistic hopes or any romantic pretence. I, and the remarkable newspaper which then employed me, was able to report with what I still regard as a proper sense of detachment on a period of brutality, intrigue and symbolic importance that has still been unmatched in the history of the province.

It was a period that began with a furious riot in East Belfast which left six people dead. It was a period that ended in the aftermath of Operation Motorman, by which in a deployment of men and large machines the British Army managed to secure the so-called 'no-go' areas of Belfast and Derry and so content their political masters that all of the North of Ireland was, after a lawless time, now amenable to the law. It was a polite fiction of course; and it was an event that has been deservedly all-but forgotten; but as a bookend to a turbulent time, it surely enjoyed a certain symbolism.

And during my sojourn there was a cascade of seminal events, as the troubles unwound and unfolded like some cruelly beautiful flower. There were riots and then bombings, and terrible murders of aplenty; there was the use of the infamous but hitherto long-dormant Special Powers Act, and then the introduction of a policy of internment without trial, and its abject failure either to still the violence or to enhance the standing or stability of the local government; the collapse of the Stormont government followed swiftly; in its place came the imposition of direct rule from London – which meant, *inter alia*, the formal ending of the role of the Governor of the province, and the official defacement (by a sword, which scored a ragged X across its surface) of the Great Seal that constitution and old custom decreed be fixed to all newly passed local laws. I always thought the very existence of a Governor suggested that Northern Ireland was run colonially: Downing Street tut-tutted at such a notion, and discouraged the suggestion that any of London's attitudes smacked in any way of Empire.

And then there was Bloody Sunday, an event that has become firmly fixed on the landscape of world events, even though the facts – beyond the fourteen fatalities, all of them unarmed and innocent Catholic men, yet shot dead by British paratroops in Londonderry on that last Sunday of January 1972 – are still in seemingly eternal dispute. There was one infamously partisan judicial inquiry later in that same year, accepted by few as approaching the truth of what happened; and now there is another inquiry, which it is said will take four more years to conclude. Whether its conclusions will or can have a signal or even a superficial effect on anything at all is doubtful: the old eight centuries-worth of hatred, chiselled into the private minds of Ireland, is unlikely to be erased even if the soldiers who fired those eight hundred shots and the commanders who ordered them to do so happen to make the most abject of apologies.

If ever one event from those times was to underscore how many layers of history are laid down to form the Irish political landscape, then it was Bloody Sunday. And yet the detached, disinterested and historically consistent views that my newspaper displayed in its coverage of the troubles in those days – 'we are going to write about this every day, no matter how tired people may get of it,' said the news editor of the time – ensured that we and our readers knew that this event was not simply a tragedy. It was just still more sediment, still more landscape, on which yet more years of bitterness, distrust and loathing would probably eventually be carved.

It is a regrettable fact this attitude of historical awareness and political detachment characterised the output of only a very few of the newspapers and broadcasting organisations that covered the story, both at that time, and still today. Most papers, on both sides of the Irish Sea, told and still tell the Irish story from within their own high-walled *laagers* of nationalism and prejudice, ensuring that the truth of the situation remains clouded, that established attitudes are relentlessly reinforced. The sense of proportion that is required by history – and which is so very desirable in so dangerous and fraught a situation as that in Northern Ireland – is woefully lacking in the press that covers the story, and which provides the information on which legislators and their voting public base the making of their legislative decisions.

But Michael Addison, with the book that follows, was until his tragic death in September 2000, an analyst who did most certainly possess all of these rare powers of detached and wise historical judgment. His analysis places Ireland in its proper historical, political and geographical context – reminding us that it is an inevitable and probably unwinnable war that must be judged as that, and not, as politicians might wish, as some kind of criminal conspiracy or treasonous escapade. All who are involved in Irish affairs would do well to read what follows – and to do so with the understanding that the dreary steeples of Fermanagh and Tyrone will be for ever there, and that no amount of wishful thinking will provide a solution today that has eluded all who have attempted one for the eight-and-a-half centuries since this all began.

Northern Ireland has now existed as a separate political entity, the wayward child of a forced partition, for eighty years – during nearly half of which time its people and its institutions have been subjected to a vicious insurgency that challenges its very right to be. Few are the countries that have been plagued by such turmoil for so great a portion of their history – Israel is perhaps one, Kashmir another, and both of them, not surprisingly, are partitioned states as well. But the very fact that so much of the Irish Six Counties' time has been spent so harshly challenged provides history with an inescapable truth: that this is not a dispute ever likely to be solved by the essentially self-interested rhetoric of temporary politicians. Only profound changes in political demography, the reality that lies at the very root of all partitions, can ever bring this fighting to an end.

Northern Irish politics – and thus by extension, all Irish politics – is pessimism writ in stone, part of the sadness of a people whose lot is a terrible melancholy. Yet, and curiously, that pessimism is a price which many are content to pay, for allowing Ireland always to remain what Ireland always has been. Michael Addison accepts this reality: and within that bleak structure, he offers serious and innovative plans for making matters a great deal better than they are today, and for offering some fresh answers at least, to help mitigate – not solve, but mitigate – a situation that has baffled and bewildered all of those who wish in vain for a short-term solution to what is in truth an ancient and quite intractable problem.

SIMON WINCHESTER

1
Violence and Politics: The Search for Meaning

The scale of violent politics

Politics is one method of solving conflicts. War is another. Violent politics – lying in the zone between peace and war – is a third.

All except the simplest political problems (and the simplest ones are managerial rather than political) are aporetic: they contain internal contradictions which prevent their ever being solved by logic. They have perforce to be resolved rather than solved: a balance achieved between conflicting interests.

This book examines what happens when the peaceful political consensus breaks down, and violent politics begins: a rather common happening.

There are now 185 countries in the world.[1] The University of Leiden[2] listed 19 high intensity conflicts during 1996 (those with more than 1000 deaths in the year), 41 low intensity conflicts (100–1000 deaths), and 74 violent political conflicts on the scale of Northern Ireland (less than 100 deaths in the year).[3] Twenty-six UN peacekeeping operations were in progress that year. Some countries had more than one conflict: India, for example, had five in the lowest category and four in the middle one. Some had none, but the total of 134 armed conflicts in 86 countries in a single year shows that it is a rather common activity.

The Stockholm Institute for Peace Research listed 27 major armed conflicts in 24 countries in the same year, compared to 30 in 25 places the year before, and 36 in 32 places in 1989.[4] Of the 27 in 1996, all but one (India v. Pakistan in Kashmir) were within states rather than between them.

Violent conflict varies in intensity from riot to civil war. The Leiden typology, which is as useful as any other, is:

1 Peace and stability;
2 Political tension;
3. Violent political conflict;
4 Low-intensity conflict, including insurgency and armed conflict between factional groups;
5 High-intensity conflict: warfare, mass destruction, massacre and population movement.

The first two shade into one another, and affect all societies; any violence is short-lived and incidental, and conventional politics is dominant. In high-intensity conflict, violence is dominant, and the side which physically masters the other wins.

This book is about the middle zone – violent political conflict and low-intensity conflict – where politics is neither entirely constitutional and law-abiding nor entirely bloody. It is not about political violence, a form of violence, but about violent politics, a form of politics.

A *tour d'horizon* of violent politics would take a lifetime: one bibliography, covering only one decade, lists nearly 6000 sources.[5] A 1997 search on 'terrorism' on the World Wide Web found over 30 000 documents.[6] A chronology of three years runs to nearly 1000 pages.[7] The RAND-St Andrews chronology lists 250 incidents of international terrorism in 1996: the lowest figure in 23 years, but causing 510 deaths, the fourth highest since 1968.[8] The *Encyclopaedia of World Terrorism* contains 314 essays by 73 contributors, and runs to 768 pages.[9] '[Terrorism is] the use of serious violence against persons or property, or the threat to use such violence, to intimidate or coerce a government, the public or any section of the public, in order to promote political, social or ideological objectives.'[10] Terrorism thus defined corresponds roughly to 'violent political conflict' in the Leiden typology. Violent politics includes low-intensity armed conflict and insurgency as well. Terrorism is therefore a subset of violent politics, but such a major subset in western democracies that the one can be used as shorthand for the other, except when it is necessary to distinguish them.

This study focuses on violent politics within states because the political aims tend to be clearer than they are in international terrorism, less far-fetched, more threatening to the stability of the state, and more difficult to deal with, especially in liberal democracies.

The Great War and the consequent destruction of the Austro-Hungarian and Ottoman Empires created many high and low level conflicts in the Balkans, the Near and Middle East. The October revolution which ended the Russian Empire created many more. Their echoes have not died out nearly a century later. The Russian Empire is estimated to have lost nearly two million from its armed forces during the First World War, eight or nine million during the Second, and 16–19 million civilians.[11] Nevertheless, its dreadful losses in war are dwarfed by those in its violent politics, in which some 54 million died.[12]

The First World War killed over 8 million in the armed forces of the participants and the Second World War some 14 million from the armed forces and perhaps 27 million civilians.[13] Nevertheless the American Civil War – an episode of internal violent politics – remains the bloodiest conflict in US history, killing as many men as all the international wars of the USA put together, including both world wars, Korea and Vietnam.[14] Communism, which preceded Fascism and Nazism and persisted long after they had been destroyed in war, killed some 100 million in times of violent politics, in the USSR, China, Vietnam, Korea, Cambodia, Eastern Europe, Latin America, Africa and Afghanistan.[15]

The concept of 'crimes against humanity' first appeared in the context of violent politics, not in war: the Anglo-French condemnation of the Turkish massacre of Armenians in 1915.[16] Some six million Jews died in the Holocaust – an act carried out during war, but essentially one of violent politics. Millions before and since have died in genocide elsewhere. More than 200 were killed in Northern Ireland in 1922, even after the Treaty which had created the Irish Free State.[17] German air raids on Belfast killed nearly 1000 people in 1941.[18] Four times as many have been killed in the Troubles of 1969 to 1998.

Violent politics kills many more people than war.

Form and substance

'Political violence' is the term conventionally used to cover the enormous variety of violent means – insurrection, revolt, terrorism, kidnapping, assassination, riot – used to achieve political ends within states. Some call it 'internal war', on the Clausewitzian analogy, although many campaigns of political violence lack the absolute nature of war and have far more limited objectives, while the dissident factions may well lack the essential elements of a sovereign state, even territory.

To describe the phenomenon that is the subject of this book as political violence implies that it is the violence which is important, and the politics merely adjectival; what we are actually examining, however, is a violent form of politics, not a political form of violence. Nor is violent politics a deviant subset of normal, constitutional, institutional, parliamentary politics. Indeed, the reverse is the case: if a state happens to possess political institutions which eschew the use of the ultimate method of resolving conflict it is how that has been achieved that requires explanation, rather than the presence of violence in politics. Institutional, non-violent politics is a subset of violent politics, not the reverse. The language of violent politics is politics, not violence. Violence is only an alphabet: the meaning of its acts – its letters – varies with the circumstances.

There are only six main ways of changing people's behaviour: by persuasion, shame or reward – the usual modes of institutional politics – and by prevention, fear or force – those of violent politics. The deliberate use of violence as a political instrument effectively prevents institutional, non-violent politics from working: prevention, fear and force trump persuasion, shame and reward.

It is the substance of each of these modes which is important, not its form. Putting a pistol in someone's back is not in form a violent act, but since it leaves the victim no practicable alternative to doing what is demanded of him, it is in substance operating in the force mode. Conversely, killing a government minister or a soldier is obviously a violent act in form, but not in substance: the killing of one particular person could not force an organisation to do anything: it certainly leaves open more than one practicable option. Such an act is in substance one of persuasion not of force.

There is no necessary connection between the violent form of an act and its political substance. It is therefore easy for violent politicians to mistake tactical success for strategic success. It is easy to believe that success in killing policemen, bombing shops, robbing banks – or for that matter killing terrorists or imprisoning them – *ipso facto* means strategic success.

People find it difficult to distinguish between an act, which is often trivial, and its meaning, which may be important. The act may seem so innocent that it would be churlish, bigoted, pompous or offensive to complain, let alone prevent it: girls wearing headscarves in French schools, or Orangemen marching to a band. The meaning, however, may well be a serious challenge: 'we can do what we like in your territory, and you cannot stop us'.

It is the simple drama of violent acts which tends to capture attention, column inches and broadcast minutes, rather than the often complex politics behind them. Images of forlorn hostages, burning cars, bombed buildings, trapped wounded and heroic rescue efforts swamp discussion of their meaning. Terrorists, and sometimes those they terrorise too, forget that deeds are not words, and underestimate the importance of using words as well as deeds to persuade the other side.

Acts of violence can either have a demonstrative effect – saying that you are not the bosses, we are, and we are giving you an order: look what will happen again and again if you don't obey; or they can have a tangible effect – the capture of territory, money, weapons, people, or other resources.

The base for success

For all the thousands of campaigns in hundreds of countries over the years and for all the millions of words written about them, the structure of violent politics is simple. The aim of the insurgents is to attack conventional politics and win. The aim of the incumbents is also to win: to defend conventional politics effectively. The manifold forms of terrorism and counterinsurgency are only means to that end. They are not ends in themselves. The distinction is crucial to both analysis and practice.

The base for success in violent politics has only four elements: will, skill, manpower and materiel, in that order of importance. These are essential to everything else – policymaking, operations, intelligence, publicity, funding, recruiting, training, finance, supplies, transport, communications. When political temperatures are high, violent political parties lack neither support nor men to do the dirty work; even so, only a few bodies within the state command enough manpower, skill, materiel or organisation to become protagonists in violent politics, and fewer still have the all-important will to win.

Will is the key component on both sides. Incumbent governments have very complex political agendas at home and abroad, huge infrastructures to manage, and heterogeneous constituencies to lead: constituencies which may well include supporters of the insurgents' aims if not their methods, and people who do not think the government's position is worth a fight. Insurgents are likely to have a much simpler agenda, a more homogeneous constituency and a much smaller infrastructure, but their problems differ in scale rather than in nature.

The base for success is the same for all sides in a conflict, but it is not symmetrical. Established governments command ample manpower and materiel, and new skills can be developed quickly if need be. Insurgents have to mobilise their base from a standing start, but with very few physical resources they can cause enough mayhem to make the government respond, and make them deploy far more resources on defence than the insurgents need for attack. These asymmetries are very important in low-level conflict: governments command so much manpower, skill and materiel that their will is the only target insurgents can hope to destroy. However often and however strongly they attack will not make a whit of difference to the amount of skill, manpower and materiel the government can deploy.

That is true of international low-level conflict too, although it sometimes appears not to be. US forces were withdrawn from Lebanon shortly after 241 Marines had been killed by a suicide bomber in 1983.[19] A decade later US forces were withdrawn from Somalia after television showed rebel Somalis towing the naked bodies of US Rangers behind trucks, and smashing up their shot-down helicopters.[20] The withdrawals were widely linked with the casualties. That may not have been the case, or only one factor among many. Whatever the facts may be, the decision clearly depended on the will of the US government, not upon the manpower, skill or materiel available to it. The attackers were simply operating through violent politics abroad on conventional politics at home, as they had in the many colonial liberation movements. Even when the colonial power was voluntarily relinquishing its rule, as many were, and the only question was to whom, violent politicians in the colony often attacked the forces and institutions of the metropolitan power with the aim of making their particular faction its successor. Here too there was usually no question of defeating the metropolitan power by armed force, by destroying its manpower and materiel; the target was its will.[21]

That tactic will not succeed when the political stakes are higher, as they are when a country or its government is fighting for survival, and it may well be counterproductive. Israel, for example, often makes dramatic counter-attacks in response to terrorist attacks: thirteen airliners for one, punitive raids causing thousands of casualties for a handful: a head for an eye.[22] When one organisation claims to be able to destroy another by force, it helps to demonstrate that the reverse is also true. When refugee camps in another country are used as terrorist bases, it helps to have an excuse to destroy them. Violent politics is a two-edged sword.

The infrastructure of small insurgent groups is very vulnerable to direct attack: the capture of a few leaders, the seizure of an arms shipment or the blockage of funds weakens their ability and may prove fatal to their will, as it has many times. Governments cannot hope to destroy the infrastructure of larger groups, but every successful attack weakens their ability, slows them down, and increases internal pressures.

Insurgent attacks are therefore aimed at will alone; death and destruction is not an end but a means. Government countermeasures are aimed at both will and infrastructure. Countermeasures are continuous and wide-ranging, and their targets are specific: to kill or capture leaders, to shut down an arms supply chain or flow of funds; to rectify maladministration, to improve services, broadcast policies, unite divided communities. Many government measures are routine and unspectacular. Insurgent operations are the opposite: spectacular, sporadic, and targeted on will, not on infrastructure; it does not matter much which particular target they choose.

If insurgents have *de facto* control of an area they may also have to administer its population as a government would; but for most that is a burden or an opportunity for corruption, rather than a willing duty. The inability of any one protagonist to mobilise a sufficiently powerful base to overcome the others may itself limit the scale of violent politics. The need for individual families to survive and for the nation as a whole to keep going may also limit the scale. The tolerable level of disruption to a society often sets an upper bound to such politics: once the damage, destruction and loss of confidence reaches this level, people tend to countenance any countermeasures that are necessary to stabilise the situation, however draconian they may be. The lower bound to the conflict is often set by the practical impossibility of preventing a low level of any activity, however criminal or anti-social.

In the many countries of the world where violent politics are endemic, the scale and methods are often limited by rules derived from custom or, in the case of the state, by law. Violent politics thus forms a spectrum with two extremes: violent politics *à outrance*, culminating in civil war, and violent politics in which the means are circumscribed, more or less tightly, by the protagonists' lack of resources, by rules derived from custom, law and prudence, or by the balance of power.

As one might expect, there appears to have been a full turn of the wheel in the theory and practice of violent politics this century, rather than a linear development. The early expectations of natural Marxist revolution were disappointed; they died in the man-made wars and were buried by the man-made revolutions which succeeded them; they slowly rose again among the New Left and revolutionaries of the natural school – Guevara, Marighela, the Tupamaros, the Montoneros – and then fell with the Berlin Wall and Iron Curtain. The deterministic view that violent politics was an inevitable, mechanical, result of objective conditions fell with it. Political will is the key.

In short, in the sort of low-level conflicts considered in this book, there are important asymmetries. Terrorist atrocities are aimed purely at the will of the government, whatever the physical target may be. Government countermeasures must be aimed at the infrastructure of the insurgents, at their will, and at providing good government: all three.

One of the principal difficulties in the study of violent politics is that its most important factor, will, is not only abstract but largely hidden. Neither governments nor insurgents publicly reveal what impact the campaign is having on their will to win, and though their public utterances state their public policy, it may not reflect their true position. Public records will reveal the latter only after a lapse of years. Insurgents may have no records, and will certainly have selective memories. Students of violent politics have perforce to rely for their interpretation of meaning on documents which are inherently unreliable: manifestos, statements, bulletins, memoirs, speeches, party newspapers, more or less partisan books and articles, election results. Only very occasionally are genuine and revealing documents captured or released. Interpreting acts is therefore important. It is tempting to invest events with a significance proportional to their casualties and destruction, and to see challenge and response in terms of events rather than their underlying meaning, which may range from nothing more than keeping the political pot boiling to setting it ablaze. The change achieved by an act may not be the one intended; but there is no going back in violent politics. Once defining moments have happened they are written into the narratives of both sides and reinforce their faith. Only rarely will they weaken it.

Will and faith

Failure of will is the most common reason for failure in violent politics – on either side.

Individual's wills, and the beliefs that drive them, are highly resistant to change. Innumerable studies have found that large groups of people believe in aliens, astrology, spiritualism, geomancy, conspiracy theories of every complexion; and are quite unmoved by evidence to the contrary. Indeed, even when specific prophesies around which people have organised their lives do not come about, most quickly find rationalisations, and carry on as before.[23] The late 1990s saw a spate of books with a common theme – the decay of discrimination (in the sense of carefully distinguishing one thing from another, the true from the false, the worthwhile from the meretricious, the good from the bad), and the acceptance of nonsense, pretension and absurdity.[24] Unfortunately for humankind, this seems to be a universal failing, not confined to any particular time or people. Many studies have shown how easily people believe fantasies, and how passionate they become about defending or promoting them. For example, the growing scientific capacity to trace the provenance of mummies and living populations through their inherited DNA has not been welcomed by those who have a unifying myth of ethnic purity to sell.

One author was roundly attacked when she was brave enough to present chronic fatigue syndrome, Gulf War syndrome, recovered memory, multiple personality disorder, satanic ritual abuse and alien abduction as hysterical: psychological rather than physical disorders. She was buttonholed by people who were sure that she herself was suffering and needed help; attacked by conspiracy theorists, who thought she had been bought by chemical corporations and mad scientists or reprogrammed by aliens during her own abduction; and stalked by avengers threatening legal or physical retaliation, despite the crippling fatigue which prevented their doing anything else.[25]

The frequency of such beliefs, their ready propagation, and their persistence and resistance to change, bode ill for attempts to break the analogous myths which so often drive violent politics. Religious imperatives are particularly resistant, but political faiths can swing sharply from hard left to hard right and back again. Secular faiths swing as rapidly and unpredictably. 'Where God appears to have died, false gods are not far away.'[26]

Spiritual belief has strengthened during the twentieth century, rather than withering away as many expected it would. The United States maintains the Christian tradition which founded it, but has added cults whose fundamentalism and millenarian beliefs yield not one whit to science; whose leaders and followers regularly immolate themselves (and occasionally others) in the name of their faith. A profession of atheism can still stop an American dinner party dead in its tracks. Many countries have absorbed the traditional religions of their immigrants, and added vast numbers of newly-invented ones: Moonies, Children of God; Hare Krishna; New Agers harking back to crystals and herbs;

druids and hamadryads; white witches and black masses; worshippers of extra-terrestrials and *feng shui*.[27] Islamic fundamentalism is troublesome in determinedly secular nations such as Turkey and Egypt, and a key source of conflict in Algeria, Iran, Afghanistan, and many more.

As the plurality of such beliefs grows, many held with great tenacity, it becomes more and more difficult to do or say anything very positive without offending at least one of them; or, if the attempt is to link irrationality with unreason, all of them. In the warm climate of moral relativism, liberal democracy and wealthy economies, groups which would not have survived in traditional societies and subsistence economies, grow and thrive. Most seek to live and let live, to find compromise. Others exploit the situation – by violence if they think it helps.

Hence, perhaps, the growing emphasis on human rights: an apparently universal declaration of principles; an anchor in the sea of relativism; a secular (or perhaps more accurately ecumenical) update of the Ten Commandments. Rights are open to conflicting interpretations, however, and can as easily become swords as shields.

In some conflicts across a religious divide, religion is an extra symbol on the tribal banners rather than a prime source of conflict in itself: Sudan, the Israel/Arab conflict, Northern Ireland, India/Pakistan, the re-Balkanisation of the former Yugoslavia, Cyprus, Greece/Turkey, Armenia/Azerbaijan. It is inconceivable that the whole world will converge on Christianity, Islam or Buddhism, or that it will converge on western-style capitalist liberal democracy as the only form of government, with the universal declaration of human rights replacing the ten commandments. The Asian economic collapse of 1998 showed that Asian family values and Japanese communitarianism do not inoculate such societies from economic collapse, and may even make it worse when it happens.

Whether religious or secular, faiths are reinforced by ceremonial: constitutions, initiations, oaths, passage rites, meetings, songs, storytellings, readings from the sacred texts, feasts and fasts, flags, uniforms, special anniversaries, rewards and punishments, processions to the graves of martyrs and other sacred places. Such things are common to all societies and to all organisations within them, from firms to football clubs. The sense of righteousness, power and solidarity thus engendered can serve fanaticism as well as civilisation. Islamic, Christian, Hindu, Japanese and Jewish fundamentalists have all been involved in terrorism, increasingly so since the death of the secular religion of Marxism, and are all the more savage and uncontrolled because they see themselves as having a mandate from their god to destroy their satans utterly. Manichaeans admit of no half measures.[28]

The French Revolution was followed by a time of Terror: tens of thousands killed in riots and in the suppression of the Vendée; twenty thousand guillotined by Revolutionary Tribunals: and later another twenty thousand killed in the suppression of the Paris Commune. But all of these were shortish episodes, justified as eggs for omelettes: the elimination of counter-revolutionaries and other enemies of the people, followed by the suppression of the crime which had flourished in disorder. *Raison d'état*; evident necessity; rational, or at least rationalisable.

The Russian Revolution, and the other Communist regimes which were installed by force of arms, sustained terror for so long and at such a high level principally because they were driven by the one true faith. Faith is at the heart of violent politics. It is the driving force of violence, so it should be the principal target of countermeasures. Faith is also very seductive, and the narratives to which it gives rise are attractive and exciting.

Religion is not a primary cause of violent politics: faith is. Both can be enormously productive of good deeds; both can be enormously destructive. Blind faith – religious or secular – admits of no compromise, but compromise is the essence of conventional politics.

Faith which drives violence often contains a mixture of historical, tribal, religious, territorial and class elements, woven seamlessly together:

> She helped convince me from an early age that the Irish had been the victims of terrible cruelties inflicted by the English and their Scots planters over many centuries ... I left Dublin [after a visit to the National Museum] with an exalted new sense of my country's history, and a new-found reverence for everything republican. [Plunkett, Pearse and Connolly] were all martyrs for our Catholic faith, the true religion: religion and politics fused together by the blood of the martyrs. I was prepared to be a martyr, to die for this true Catholic faith ... It dawned on me that I was not just looking at a dead history of insurrection, I was looking at an alternative society, government and army.[29]

Analogous themes were presented by the neo-Nazi movements which grew after the collapse of the East German regime, unification, and the surge in immigration from poorer countries:[30]

> We stand a humiliated nation... The root of this humiliation is in the Thirty Years' war, the treaty of Versailles and St Germain, 1919,

to the last great war which entwined the best and most beautiful... The reparations to insatiable Israel. The traitorous 'eastern treaties'. Credit to communist Poland. The expulsions of the Germans from the eastern territories ... The stationing of foreign missiles on German soil ... Yesterday points to today, today points to tomorrow. Never must we forget the monstrous humiliation.[31]

And excitement:

Everywhere there were young activists. We were really a movement. Young comrades who come today to a known and organized movement will never really understand what that meant for us.[32]

The faith of single-issue fanatics is no exception:

What they don't realise is that they are fascists. They believe the cause of animals supersedes that of humans. The feeling is that you have to be purer and purer, then you get more extreme and end up bombing people ... They are not really animal lovers. They don't watch wildlife programmes, or read books on animals. They know nothing about wildlife. They are anarchists who view the use of animals as a political conspiracy and human cruelty ... It is a mindset that allows you to bomb people with impunity [sic] ... Liberation is all. That is as far as they think.[33]

A similar element has arisen even within the Mormons: since the early 1990s so-called Straight Edge gangs have been operating in the traditional Mormon areas of the US, abiding by their traditional codes – no drink, no premarital sex, no drugs; adding others – no vandalism, smoking, meat-eating or fur; and enforcing their code with firebombs, beatings, razor-slashing, knives and firearms. The mindset of Straight Edgers is uncannily similar to that of the young Nazis described in Chapter 3:

Maybe we feel the world thinks of us as good little Mormon boys, so we act out to get away from that image. I was prone to violence because everyone gave me crap about that. And I had friends who backed me up. My parents were cut up when they found their dear son was into it but I can't stop being Straight Edge for them. I can't compromise.[34]

The focus of protesters tends to shift from target to target: nuclear disarmament, American bases (and wars) abroad, trees, roads, airports, nuclear tests, acid rain, global warming, the ozone layer, arms sales, hardwood furniture, animal liberation, foxhunting, fur coats, seals, whales, genetic modification, globalisation. The same faces appear in one protest after another.[35] The same voices are heard demanding the punishment of dictators and the release of terrorist leaders, both accused of exactly the same crimes.

Protest is at the lower bound of violent politics. Many direct-action protesters are specifically and determinedly non-violent against people, although some cause spectacular and costly property damage.[36] Others invite the use of force to remove them from runways, roads, trees or buildings. Either way the human (and therefore media) fascination with violence comes into play, and the political message is reinforced. Either way, uncompromising faith leads to violent politics.

Since the aim of the violent politician is to weaken the will of his opponents, he chooses his targets by lot: it could be you. In rough order of 'acceptability':

- 'economic' targets: electricity supplies, oil pipelines, railways, bridges, road-building machinery, laboratories, factories;
- high-visibility public places: banks, financial institutions, post offices, ports; and glass-clad tower blocks and railway stations, since they appear spectacularly damaged in photographs;
- armed opponents of the terrorists: soldiers and police;
- civilians in direct support of the security forces: 'collaborators';
- other servants of the state: politicians, civil servants;
- families of 'occupation forces';
- members and supporters of opposing communities;
- places where only opponents go: community centres, pubs, clubs, barracks, police stations, animal laboratories, abortion clinics;
- dissident members of the terrorists' own community, and their supporters;
- members of highly visible groups, which might be expected to react on their behalf: priests, nuns, schoolchildren, churches;
- places where everyone goes: shopping centres, bus and railway stations, sports stadiums. Non-lethal blast bombs show the terrorists are compassionate but serious; lethal ones that they are deadly serious, and that the authorities are powerless.

If there are 'accidents' the violent politician easily excuses them: warnings have been ignored to cast blame, or through incompetence; regret about injuries to innocent civilians and children, implying that there are civilians or children who are not innocent; or that the state is the guilty one and its servants thus legitimate targets.

As was shown earlier, there is only one key target for violent politicians: the will of the state. States have three targets: to destroy the will of terrorist organisations, to weaken their capability, and to maintain good government. The will of insurgent organisations is driven by faith, by a creed reinforced by ceremonial and bonding rites, so it is highly resistant to change by any of the three modes of conventional politics: persuasion, shame or reward. It is not possible for the state to avoid using the modes of violent politics – prevention, fear and force – if its opponents do so.

The aim of both sides is to convert the other: to change their faith. Conventional politics seeks compromise, toleration and moderation. Violent politics seeks only to win. Many find that appealing: zealotry is fun.

Symbolism

The post-modern (or perhaps anti-modern) technique of regarding argument as a discourse between people whose beliefs are equally valid and equally true, none of them being privileged as justified, is useful in the study of violent politics because it forces concentration on the meaning of the acts rather than on the acts themselves. It also allows for the meaning of some acts to be spiritual – in the broadest sense, including mythical, symbolic and emotional meanings – as well as rational. Its most useful contribution may well be that it deals very well with the complexity of violent politics, where different acts have different meanings at different times, and where the 'narratives' of the discourses on both sides (or all of them) change as events change. It breaks away from deterministic views, where effect follows cause along a single timeline, and normative ones, where violent politics and countermeasures are seen as aiming at a model, be that liberal democracy, communism, or a religious state, with deviations from the norm being regarded as pathological, and therefore to be destroyed.

Seeing politics as a debate – a dialogue between traders rather than as a pragmatic battle with Harold Macmillan's 'events, dear boy, events' – is probably at the root of the oft-made observation that more can be learnt from fictional accounts of violent politics than from historical ones; in other words that they are more coherent, more understandable, more comfortable to live with. The oversimplification of narrative necessitated by journalistic reporting may also contribute to the impression of determinism; stories do not make sense unless they have heroes and villains, just causes and psychopathic killers. That is not to say that seeing politics as a dialogue is methodologically superior to a normative or deterministic approach, or that it will yield better results. Dialogues can be of the deaf; and since violent politics relies on simple messages for simple people, they can become repetitious monologues.

The importance of symbols in violent politics is often not realised, even by those who are used to them in conventional politics: remembrance day; the trooping of the colour, the state opening of parliament, the monarchy itself, state visits; ceremonials repeated in county councils, villages, masonic halls and churches across the land; Orange marches, African stomping chants, Arab ululations; rituals of sacrifice in all religions, and flagellation and self-mutilation in many; commemorations of defining moments in history; flags, colours, venerated icons and crosses; days of atonement, birth and death; rites of penitence, triumph and celebration.

Violent politics has its own heroes, martyrs and demons – perhaps even more so than war, because of the intimacy of violent politics. While the martyrs of war are commemorated, they are rarely avenged. Victory is the reward of those on the winning side, and the defeated accept their fate. In violent politics martyrs are saints and battle banners, their memory kept fresh by stories and songs, and their example kept alive by violence against their enemies. Enemies are not figures of scorn to be hung out on the Siegfried Line but wicked demons to be killed and mutilated; hung, drawn and quartered, so to speak, to exorcise them and punish their evildoing.

Mutilation in violent politics is, sadly, not at all rare, especially compared to war. Somehow, death in war is enough. Its weapons cause mutilation too, but that is incidental rather than an end in itself, and brings sadness rather than rejoicing. There but for the grace of God....In violent politics it is often a different story:

> The first body was ... a girl of maybe four or five, with her throat ripped open by a knife wound that stretched to the edge of her mouth ... There was another woman, then another two children, with their heads blown apart ... Beneath them was an elderly man who had been shot in the head and his wife, also shot and with her left foot nearly severed at the ankle ... the body of an elderly man with his throat cut and half his head removed.[37]

Militiamen hid in abandoned buildings along the line of demarca-
tion, the existence of which they reinforced by blindly shooting
rounds of ammunition at anyone they spotted on the 'other side'.
Their shooting sprees punished by death any violation of newly
defined borders. Rule was further enforced by the omnipresent sight
of summary executions of captured enemies: naked corpses strewed
street corners, others were dragged behind automobiles, and in
newspapers one could see the photos of the victims of kidnappings
or summary executions.[38]

Similar mutilations appeared during the intercommunal fighting in
Cyprus, in Rwanda, everywhere. They were so common in Colombia
during *la Violencia* of the 1950s that each had a special name: *picar para
tamal* for cutting a living victim into small pieces, and *bocachiquiar* for
bleeding to death from hundreds of stab wounds, for example.[39] It is
difficult to explain these except in symbolic terms; rationally, a dead
enemy is no longer a threat of any kind to anyone: but a demon has to
be torn apart, and shown to the world.

Mindsets are reinforced or modified by events. The background built
up by many small incidents is an important factor, because it conditions the interpretation of major events which are later seen as
'defining moments'. History is not the only subject 'in which things
happen one after the other':[40] mindsets and narratives are built that
way too. 'When the facts change, I change my mind. What do you do,
sir?' People may well agree with Keynes in principle; in practice they
are quite likely to change the facts to fit their mind. What matters in
violent politics is not the truth, but what is believed to be the truth.

The truth of what happened during defining events, and what came
where in the causal chain, will be endlessly debated. From the point of
view of the student of violent politics rather than of history, what
matters is not the truth but what people passionately believe it to be:
that is what affects their will. Once a defining event has happened,
therefore, the facts matter less than the interpretations: the 'narratives'
in postmodernist jargon. What is important in violent politics is that
every past, present and future event can be woven by each protagonist
into a totally coherent, consistent and convincing narrative, albeit one
which is totally incompatible with those of the others.

It is not surprising that the bigger the event the bigger the impact.
Skilled violent politicians avoid big events if there is any possibility
that they may cause a big adverse shift in narratives, and therefore in
will. The Canary Wharf bombing that ended the IRA ceasefire in 1996[41]

was a big event by any standard, but it did not do the republican image any harm; others, of which Omagh is the most obvious, certainly did.[42]

The nature of violent politics

Political conflicts which would have been resolved by war when it was economically and politically affordable, now bubble on in a more or less hostile state, including the use of violent politics short of war, often supported openly or covertly by other states; by non-violent measures such as embargoes; and by maintaining large standing armed forces and other deterrents.

Paradoxically, while full-scale war has become ever more costly and dangerous, low-level violent politics has become steadily cheaper and safer. The have-nots (whether of money, status, religion, territory, independence, class, nationality or colour) can easily find the weapons necessary to attack the haves and, for the first time in history, they actually have a realistic chance of winning or at least gaining ground. Human rights legislation, sympathy for underdogs, aversion to their being hunted down, moral relativism, easy communication and publicity, cheap arms and explosives, global banking and free capital movement, are all on their side.

Terrorism is cheap: huge amounts of casualties and damage can be caused by bombs which anyone can afford to make from readily available materials: car bombs killed 317 in Bombay in 1993; a truck bomb in a Jewish community Centre in Buenos Aires in 1994 killed 96; the Oklahoma City bomb in 1995 killed 168; the suitcase bomb on PanAm 103 over Lockerbie in 1988 killed 270; the truck bomb in the World Trade Centre in New York in 1993 which killed six, injured 1,000 and caused over half a billion dollars in damage cost four hundred dollars to make.[43] The IRA fertiliser bombs in London and Manchester in 1991, 1992 and 1996 caused hundreds of millions of pounds in damage, and as much again in lost business and additional security measures.

It is not surprising that acute conflict which used to be resolved by war or *force majeur* has now become chronic; nor is it surprising how slow, uncertain and ineffective the evolution of its law and practice has been.

Violent and conventional politics

Conventional politics aims to heal divisions. Violent politics aims to reinforce divisions, even when they are trivial; to polarise; to sharpen differences; to promote intolerance, to mark boundaries, to separate classes, colours, races, religions; to fight for a single issue. In David Apter's phrase, violence is the original sin of politics.[44]

Conventional politics deals with thousands of problems, great and small: tax rates, subsidies for this and that, health services, education, monetary policy, inflation, devolution, constitutional reform, genetic engineering, transport. The problems it deals with tend to be large, important, well researched, endlessly discussed, and examined from many different points of view. Violent politics has only one aim, to which it offers only one solution; take it or pay the consequences. It brings a sense of urgency to political change, but not necessarily change itself. It may of course accelerate the pace of change when the fact of change is already there, and it may well alter the direction of change.

There is no first-past-the post system within violent political organisations to resolve, or at least suppress, internal conflict: it is open to anyone to start their own terrorist organisation, recruit skill, manpower and material where they can, and play their own violent politics, even with those ostensibly on the same side, even within their own organisation: witness the feuds between the Official and Provisional IRA, the Palestine Liberation Army and Hamas, Collins and deValera; the various Kurdish factions.

Reaching an agreement with one faction is not enough. The Social Democratic and Labour Party and Sinn Fein may claim to speak for all nationalists in Northern Ireland, or the PLO grow into the Palestinian Authority, but minority terrorist groups remain, free to pursue their own ends either in concert with those who have signed up to a peace process, or against them. Attributing each atrocity to the faction which committed it is only a start. What matters is what the pattern tells us about the totality of the groups with a common aim: their leaders, their objectives, and the kind of things they are prepared to do to achieve them.

Sinn Fein, for example, might well be prepared to let bygones be bygones and reach an accommodation in Northern Ireland which accepted the existence of the province, despite their predecessors and those of the present-day Fianna Fail (which courageously, and significantly, signed the 1998 Good Friday agreement) not having done so.[45] However if the 'Real IRA' for example, and the '32-County Sovereignty Committee' which is its political arm, refused to accept the 1998 agreement and referendum result, and were able to recruit support from those at home and abroad who had previously supported the Provisional IRA, they could continue the campaign of violence on the same scale as before; only the name of the main actor would have changed, in the same way as it did when the Provisional IRA succeeded the Official IRA.

So what is important in violent politics, as in the conventional form, are the political factions which exist, their aims, objectives, leaders, supporters, and relative strengths. Engaging one only will never be enough.

Violent politics will increase if it is made easy or rewarding; or if it is not made difficult and unrewarding. Rich societies are disadvantaged here because they can afford security measures which are not in fact secure, but give the comfortable illusion that they are. When the terrorists breach the 'ring of steel', their effect is all the greater. The aim of counter-terrorism is not to protect all potential targets – there are far too many of them for that – but to counter the perpetrators, particularly their leaders. Footsoldiers are easy to replace; leaders are not.

Here again, there is a lack of symmetry which greatly benefits the terrorist: he is a needle in a haystack of ordinary people, but he can choose any one of a vast number of targets. Conversely the counter-terrorist has a huge infrastructure to defend, and a tiny target to find. It is easy to neglect this fundamental constraint and use techniques that look good but simply do not work: that way lies prolonged conflict and stalemate. After the Omagh bomb, for example, both governments vowed to 'destroy the Real IRA'. Those who asked why 28 murders in one atrocity had spurred them into that promise, when 3000 killed over 30 years had not spurred them to destroy the IRA that had done 2000 of the killings and triggered many of the rest, had a point.

On the one hand, since terrorists strike one target among thousands, most people are not individually afraid that they will be killed or maimed, any more than they are when they travel by car, which in all but the worst year of the Troubles in Northern Ireland killed many more people than terrorism. They take sensible precautions, the equivalent of wearing a seatbelt and not driving too close, but otherwise terrorism has little effect on their everyday life. Counter-terrorist precautions, such as searches, parking restrictions and walls round city centres, affect them far more. Those who live in areas controlled by terrorists, on the other hand, are subject to their rule, arbitrarily taxed and punished, and genuinely terrorised, even though they are ostensibly on the same side.

A hunted terrorist knows he is hunted – and the better the hunters the more effect it has on his daily life. He has to keep his head down, his contacts limited, and his hands away from his weapons. His hunters only have to be lucky once; he has to be lucky all the time.[46]

Violent politicians often cannot appear on a public stage in person, as a conventional politician would; so their published and broadcast words are all the more important. Hence the section on violent politics and the media later in this chapter.

Violent politicians aim to legitimise themselves, to put themselves on the same plane as the incumbents; and simultaneously to deny legitimacy to the incumbents, by claiming that they are violent too. If the state says violence is evil, then it is as evil for the state to use it as it is for those countering the state; the police firing tear gas and rubber bullets are therefore as violent as the rioters; soldiers shooting terrorists are therefore terrorists themselves. The doctrine of the state's monopoly of force is a difficult one to sell, particularly to those with memories of Stalin, Mao and Pol Pot.

Violent politicians need a manifesto as much as conventional politicians do – perhaps even more so. They are not in power, so their manifestos lack the practical details which conventional politicians have to include. Instead, they aim to create a quasi-religious creed based on a unifying myth: a clear, simple and compelling story which may have little to do with reality, but is nonetheless believable. Successful movements need a unifying leader too, as the author or interpreter of the unifying myth.

Principles and aims

Rationality

Is violent politics rational, a way of opening channels blocked by conventional politicians, for good reason or bad? Or is it pathological, a symptom of a sickness in society, or in individuals? Can it be creative, or is it always destructive? Does it ever deserve to succeed, or should it always fail? If it ought to fail, are the reasons for that judgement fundamental or prudential?

The awkward answer is that it can be each of these in different circumstances, and all of these at different times in the same circumstances. The judgement often depends, as it would not were the objections to it fundamental, on the methods used, their scale, their timing, their targets and their results. Terrorism can be rational, deviant, pathological, atavistic; and all of these at different points in the same campaign.

Violent politics is by no means always illegitimate: the English, French and American revolutions were undoubtedly legitimate – and the Russian one too, though most would now hesitate to put it into the same benign category. Few would regard Solidarity in Poland, the ANC in South Africa, Czech resistance to Soviet occupation in 1968 and Hungarian resistance in 1964 as illegitimate in moral terms – unwise perhaps in the circumstances, undesirable perhaps in principle, but certainly deserving support.

In all violent politics, however, there is a boundary between the acceptable and the unacceptable; in fact several boundaries, because those defined by the insurgents will certainly not be the same as those of the incumbents, at least at the outset.

Neither side can afford to alienate its supporters, and both may find it unwise to defy international opinion. So there is a tendency for the boundaries to converge, and for the ground between them to narrow, although it will never disappear. Action of one kind is then held to justify action of another kind; strong action, strong reaction; mild action, mild response; new measure, new countermeasure. Both sides are trapped in these unwritten rules. So stasis in violent politics is not hugely different from stasis in conventional politics; the problems may simply be too difficult to solve, and the intervention of violent politics, though it certainly gets attention, may well make them even more difficult to resolve.

Unlike warfare, violent politics rarely becomes a trial of strength. This is only partly because violent politics *à outrance* would redefine itself as war. The main reason is that the aim in violent politics is not conquest by force but by persuasion – aided by prevention, fear and force as necessary tools when all others have failed.

Morality

The rules of religions, law and conventional politics are practical distillations of where the boundaries of socially acceptable action should lie, and what should be done if they are transgressed. They are far from absolute, as national differences between them show. They are closer to being rational, but differ in rationale. Which rules: the principle of non-intervention between sovereign states, or the prevention of genocide?[47] National self-determination, or the prevention of fragmentation and ethnic cleansing? If the right of conquest was legitimate then but not now, who now has title to land acquired by conquest? If the clock is to be turned back, where does it stop? Should morality take precedence over *raison d'état*? If so, whose morality? Is revenge moral or immoral? Or are some forms of it moral (reparations, the execution of war criminals, disarmament, occupation) and others immoral (executions *pour encourager les autres*, forcible relocation, deindustrialisation)?

How long can the moral forms of revenge go on before they become immoral? Is abortion, or euthanasia, or the death penalty, moral, immoral, or a matter of practical choice? Is the possession of property an absolute human right, or are there limits? Is trespass a violation of human rights? If property (or excessive property) is theft, is it moral to steal it? Is free trade moral, or protectionism, or are both morally neutral? Is it right to prevent immigration from poor countries to rich ones? Is war moral, immoral, or a morally-neutral practical necessity? Is it moral to conscript people to fight and die, even in a just war? Is there any moral difference between punishing an individual for transgression and punishing a nation? Is an Islamic *jihad* or *fatwah* moral or immoral? Is justice natural, a matter of practicality; or of morality? Do different principles, or different moralities, apply to international and national law, or should they be consistent? If consistent, which adapts to which?

In John Gray's words:

> Even if liberal political morality is universal [which he argues it is not], applying its principles involves confronting fundamental conflicts of values. Such conflicts are tragic in that wrong will be done however they are resolved. Advancing democracy does not always foster political stability. Preserving peace does not always coincide with the promotion of human rights. These are not transitory difficulties which we can one day hope to leave behind. They are permanent ethical dilemmas, deeply rooted in conflicts that states will always confront, which will never be fully resolved.[48]

Human Rights campaigners act as though there is an unchallengeable moral obligation to follow them in all circumstances, everywhere, at all times, and to the letter. Real life is more complicated than that, if only because violent politicians and criminals do not accept that premise. The domains of morality, human rights, politics and the law overlap like circles in a Venn diagram; they do not coincide. Still more inconveniently, they change as circumstances do, and as people view those circumstances from their different angles. There are no absolutes.

Aims

Violent politicians may aim to achieve independence or national liberation; to overthrow an existing regime; to impose ideological or religious beliefs or destroy those of others; to force the resolution of problems; to rectify injustices; to build support among believers; to punish or destroy unbelievers. Their rationale is straightforward:

- conventional politics is slow and ineffective;
- however loudly we shout, the government remains deaf;
- ends justify means;
- the more worthy the end (of which we are the judge), the more justifiable the means;
- unrectified wrongs justify violence;
- the greater the wrong, the greater the violence;
- you claim your politics are democratic, but that actually means the hegemony of the majority and the oppression of minorities;
- you claim that you act under the rule of law, interpreted by an independent judiciary, but you change the law whenever you wish, and appoint your sympathisers as judges;
- you suspend the right of trial by jury whenever it is expedient;
- you claim to protect your people but you cannot; we'll prove it.

Violent politicians could even claim that theirs is a superior form of politics: they risk life and limb, not just unpopularity and loss of office; they must recruit support day-to-day, without the aid of institutionalised treasuries, tax-gathers, agencies and armed forces; they do not even have the security of tenure afforded by elections; they can be deposed by a shot to the head.

Their rallying flags are tribe, race, ethnicity, nationality, territory, class, language, religion, ideology, principle; in short: difference. They tend to have clear boundaries, and where they do not they are reinforced at every opportunity.

Simplistic geopolitical and historical beliefs often underly their creed:

- any territory in which nationals live is national territory;
- any territory contiguous to a national territory but not separated from it by a natural boundary is national territory;
- any contiguous territory which once belonged to the nation is national territory;
- inequities stemming from past conflict must be rectified by turning the clock back.
- Society is on the edge of catastrophe; the existing regime has either caused it or failed to prevent it. It has no answers; we do. The time is ripe, and we must act before it is too late. A new and better society will follow the overthrow of the old.

So violent politicians tend to have a single aim, a coherent creed, and a clearly-defined constituency, large or small. They choose violence when they cannot sell their ideas through words because conventional politicians and their electorates will not buy them. The propaganda of the deed then becomes as important as the propaganda of the word. Both are reflected by the media.

Violent politics and the media

Acts of violent politics are literally meaningless without an explanation of why they have been done. Once a campaign has become established, of course, acts take on a conventional meaning of their own; people interpret them in the same way as they did the last atrocity. Nevertheless, each new one demands new explanations from both sides. Why the terrorists chose that particular time, place and act. What they aimed to achieve by it. Why the incumbents still refuse something which has been demanded with so much force, and what they plan to do now. It is meaningless to bomb and be bombed; there must always be words too – and they are just as much part of the violent political process as the violence itself. Sadly, the words on both sides are often ritual phrases. It is not surprising that violence and countermeasures become rituals too.

The effect of the media on political conflict – violent or conventional – is a subject of endless debate, without firm conclusions about whether it is an amplifier, an attenuator, a catalyst or a spectator. It is commonplace that media coverage of famines, disasters, health scares, scandals, bombs and bullets raises public concern, not simply awareness; and that politicians react accordingly, so the spectator thesis is weak.

The US Secretary of State of the Clinton administration Madeleine Albright, called television the sixteenth member of the Security Council. Nevertheless, there are very experienced people who argue that politicians' response to media hyperbole is superficial and only for show; that news does not skew policy; that there is no 'CNN effect'.[49] Some argue that the media can act as a catalyst, but only when politicians allow it to do so.[50] Others maintain that it does affect policy, and that reporters are key participants in decision-making and policy-making, however much we may wish they were not.[51] One agrees that journalists assist in testing political policies to destruction, but warns of the dangers of initiating a popular over-reaction which will demonise dictators and strengthen their position at home, or an under-reaction, leading to paralysis.[52]

The importance of the media in violent politics is clearly indicated by its extensive bibliography.[53] Paul Wilkinson shows how terrorists exploit the media, and how, in their attempt to gain audiences, the media may reinforce terrorists' messages and hamper countermeasures. The media are actors in violent politics, for good or ill, not passive reporters.[54] However, television, and to a lesser extent print journalism, is highly selective, favouring pictures over words, descriptions over concepts, drama over importance, presentation over explanation, image over substance, immediacy over depth, sound bites over analysis; the new, however trivial, over the old, however important; the local over the international. The facts of what happened are usually well conveyed, and vividly illustrated by eyewitnesses who describe how things felt. The reasons for the event are either taken for granted or briefly explained, moral judgement is quickly passed, and recommendations about what should be done sketched in. Presentation swamps analysis, images hide abstractions, the events of the day loom greater than the long-term context.

Moreover, even the most analytical and thought-provoking television programmes are limited by the medium; the script of a thirty-minute programme would occupy barely one page of a broadsheet newspaper. Repetition dulls the senses; faced with blood and death on screen every day, it is easy to write off long-lasting conflicts as insoluble, their nations as basket cases, and their leaders as savages:

Television has unfortunate strengths as a medium of moral disgust. As a moral mediator between violent men and the audiences whose attention they crave, television images are more effective at presenting consequences than in exploring intentions; more adept at pointing to the corpses than in explaining why violence may, in certain places, pay so well. As a result, television news bears some responsibility for that generalized misanthropy, that irritable resignation toward the criminal folly of fanatics and assassins, which legitimises one of the dangerous cultural moods of our time – the feeling that the world has become too crazy to deserve serious reflection.[55]

There are far fewer radio and TV news services than newspapers and current affairs journals, and because the number of broadcast presenters and editors is so limited, the views and problems discussed are limited too; as indeed is the range of views selected for broadcast from those who contact the stations. Rarely is any outside speaker allowed to raise a new subject, or produce an unhackneyed line on an old one.

Violence is an easy way to capture television time, and for the political arms of terrorist organisations to get as much air time as government politicians, at least on their particular agenda.[56] Indeed, neither can remain silent after an event, lest they are thought uncaring or incompetent. Terrorist spokesmen are practised and glib. Even the worst atrocities can be justified by double-speak – the paramilitaries did it, and we politicians don't control them; the police had a clear warning, but it was ignored; the massacre was done by dissidents within their own community; we don't condone the shooting, but it was an understandable reprisal for the other side's shooting last week.

The initiative lies with the violent politician. He can time events for maximum effect. Government spokesmen have to clear the line they will take, making their response appear slow, shallow, formulaic or repetitious. Publicity during hostage-taking or hijacking incidents may allow terrorists to turn up the emotional heat by setting deadlines for killings or sending out the ears of their victims, and make it difficult to hold the line on a no-concessions policy. Grieving relatives and their viewers want deeds rather than words, but it is difficult to find new reactions to repeated incidents. It is easy to make the government look incompetent by committing a series of similar atrocities – claiming that the government has caused them by not listening, or has not moved fast enough, or has reneged on an agreement. Politicians and police dare not say that they cannot be everywhere at once, and can no more prevent every bomb than they can prevent every burglary or catch every drug dealer. Both sides produce the ritual soundbites, and their supporters become even more polarised.

Furthermore, the more sensitive a government is to public opinion, perhaps as it approaches an election, perhaps when it needs to earn its spurs immediately after one, the more likely it is to be trapped into taking action when inaction might be better. That can lead to gesture politics such as the strategy of the latest bang, in which the latest target becomes the best protected though it is the least likely to be hit again, or the handgun ban after Dunblane though the weapon was incidental to the killer. But if no action were taken the terrorist *would* strike at the same target again, to much greater political effect the second time round; and since the possible imitators of the Dunblane killer are unknown, his weapon is the only practicable target. The form is removed because the substance cannot be; the something-has-to-be-done trap.

The need for governments to act in response to incidents of violent politics can be also very costly. It is not easy to heed Napoleon's warning about torrents of precautions exceeding the real danger.

The media also help to create a climate in which crime and violence are believed to have physical or environmental causes beyond the control of the individual. People are depicted as powerless to help themselves, or to behave in a civilised way: they have no choice. Attacker and attacked are therefore both victims of circumstance: their suffering is equal.

The violent politician has a simple message to sell: the violence has a just cause; it is bound to continue until there is a political settlement; there is nothing he can do to prevent it, but he can tell the government what the men of violence would say if they could speak for themselves; he can negotiate on their behalf, not because they are under his command but because they are of one mind.

By contrast, the conventional politician has a much harder job: explaining to the injured why they were not protected by the security forces. Why they accept that violence is a lesser evil than compromise. Why they do not take stronger countermeasures. Why, if they are taking new initiatives, they are taking them now rather than earlier, before so many were killed and injured; or, if they are not changing their policy, how long things will be allowed to go on before they do.

In short, the violent politician has a simple demand and the conventional politician a complex response; television, radio and the popular press greatly favour the former. This structural bias is more important where people are not generally aware of the complexities of the situation. Those who live in Northern Ireland, for example, are well aware of the background to every act, and can place it in context. Those further away, and less involved, can readily have their judgements formed or prejudices reinforced by the media. They may well follow them up by contributing funds or support, especially if they are expatriates. Pay-to-view terrorism, so to speak, delivered from the comfort of your own home.

The violent politician is helped by the very simplicity of broadcast media. Complex conflicts are reduced to moments which are far from defining in the political sense, but certainly are in folk memories: the Bastille, the storming of the Winter Palace; Sharpeville; Oklahoma City; Bloody Sunday; Enniskillen; the bombing of the World Trade Centre; the assassinations of the Kennedys, the Gandhis, Mountbatten, Rabin. The clips disappear into the archives until the conflict surfaces again, when they are run again. When the problem disappears from the screen or the airwaves, it ceases to exist.

On the other hand, media coverage can have positive effects for the incumbents and negative ones for their opponents. The political message ranks well below the violence and victimisation. Few support violence, and those who do support it lose support themselves. The results of violence have to be moderate if they are not to be counter-productive; terrible violence justifies condign countermeasures. Incidents give both sides an opportunity to speak; the spokesmen for violence may appear evil, hypocritical or unconvincing: condemned from their own mouths. Suspects may be identified from news footage, or traced through re-enactments or the publication of photographs. News blackouts may deny useful information to suspects. Governments can arrange for good news to be presented: new housing, jobs, roads, services; children from divided communities going on trips together; the injured being treated and damage rebuilt.[57]

It is doubtful whether the great proliferation of TV and radio chan-nels, and the great improvements in the technology of information-gathering and dissemination will have much effect on serious political debate: there is a limited market for it compared with sport and cinema, unless politics apes them. That is not unknown, or indeed uncommon, but the simple story lines of 22 men and a ball, or several dead bodies and a puzzled detective, can never be matched by real pol-itics. The US experience has been that news cannot compete with situ-ation comedy on multiple channels, and tends therefore to be concentrated into special news channels which become more and more parochial in the battle to attract viewers and advertisers.[58]

It may be that internet news groups will fill this void; they are dia-logues of equals, where the status of each speaker is unknown, and there are no bylines, no known faces; received ideas are given a thor-ough critique, crazy ones ignored, flamed or deleted. No-one can claim that they only have to shout so loudly because no-one listens: every-one has a voice, and if they use it well they will be listened to. It may be starry-eyed to think that the internet could be a modern day Athenian Forum, but it is unlikely to have no effect on politics. It would be unwise to leave the ground to opponents.

Causes and cures

It is easy to list all the possible factors which might be thought to cause violent politics – or at least the circumstances in which it often arises. If there were a causative basis for violent politics (or conventional poli-tics for that matter) one would expect to see theoretically-based solu-tions to problems – perhaps not as firm as the physical calculations that put spacecraft into orbit, but perhaps as firm as medical treatment or economic prescriptions. The next chapter describes the search for such theories.

2
The Search for Theory

There is clearly a common structure underlying the activity of violent politics: there are common sets of circumstances which can be expected to involve violent politics, and they can be ranked roughly in an order which reflects the likelihood of their 'causing' disorder. Different people react in broadly similar ways to these problems, and the same people react at different times in closely similar ways. There appears to be both a bandwagon or echo effect – kidnapping or riots in one country being copied in another, and a folk memory: people using the same technique in one conflict as they did in another, though they occurred generations apart. The sense of *déjà vu* when reading campaign reports is so overwhelming that it is obvious that there must be an underlying structure to this activity. However, all attempts to determine what it might be and to determine its interactions in any scientific way, have failed.

Structural analysis

World Conflicts lists 113 major wars and insurrections since 1945, causing 15 to 20 million deaths; there have been 300 coups and revolutions, and nearly the same number of assassinations.[1] There were international wars between Israel and its neighbours; North and South Korea; North and South Vietnam; India and Pakistan; Britain, France and Egypt; Iran and Iraq; China and Vietnam; the UK and Argentina; Iraq and Kuwait plus its allies; and civil wars in Greece, China, India, Pakistan, Afghanistan, Cyprus, Lebanon, North Yemen, South Yemen, Ethiopia, Sudan, Somalia, Liberia, Mozambique, Chad, Uganda, Angola, Congo, El Salvador, Cambodia, Bosnia, Georgia, South Ossetia,

Abkhazia, Chechnya and Tajikistan. Some of them have some things in common, but at least as many have not.

At the other end of the scale it would be very easy to compare the form of the assassinations of the Archduke Franz Ferdinand, John F. Kennedy, Lee Harvey Oswald, Malcolm X, Dr Verwoerd, Lord Mountbatten, Indira Gandhi, her son, and Yitzak Rabin, for example; quite easy to compare and contrast the motives of their killers; but very difficult to analyse the outcomes of these acts in a way which said anything sensible about the use of assassination as a technique in violent politics.

In between is a host of uprisings, insurrections, invasions, insurgencies, rebellions, revolts, revolutions, genocides, tribal conflicts, civil disturbances, domestic and international terrorism and banditry. This level of conflict is the one most often subjected to comparative analysis, and indeed rightly so, since the campaigns tend to be driven by similar aims, share a limited number of ideologies or creeds, have the same types of leaders and followers, use similar strategies, tactics and techniques, affect most countries in the world, and be numerous, long-lasting and recurring.

A new danger arises from the physical ability of anyone with a grievance to produce weapons of immense effect with few resources, because of the ready availability of the raw materials for bombs and poisons, the simplicity of making them, the ready availability of instructions via the internet, the multiplicity of high-profile targets, and the ease of access to them.[2] The IRA, ETA, PFLP, groupuscules of left and right, chronic violent politicians so to speak, are restrained by the necessity to make their violent acts serve their political cause rather than lose them support or legitimise counter-action against them. Nihilists are not restrained in the same way: they tend to be loners and religious fanatics who are answerable only to their gods, not to men.

The University of Leiden's assessment that there had been 134 conflicts in 86 of the 185 countries in the world in 1996 was quoted in Chapter 1. There are two problems in trying to analyse this number of armed conflicts into coherent categories. The first is that the number of dimensions is so large: the aims of each conflict; its driving creed; its nature – civil war, guerrilla warfare, coup, insurrection, revolt, massacre, assassination, terrorism – its historical, geopolitical and social background, the scale of death, destruction and the number of refugees; the forces involved on both sides; their strategy, tactics, techniques; the cost, the disruption to everyday life, the duration, the international impact, changes over time.

The second is that the nature of conflict is independent of the reason for it: separatism, tribal domination, religious fundamentalism, national independence, ethnic cleansing, anarchism, millenarianism, fanaticism. The same aims may be pursued in quite different ways, and the same sorts of conflict have completely different aims and backgrounds. Sorting conflicts into a grid with perhaps a dozen forms on one axis and a dozen functions on the other would only have one or two of the 130 conflicts in each box, and even then there would be obvious differences between ones in the same box or on the same axis.

It could of course be argued that all the reasons for conflict can be rolled into one: the urge of one set of people to get what they want from another. That is true, but analytically unhelpful. Equally, it could be said that the actual form of the conflict is immaterial; violent politicians will do whatever works. That is also true, but equally unhelpful to the analyst of strategies, tactics and techniques – and their countermeasures. Either way, our grid collapses into a single box containing all types of conflict and all reasons for them, so we are back where we started.

Similarly, the level of deaths is a useful indicator of the actual state of a conflict, but not of its past or potential. For example the category with the lowest numbers of deaths spans a range from the banditry endemic in many countries, through the remnants of serious conflicts such as those in Serbia, Bosnia and Croatia, to simmering, potentially serious conflicts such as those between India and Pakistan, North and South Korea, Greece and Turkey.

However, the focus for students of violent politics must always be on political substance, which is infinitely subtle, and not on violent forms. If violence is routine, its political effect will be small: people get used to it as they get used to winter and its seasonal storms. Out-of-the-ordinary violence is likely to provoke out-of-the-ordinary political reaction, but the result may be dramatically different from the one intended. Acts of violence are not tools like hammers and chisels, carving out new policies in predictable ways.

Causal models

It is a common belief that conflict is an unnatural process, that it is caused by defects in society, and can be cured by rectifying them:

> Since the frequency of war in a particular population can vary over time, it is generally assumed that war is learned behaviour ... It may

even be realistic (as well as idealist) to think that if we can understand why war and other social problems occur (if we can discover the conditions that produce and perpetuate them), we may be able to do something about these causal conditions and therefore reduce or eliminate the problems.[3]

If war is learned behaviour, then it is so frequent that it might as well be innate. If the deterministic theory of cause and cure is correct, however, it would not matter which it was; war could be eliminated by making the right diagnosis and prescribing the right medicine.

Roderick von Lipsey, for example, offers a conflict model with three phases: prevention, mitigation and resolution, followed by prevention again; with enfranchisement being the key factor: all parties being confident with their stake in the political, social and economic milieu. The model is sound in itself and fits most real-life situations, provided that it allows for any situation containing multiple cycles, and for their not necessarily being in phase with one another.[4]

Like many such models, however, it is an aid to clear thought rather than a guide to action, as James Gow rightly points out:

> While this intellectualisation of empirical experience is of some use towards further thought, it does not, in itself, provide any answers ... There is little... which would help the legions of diplomats, academics and others overtaxed with trying to prevent, mitigate or resolve the conflict between the Serbs and Albanians in Kosovo: all might agree on the need for resolution based on enfranchisement, but cannot see a solution which will mutually satisfy the need for enfranchisement given existing parameters.[5]

Another fundamental difficulty in building theories of violent politics is its inherent unpredictability. For a theory to have explanatory value, let alone predictive value, similar actions must cause similar reactions under similar circumstances in different societies, places and times; in violent politics they do not. That makes it difficult to say whether a given action or policy will produce change in the desired direction, the opposite direction, or no change at all.

Determinism – the contention that the same causes produce the same effects – is the foundation of basic science, and of much in everyday life. No-one seriously doubts that the light will go on when they press the switch, but if it does not, they know where to look for the cause, and what to do to put it right. They expect the sun to rise and set in a pretty predictable way, the tides to rise and fall, and their car to run on petrol every day rather than milk one day and water the next. The weather, however, is not nearly so predictable; every element of it obeys the deterministic laws of physics, but there are so many elements, so many interactions between them, and so few observations in space and time, that forecasts become worse as they look further ahead, and complete surprises become more common.

Individuals are much less predictable, and societies even less. But unpredictability does not mean non-determinism, so the search for social laws paralleling those of the physical sciences is not inherently unreasonable. Marx's historical materialism drove half the world for half a century before the Great Experiment failed.

But predictability does not mean determinism. The whole of history is a search for the causes of events: a rational and believable explanation of how things happened. There are many histories of the same event, and though it may well be evident that some are better than others, it is not self-evident that any one of them can ever be 'true' – not because the explanations are implausible, but because they are syntheses of horrendously complicated events, which can be interpreted in mutually contradictory ways.

It is extremely difficult to define the building blocks of a causal model objectively, or even in a way that commands a reasonable measure of agreement. How are inequalities in wealth, education, or still more difficult, status, to be defined? How is the degree of legitimacy of a government to be graded when democrats would deny the legitimacy of any authoritarian government and some would deny the legitimacy of any capitalist state?

It is of course possible to arrive at imperfect but workable definitions of the parameters of political violence, but there would be a great many of them, most extremely difficult to quantify. It is difficult enough to define what is meant by the historical antipathy between catholics and protestants in Northern Ireland, for example, though it obviously exists. It is still more difficult to rank its strength on a scale, or even to say whether it is greater at one time than another. It is impossible to find out how much antipathy existed on a given day, as one might look up weather records to see what the rainfall was. Antipathy can only be inferred from records of people's behaviour, which in turn poses questions of interpretation, and creates circular definitions.

After the problems of definition and quantification, the problem of exploration – of finding out exactly what did happen in each of the situations under examination in sufficient detail to define the role of each of the key parameters, their interactions and the changes over time: a daunting prospect. The number of parameters cannot be reduced without destroying the usefulness of the model – though this is an approach often adopted. Their interactions cannot be left unexplored, because there would then be no way of knowing that vital ones had not been left out – though again this is not an unusual approach. Furthermore, facts are notoriously difficult to come by in times of conflict, when secrets must be kept and reputations preserved.

Finally, the problem of modelling, again horrendous, again often ducked. It is striking how few technical analyses of political conflict conclude with anything more than a page or two of banalities. The writers may claim that they did not set out to build models, or theorise, but nevertheless that is what they are doing – like *le bourgeois gentilhomme*, they speak prose whether they know it or not. Every explanation or judgement rests on a network of assumptions – explicit or hidden – which constitutes a model. For a model to be useful, it must be able to predict, and thus to act as a guide to the likely consequences of various courses of action. It must not leave out any of the key parameters or fail to specify their interactions correctly, which means that it must be huge, and very complex. This is more easily illustrated in the case of economics, where the parameters are more readily quantifiable, and model-building a more usual way of going about things.

In the days when brain and pen were the only tools for dealing with complexity, quite complicated economic theories could be built up, but their predictive value could not be tested because the facts could not be collected and processed before they were overtaken by events. Now that computers have made this possible, forecasts are becoming more accurate, though they still remain far from perfect. This has been achieved, not by the discovery of some great unifying principle which makes everything simple, but by building ever more complex models which approximate ever more closely to real life. The vast models which computers make possible have greatly improved the accuracy of weather forecasting – as have satellites, which give a new view of the world, quite literally.

However, no-one engaged in the analysis of the economy or the weather would seriously suggest that a breakthrough into simplicity is at all likely: all the advances are likely to come from their being able to handle ever more complex and thus ever more realistic models. The prospect of being able to do this in the political sciences is dim.

The perils of prediction in politics are easily illustrated. In 1968, one study concluded:

> In the Middle East, revolutionary turbulence can well be expected in Algeria, Libya, Egypt, Sudan, Jordan, Saudi Arabia, Aden and South Arabia, the Oman conglomerate, Iraq and Syria. Such turbulence will occur for a galaxy of reasons. But expectations of this kind certainly do not preclude revolution in other areas, such as Afghanistan and Tunisia, whose current stability is above that as a whole ... In Latin America, Mexico, Costa Rica, Uruguay and Chile seem most likely to avoid revolutionary upheavals. Haiti at the other extreme appears to be on the point of explosion. A few countries like Venezuela and El Salvador have achieved at least temporary settlements of internal political quarrels and can be expected to maintain their regimes constitutionally for the moment. Others like Cuba, Paraguay and Nicaragua, will avoid serious trouble through iron control by police and military forces.[6]

By 1980, of the twelve middle eastern countries mentioned in the first sentence, none had entirely escaped 'revolutionary turbulence', but Libya's monarchy was the only one of them to have fallen – to a coup; so had the Emperor of Ethiopia, who was not tipped. Sudan's civil war, which was in progress when the study was written, ended with the state intact, while the Oman successfully defeated an insurrection in Dhofar. On the other hand, unlisted Iran had had a full-scale old-fashioned revolution, while equally old-fashioned wars were in progress on the Iraq/Iran border, the Horn of Africa, the Western Sahara and the Lebanon, to name but four. Afghanistan had had several coups, followed by a Soviet invasion. In Latin America, five out of the authors' ten guesses were wrong: neither Chile nor Uruguay had avoided 'revolutionary upheavals', but Haiti had. Nicaragua had had a successful revolution, and one was in progress in El Salvador.

The authors were therefore wise to conclude 'but precise predictions will remain difficult to make'.

Although the search for a mechanism, a model, has perfectly respectable antecedents; it is almost certainly doomed to fail – not just because of the difficulties of definition, quantification, exploration and modelling which have already been discussed, but for a much more fundamental reason – the presence of will, of choice.

The mathematics of game theory affords a way of dealing with choice, but only when the options and goals can be clearly labelled and, perhaps equally importantly, when there are very few of them. It has proved remarkably difficult to apply game theory to social issues, and it has certainly produced no results which show any promise of its being any more useful in the future.

However, will could be regarded as mechanical in itself, since humans are themselves biological structures, and their memories, decision-making, feelings and actions are all mediated by physical and chemical processes in their bodies. Even so, it is a long step from a social concept to the physical representation of that concept in the brain, and even if the mechanism of mind were understood, it is far from certain that the mechanism of minds, in the plural, would simply be an extension of this.

So the conclusions we can draw are simple, if depressing: the search for a general theory of political violence, or even for theories limited in time and circumstance, although pursued with great vigour, has not been successful. More work might yield results, but it seems likely that the difficulties of identifying the key parameters, defining them in a universally acceptable way, quantifying them, extracting them from real life, determining their interaction, dealing with the complexity of the real world and building hypothetical models from them, will prove insuperable in practice. The search for theories in social science which parallel those of the natural sciences, however poorly, is likely to founder on the fundamental difficulty introduced into the social sciences by will, or 'reflexivity': the fact that people think for themselves, and react to things differently and unpredictably. The objects with which physical sciences deal do not do that. The physical basis of will may one day be found, but when it is, it is likely to involve totally new concepts rather than extensions of the present sciences. Workers in the field of machine intelligence, however good they are becoming at imitating the functions of the brain with computers, show few signs of discovering the actual workings of the brain. The mathematics of mind is unlikely to be the mathematics of mathematicians and machines.

The fall of the Berlin Wall, and the revolutions of 1989 onwards, led to the fall of Marxism as an ideology in all but the few remaining communist countries – and perhaps it had died even there. In the 1970s it was said, not entirely in jest, that there were more Marxists in the University of Oxford than in the whole of the USSR. Hegel had argued that history, in the sense of a broad evolution of human societies advancing toward a final goal, would end in communism. Many believed he was right, especially after the failure of protectionism, fascist corporatism, absolute monarchy and other dictatorships.

However by the 1990s it was clear that he was not; Francis Fukuyama argued that it would instead end in western liberal democracy, market economics and global capitalism.[7]

Post-modernism

The death of rational, 'scientific', Marxism has given birth to counter-scientific post-modernism, where every 'narrative' is as valid as any other, and none are 'privileged':

> Instead of defining it as true belief – or perhaps, justified true belief – knowledge for the sociologist is whatever people take to be knowledge. It consists of those beliefs which people confidently hold to and live by ... Of course knowledge must be distinguished from mere belief. This can be done by reserving the word 'knowledge' for what is collectively endorsed, leaving the individual and idiosyncratic to count as mere belief.[8]

> For the relativist there is no sense attached to the idea that some standards or beliefs are really rational as distinct from merely locally accepted as such.[9]

It is hard to see how a postmodernist ideology could guide conventional political action, as Marxism did. If truth is relative, and what is actually believed in a given situation is just as valid as justified true belief, then there is no rational way of countering such a belief by persuasion, shame or reward: the modes of non-violent politics.

On the other hand, violent politicians can take comfort from the acceptance of their view of the world as being as valid as anyone else's, and therefore a legitimate reason for action. Violent political dissidents taking this view could not actually say so, however, without inviting their opponents to make a parallel claim to legitimacy for their own world view, and their own countermeasures.

Postmodernism and moral relativism have nothing to contribute to conventional politics, since they deny the legitimacy of its modes: persuasion, shame and reward. They have a lot to contribute to violent politics, because they enhance the legitimacy of its modes: prevention, fear and force; an effect unlikely to be intended by their advocates, but nonetheless unavoidable.

Psychological correctness also contributes more to violent politics than to the conventional kind. Its belief that human culture simply writes on a biological slate blank except for five senses plus a few basic drives such as hunger, thirst, aggression, fear and sex leads, for example, to the Seville Statement on Violence, later adopted by UNESCO and several scientific organisations:

> It is scientifically incorrect to say that we have inherited a tendency to make war from our animal ancestors.
> It is scientifically incorrect to say that war or other violent behavior is genetically programmed into our human nature.
> It is scientifically incorrect to say that in the course of human evolution there has been a selection for aggressive behavior more than for other kinds of behavior.
> It is scientifically incorrect to say that humans have a "violent brain".
> It is scientifically incorrect to say that war is caused by "instinct" or any single motivation... We conclude that biology does not condemn humanity to war, and that humanity can be freed from the bondage of biological pessimism and empowered with confidence to undertake the transformative tasks needed in the International Year of Peace and in the years to come.[10]

This belief, that violent conflict is an unnatural act which arises only in unnatural circumstances, leads to at least three unfortunate consequential beliefs: that eliminating the putative causes of conflict is the only correct treatment; that 'state violence' does not differ in principle from violence against the state and indeed may be worse since it seeks to preserve what ought to be changed and may grossly violate the human rights of its citizens; and that since there is no natural, good, or even acceptable form of violence, there are no natural, good or even acceptable rules which ought to be applied to it.

The cause of countering violence would be better served, not by denying reality, but by understanding how faith arises which is so strong that people who do not share it can be killed – in good faith, so to speak.

Evolutionary sociobiology

Man has evolved over thousands of generations, not the hundred or two since the dawn of civilisation. For all but one percent of our existence, humans lived as foragers in small nomadic bands and our minds evolved accordingly: for the Stone Age, not for the Age of Aquarius; writing, schools, governments, social institutions, medicine, law and policemen are newcomers. Nevertheless, natural selection does not pull the strings of behaviour directly; it is 'the outcome of an internal struggle among many mental modules, and is played out on the chessboard of opportunities and constraints defined by other people's behavior. Behavior itself did not evolve; what evolved was the mind'.[11]

The theories of evolutionary psychology and social biology have more to offer the student of violent politics than determinism, historical materialism, or the wishful thinking of political or psychological correctness that culture is inherently separate from human nature, and not a complex and difficult product of it. That way lies not just liberation theology, but the re-education camps of the Gulag. To quote Pinker again:

> But when we look around us, we sense that these simplistic theories [about people being conditioned, taught, brainwashed] just don't ring true. Our mental life is a noisy parliament of competing factions. In dealing with others, we assume they are as complicated as we are, and we guess what they are guessing we are guessing they are guessing. Children defy their parents from the moment they are born, and confound all expectations thereafter: one overcomes horrific circumstances to lead a satisfying life, another is granted every comfort but grows up a rebel without a cause. A modern state loosens its grip, and its peoples enthusiastically take up the vendettas of their grandparents. And there are no robots.[12]

Survival of the fittest is not survival of the fiercest, because all human societies, and indeed most animal ones, require co-operation too. Both have survival value. Both have therefore been built-in during evolution, and have become part of our inheritance.

Violent politics (and indeed war) does not arise automatically from people genetically or culturally programmed to behave thus. The antagonists do not differ in any fundamental way from one another; indeed, they are often neighbours, and rather similar. Their main difference lies not in their biology or their culture, but in the ideas in their heads. It might be, of course, that *those* are biologically or culturally determined, as many have argued, particularly those wanting to excuse evildoing, but the chain between cause and effect is too tenuous to be credible.

Sociological theories

Much work has been devoted to building theories about political violence, attempting to trace the causes of violence in society to frustration, relative deprivation, oppression and so on, and to determine the parameters which make for stable societies. The search for a model is indispensable to a theoretical approach, for without one no situation can be compared with another, no conclusions drawn, no lessons for the future extracted. The modelling may be very rough, many elements in real life being grouped together into one element of the model, but every judgement on the cause of a given situation, or the effects of a given set of circumstances, presupposes the existence of a model: at least one which existed in those particular circumstances, if not more generally.

However, if the model only applies to a particular time and place it is not a contribution to a general theory, economic, political or whatever. If the scholar is to make a step towards a general theory, he must show that his theory applies to every circumstance, or at least to a well-defined set of circumstances.

Success in this field is hard to come by. An explanation of political violence will be regarded as successful by historians of the period and by those who lived through it if it conforms to their experience and judgement, but *quot homines, tot sententiae*. On the other hand, to the practising violent politician, be he insurgent or counter-insurgent, a successful explanation is one which yields the results he wants when it is applied. Success in these terms, too, has so far eluded the theory builders, though not for want of trying.

Many theorists have tried to extract models from real life, examining one or more campaigns and arriving at sensible-sounding and practical conclusions. Unfortunately, these all turn out to be wrong, at least in the sense that however true they may be about the circumstances investigated in the study, the opposite can be shown to be true in a different time and place, or even worse, in apparently similar times and places. If there are two different models, how can a rational choice be made in a third set of circumstances?

The intellectual and practical difficulties of adopting such an approach were well illustrated by the failure of Project Camelot, a very ambitious American attempt to:

> determine the feasibility of developing a general social system model which would make it possible to predict and influence politically significant aspects of social change in the developing world.[13]
>
> Camelot is approaching the problem of internal conflict from the standpoint of developing an explicit framework for the extensive collection of historical and contemporary data necessary to

scientifically and systematically analyse the process by which strains and tensions in a society may lead to internal conflict.[14]

Project Camelot was envisaged as lasting three to four years, costing one-and-a-half million dollars a year, and taking place in half a dozen Latin American countries. The idea was floated in a circular to a number of academics in December 1964, and the research design was begun. In March 1965, however, the US Marines landed in the Dominican Republic to restore order, and when opposition groups in Chile discovered a couple of months afterwards that Camelot researchers were working in their country, there was such an outcry that the Project was cancelled. The Americans were accused of espionage; suspicion and mistrust spilled onto American agencies which were not involved with the Project at all, and raised the political temperature in Chile, creating, in the words of one of those involved, 'a self-fulfilling research objective'.

The researchers could not gain access to the data, nor to the people involved in disorder, without themselves becoming, in essence, part of the problem they were researching. The boundaries of the system to be studied proved never-ending; nor was there any obvious limit to the number of parameters, nor indeed common agreement on what they were. The Project had been organised by the Department of Defense, and it was frustrated at every turn by the Department of State, partly in defence of its bureaucratic territory, and partly out of fear (which proved justified) that the Project would cause the very trouble it was seeking to cure. For their part, the social scientists employed by the DoD suspected that they were being manipulated by intelligence and foreign affairs agents; many would not join the Project because they saw that they would inevitably become 'scholars in armour' and partisan.

Even so, the work that was done on Camelot and similar projects (for example Project Simpatico on rural politics in Colombia, Project Revolt on Francophone Canada, and Project Michelson, an analysis of the goals and goal structure of the US, USSR and China) showed no promise of yielding anything approaching a workable theory of internal violence, while the pre-eminence of the systems approach led to exaggerated model-building techniques that obfuscated the issues instead of clarifying them.

Other theorists have therefore started at the other end, building a hypothetical model, then trying to refine and adjust it to fit real life. The actual results produced by such attempts to build models from the bottom up have been meagre. Ted Gurr's sociological work on rebellion ends with a few pages of advice on strategies which governments and insurgents should adopt against each other, but it is advice that is so self-evident that any protagonist who had not thought of it for himself would deserve to lose, and so general that it provides no practical guide to action.[15] Such reductionism has not yet paid dividends on the intellectual capital invested in it.

Yet other theorists, recognising the shortcomings of the top–down and bottom–up approaches, start somewhere in the middle, selecting not a particular campaign but a particular phenomenon, a sample from the spectrum of political violence, such as terrorism. This certainly brings together a number of common factors that are selected out by the other two approaches, but it also creates new problems. Is it sensible to talk of terrorism as a single phenomenon when its protagonists range from large groups, such as the PLO, which operated transnationally with international recognition and much international support, to tiny nihilist groups, and the countries affected range from West Germany to Bolivia? Such selective studies may illuminate the problem from a different angle, but they have been no more successful at generating theories than the others.

Four major difficulties underlie all of these attempts to create theories of political violence:

- selecting and quantifying the key parameters;
- exploring the complex interactions between them;
- constructing a model which represents both the parameters and their interactions accurately enough to explain and predict;
- dealing with human will.

Sociological theories have provided useful insights into political violence, of an inductive kind; the difficulties of running the process the other way round, and deducing what should be done in a given case remain overwhelming. Lord Dahrendorf's statements about political structures were made *à propos* the revolutions of 1989, but apply equally to those of 1968, and to the genesis of the Northern Ireland conflict in particular:

- Monopolistic classes may suppress opposition but this merely turns manifest conflicts into latent conflicts.
- The more rigidly monopolistic classes enforce their rule, the more absolute will opposition demands become.

- Latent conflict becomes manifest once certain political conditions of organisation are given.
- In a monopolistic structure a spark of hope for change will set the powder keg of revolution on fire.
- (In such a situation, *glasnost* and *perestroika* are incompatible: freedom of speech and association means revolution, and restructuring can only be achieved with a high degree of control.)
- Revolutionary change leads to the replacement of ruling groups but also to the dismantling of the machinery of government.
- The revolutionary process involves the collapse of the centre, thus a tendency towards anarchy and anomy.
- Anarchy and anomy lead to calls for the (re-)establishment of effective power, even by groups or individuals which make (old or new) monopolistic claims.
- There is no straight and painless road from monopolistic structures of power to pluralism and democracy.[16]

It is obvious that humans are inherently violent animals, and equally obvious that this is part of our genetic heritage. We could not otherwise have become who we are: evolution would have eliminated us. But evolution has also endowed us with the ability to over-ride our instinctual behaviour as a deliberate act of will – or indeed to give way to it, which is no less an act of will, however much we may deny that when it is convenient to do so.

Nature is savage.[17] Civilisation seeks to master both the physical inconveniences of nature and the atavistic inheritance of man: no societies, no institutions, no protection. We cannot be utopian about this (or rather we can, but it fails), because the basic concepts of a civilised society – *liberté, égalité, fraternité* – themselves conflict. Political problems are aporetic – they have no logical solutions. Morality, politics, rights and laws overlap. They are not coterminous.

Millions of words have been written about the nature of man and society, and millions more will be. There is no need to add to them here, but what is necessary is to set out the themes on which this book is based.

Conflict is both natural and necessary, however much utopians maintain that it is not, or that it could be made unnecessary:

In *Human Universals*,[18] the anthropologist Donald Brown has assembled the traits that as far as we know are found in all human cultures. They include prestige and status, inequality of power and wealth, property, inheritance, reciprocity, punishment, sexual modesty, sexual regulation, sexual jealousy, a male preference for young women as sexual partners, a division of labor by sex (including more child care by women and greater public political dominance by men), hostility to other groups, and conflict within the group, including violence, rape, and murder. The list should come as no surprise to anyone familiar with history, current events, or literature. There are a small number of plots in the world's fiction and drama, and the scholar Georges Polti claims to have listed them all.[19] More than eighty percent are defined by adversaries (often murderous), by tragedies of kinship or love, or both. In the real world, our life stories are largely stories of conflict: the hurts, guilts and rivalries inflicted by parents, siblings, spouses, lovers, friends and competitors.[20]

Life contains both conflicts of interest and coincidence of interest, so it contains both conflict and co-operation. Neither can be avoided, or should be if they could; both are necessary for individual and collective prosperity. 'Conflict is the great stimulus of change, and our task in a world in which change is our only hope is to domesticate conflict by rules, by the constitution of liberty.'[21]

However, change is dangerous; it can as easily result in unexpected turbulence as in steady evolution; it can be the trigger for an explosion. An East German bureaucratic muddle over the arrangements for visits across the Berlin Wall after the Soviet withdrawal was the trigger for the fall of the Wall itself, and reunification. It is reasonably easy to explain why after the event, but few predicted it, and they were ridiculed when they did.

It is not surprising, then, that the evolution of terrorist – and counter-terrorist – doctrine is so slow. Every new move is a gamble, which may pay off or may backfire. Hierarchies on both sides inhibit new ideas because of this, and few are willing to try and perhaps be proved wrong. Military and police training is usually based on applying doctrine rather than evolving it – and in the early stages of a campaign, so many resources are deployed on expansion, recruitment and training that thinking about effectiveness takes second place.

Soldiers and policemen may also be inhibited because politicians and other civilians are inherently suspicious of them: they live dangerously, and are thought to be dangerous themselves. Their life is tough, and they are thought to be tough on life. There is a bit of envy for the man or woman who has heard the crack of bullets. People in the security forces are sensitive to this, and know that if they propose dramatic action the reaction is that 'they would say that wouldn't they' – so they do not. In any case strong action may well have strong and unpredictable consequences, so there are prudential reasons for avoiding it too.

But that makes the lot of the terrorist easier, less dangerous, more rewarding. He can make the incumbent government look foolish, leaden-footed, weak-willed, indecisive, ineffectual and passive. To prevent that, governments have to take action, preferably lots of action, preferably highly visible action; whether it is effective or not can be left until later. For example, a standard – and effective – tactic of the Buddhist nationalist JVP[22] in Sri Lanka was to assassinate members of groups, including Buddhist priests, *pour encourager les autres*, and to send death threats to the powerful, requiring them to act in its favour.[23] It was used to being obeyed. Then, in what was to have been its final drive to take over the government in late 1989, and in what may have seemed a natural extension of its hitherto successful measures, the JVP announced that it would attack their families if the armed forces did not disobey government directives to move against it.[24] Instead, the armed forces violently counter-attacked the JVP. Its principal leader was captured in November, and shot. The last surviving leader was killed in December, and the revolt collapsed, having cost over 8500 deaths in six months, and tens of thousands since the JVP insurrection began in 1983.[25] The family of the Deputy Inspector General of Police was destroyed by a JVP mine; he became a hero of the destruction of the JVP, and was portrayed in the press as a victim executing a righteous revenge.[26]

Political drama often sneaks up unseen: *les événements de mai* and the outbreak of the Troubles in Northern Ireland, the fall of the Shah and the rise of Ayatollah Khomeini, the Argentine invasion of the Falklands, the rise of Gorbachev, the Soviet withdrawal from Eastern Europe, the breakup of the former Soviet Union and the re-balkanisation of the Balkans, the dramatic economic collapse of the Asian Tigers and Japan in 1998. Once such things have begun, it is as difficult to see an end to them as it was to foresee the beginning. What is the trigger that will make everything fall back into place again? What are the policies that will bring a steady state of order out of a steady state of conflict?

People are unused to such uncertainty in everyday life: they may not know exactly what the weather will be next week, but they do know that winter will be colder than summer, the sun rise later and set earlier. If they follow the recipe for a cake it does not turn out to be shepherd's pie. Why no recipe for peace and good order?

The answer is that the huge number of parameters in violent and conventional politics, economics, international relations, national and international law, and the immense complexity of their ever-changing interconnections, means that the search for grand, comprehensive, coherent and verifiable (or, to be thoroughly scientific, non-falsifiable) theories is forever doomed. There are sound(-ish) theories aplenty in subsets of this complexity. The relationship between interest rates, inflation, monetary and fiscal policy, for example, is well enough understood to guide action in real life; but there are still enough uncertainties to keep lots of economists hard at work.

It is not possible to assemble a grand theory of violent politics. It is indeed possible to build coherent theories from abstractions such as identity, power, threats, needs, deprivation, norms, beliefs, ideologies, values, perceptions and intent.[27] However these are not physical entities like mass, velocity, temperature, pressure, resistance or energy. The physical theories which link those, and have enormous predictive power and practical application, cannot be transposed into the social sciences, because people are not inanimate objects which react in predictable ways when affected by forces of one kind or another.[28] They think for themselves. They act independently. There are no Newton's laws of emotion.

Every abstraction such as 'enfranchisement' is a box which will accommodate lots of disparate, indefinable, contentious or even contradictory facts and figures without strain, and elements can be moved from box to box if they look untidy where they are, maintaining the structural integrity of the reductionist model, albeit at the expense of its intellectual integrity.

The analogy of a butterfly's wing triggering a hurricane is often made as if there would have been no hurricane had there been no butterfly. That could be true for chaotic systems in nature, where 'chaotic' takes its scientific sense of extreme sensitivity to starting conditions, rather than its everyday meaning of 'disorganised'. In violent politics the butterflies' wings tend to be sledgehammer blows, which everyone remembers afterwards. It is true that some small events do cause (or are followed by) great changes, and have lasting effects. It is also true that some great events are not followed by great changes, and are remembered, if at all, as milestones along the road rather than as signposts to a different destination. By contrast, defining events tend to happen in times of great uncertainty and confusion – 'chaos' in its ordinary sense. But it is a mistake to extrapolate this to 'chaos' in its scientific sense, and to attribute too much causation to the triggering event, because in such conditions any event would have done, just as touching any card, not a particular one, can cause a house of cards to collapse. The analogy here is not the butterfly and the hurricane, but an avalanche triggered by a single skier.

Theory-building is a useful way of dissecting real life, providing different views of all its complexities, and encouraging insight. It can certainly be a guide to action, but never a prescription. Nor can it ever be. Nor should anyone think it so.

Lessons from experience

Having ruled out, at least for the foreseeable future, the possibility of producing a theory of political violence with any predictive value and thus of any practical use, what can be done to help those who have to decide what to do for the best – the civil power: the government of a state; its security forces, or of course the insurgents themselves. For there must be some lessons from experience, and any guide is better than none.

A number of broad principles have emerged from the mass of studies over the years. Even these, however, suffer from two main faults: the principles extracted by most writers from their experience or study are so general that they afford little guide to concrete action, while the detailed lessons are so specific to the area or period of the campaign that it is impossible to transplant them.

To take Sir Robert Thompson's excellent book on defeating communist insurgency as an example. From his experience in Malaya and Vietnam he set out five principles.[29] The first of these is that the government must have a clear political aim: to establish and maintain a free, independent and united country which is politically and economically stable and viable. Unexceptionable – but what government would not have such an aim, or would deserve to retain the loyalty of its subjects if it did not?

Thompson's second principle, that the government must function in accordance with the law, suffers from disadvantages of a different kind. He makes it quite clear that the government is free to change the law to its own advantage, so cynics would not be unjustified if they argued that this principle, at least in the form in which it was expressed, was sophistry. The governments in Malaya and South Vietnam were in a position to enact practically any law they liked; this is far from being the case in many democracies. Nor does he allow for a breakdown of the judicial system of the sort that happened in Palestine before the end of the Mandate or in Ireland in 1919/20,[30] nor for it simply failing to deal swiftly enough with lawbreakers. Furthermore it is evident that many countries have dealt with insurgency very successfully using techniques outside any law, so operating within it cannot be a precondition for success.

Thompson's third principle, that the government must have an overall plan, is open to the same objections as the first. What government would not have such a plan, or would admit it if it had not? The aim is not to have a plan, but to have an effective one; how does the government determine its priorities? How does it solve the innumerable problems which arise because change does not benefit people equally, even when it does not actually rob Peter to pay Paul?

The fourth principle, that the government must give priority to defeating the political subversion not the guerrillas, is again common sense – but how much priority? What proportion of its scarce resources dare it devote to the long haul of defeating subversion, which is invisible, kills nobody and inconveniences few, while its people are being killed in the streets and the hills?

Thompson's final principle, that in the guerrilla phase of an insurgency, the government must secure its base areas first, is qualified in his very next sentence 'This principle should to a large extent be reversed in the build up phase, before open insurgency starts.' What if there are no such phases; if they are unrecognisable; if they come at different times in different areas; if they ebb and flow? So, even sound broad lessons are less than adequate guides to governments or rebels seeking a strategy; they simply tell them that they must keep their balance – and that they knew already.

Political theories are inductive, but political practice is deductive. The richness of detail removed by the inductive process cannot be recreated by the process of deduction, which greatly limits the value of theory to the practising revolutionary or counter-revolutionary.

Sadly, statements of principle are valueless in themselves. They have to be vastly expanded in order to be to be translated into action. Much of Lenin's writing, for example, was devoted to highly practical, detailed and specific advice – matters of day-to-day tactics. *What Is To Be Done?* contains at least 15 000 words on newspapers alone.[31]

The difficulty of actually putting into practice simple, and politically irresistible, principles such as 'land to the tiller' or 'land or work' can be illustrated by the situation in Cuba after Castro's revolution. Before 1959, 80 per cent of Cuba's export earnings came from sugar, 90 per cent of which was grown on moderately-sized farms owned or tenanted by the Cuban occupier, who employed wage labourers.[32] The agricultural sector accounted for about 100 000 landowners, about the same number of tenants (both groups very much too large and powerful to have their land expropriated) and 500 000 agricultural labourers: 35 per cent of the working population.

The 1959 Agrarian Reform Law gave ownership rights to all types of tenants, and restricted the amount of land which could be owned by any one farmer to 400 hectares. The remaining land was to be formed into co-operatives worked by the former labourers. The owner occupiers were allowed to choose the land they wanted to keep, so the land available for the co-operatives was scattered, and of course the least productive. Agricultural work, which had been seasonal even at the best of times, now fell away sharply. The farmers had less land, and therefore less need for labour, while the ex-tenants found that they could not get credit from the banks because of the uncertainties created by the revolution, and could not afford labour, nor to invest without return for the five or six years required for the other cash crop, coffee, to grow to maturity.[33]

The new co-operatives were inefficient, since there were no skilled farmers to run them properly; they were unpopular, because the government refused to divide them into smallholdings, as that would have created a totally private agricultural sector. Nor would they allow the former peasants to grow what they liked, since enough sugar had to be produced to keep up export earnings, and grown in specific places so that it could be reaped efficiently, unmixed with other crops. The peasants thus lost effective control over what was supposed to have been their land.

In politics, simple problems do not have simple solutions.

Another frequent fault in the study of political violence is an obsession with the violence itself, whether it be rioting, guerrilla warfare, or terrorism. Violence is unusual, dramatic and exciting – it is often possible to spot the quickening of the pulse, even in cold print, when the details of violence are discussed. Excitement narrows horizons, and the greater the excitement, the more the narrowing of perception. That may be why much popular writing on political violence is hagiographic in tone. The writers yield to drama and emotion, and cease to be analytical, or even to use their common sense:

There is only one means of defeating an insurgent people who will not surrender, and that is extermination. There is only one way to control a territory that harbours resistance, and that is to turn it into a desert. Where these means cannot, for whatever reason, be used, the war is lost ... [Guerrillas] have found an effective counter-strategy against the tyranny of wealth and the tyranny of power. Because of it ... the privileged castes of any society [cannot] oppress the poor or the disenfranchised within it. Because of it, the war machines grind to a halt, and the ideal of a human society that is both just and free is brought a step closer to reality.[34]

Conclusions

The extreme complexity of the conduct of violent politics, whatever the simplicity of its objectives, is the greatest single obstacle to success in it: it is self-evident that over-simplified perceptions of a situation must lead to over-simplified prescriptions for it. It takes a long time for an outsider to construct in his mind a model of the political realities of an unfamiliar situation which is sufficiently rich to enable him to make reasonable judgements of what will work and what will not. Furthermore, it is doubtful whether the complexity of the ways in which the political situation has changed over time can really be understood except by people who have themselves lived through the key events of the period. Outsiders have not been conspicuously successful in understanding or resolving internal conflicts.

There does not appear to be any practical possibility at present of modelling the factors involved in violent politics, or any other sort for that matter, sufficiently well to form a valid guide to action in particular circumstances, except inside people's heads, which may be why statesmanship, by and large, is an old man's game. No external model – mathematical, logical, conceptual; quantifiable or non-quantifiable – is anything but a gross oversimplification. Nothing much should be expected of them.

Although the best possible models exist in the minds of people who have studied their own society and have lived through its politics, it does not follow that the decisions they make from these models will always be right. They may be biased by ideology, upbringing or experience, or disabled by lack of intelligence. Or by luck: time and chance happeneth to them all.

The next step

Chapter 3 outlines the search for practical strategies for waging violent politics. Chapters 4, 5 and 6 examine the politics, violence and countermeasures in a case study: Northern Ireland during the thirty years of the Troubles from 1968 to 1998. The succeeding chapters examine six options for dealing with violent politics: treating it as common crime; treating it as treason, sedition or other offences against the state; declaring martial law; using emergency legislation; treating it as internal war, or dealing with it outside the law.

3
The Search for Strategy

Introduction

The strategies of violent politics that are in vogue at any particular time are clearly conditioned not only by the circumstances of the time and place but by contemporary received ideas.

The key doctrine of this century has been Marxism – for its startling new look at the world, its fertility in generating offshoots and variants, and for opening up the armed dialogues which gave rise to the socialist revolutions in Russia and China and the fascist revolutions in Italy and Germany, to name but four.

In examining strategies, a distinction can be made between the deterministic theories of classical Marxism, and the voluntaristic doctrines exemplified by Leninism: between a belief in the historical inevitability of revolutionary change, driven by the economic base, and the belief that revolutions are made rather than born. It is a useful distinction, because deterministic doctrines, whether those of Marx himself, of the New Left, or of Guevara and Debray, have conspicuously failed to fulfil their promise. The voluntarist schools of left and right, on the other hand, have had a fair measure of success, fair in that when they have failed, it was not because their principles (such as they had; they were often remarkably short of them) were wrong, but because in practice they were unable to mobilise a base sufficient for them to win.

Marxism

The success of the Bolshevik Revolution, unexpected though it was, gave heart to believers in the inevitability of Marxist revolution.

However, it is now abundantly clear that in the western countries in which capitalism is most advanced, it has adapted to socialism in ways which make revolution ever less likely. The more primitive and unsubtle the form of capitalism, the more likely it is that there will be economic stresses which may – but not must – precipitate revolution, or at least be a contributory factor, for there are others, nationalism, tribalism and religion for example, which have proved at least as important.

As capitalism has not proved inherently incapable of reform, a revolutionary wishing to destroy it must work against it, not for it, in order to aid it towards its Armageddon. Even when capital has behaved as Marx and Engels thought it would, and has become concentrated in fewer and fewer hands, as for example in Nicaragua and other Latin American countries, the successful revolutionaries have been those who fought the system, not those who joined it to help it on its way to its historically inevitable collapse.

In a very real sense, the industrial democracies of today, even those which most recoil from the label, *are* socialist, while the few remaining states which achieved Marxist socialism by revolution or conquest, and which do have near-universal public ownership of the means of production and exchange have demonstrably failed to eliminate exploitation and privilege thereby. Furthermore, the present-day standards of democratic freedom, social welfare and equity in the neo-capitalist societies of the West compare favourably with those in the neo-socialist states, while past experience of war, purges and other inhumanities reflect no credit on either system.

The assimilation of democratic socialism by the West, the increasing diffusion of capital and class, and the political inflexibility and social poverty of states constituted on Marxist lines, destroyed the intellectual basis for Marxism. As Kolakowski's monumental review concluded:

> The influence that Marxism has achieved, far from being the result or proof of its scientific character, is almost entirely due to its prophetic, fantastic and irrational elements. Marxism is a doctrine of bland confidence that a paradise of universal satisfaction is awaiting us just around the corner. Almost all the prophecies of Marx and his followers have already been proved to be false, but this does not disturb the spiritual certainty of the faithful, any more than it did in the case of the chiliastic sects: for it is a certainty not based on any empirical premises or supposed 'historical laws' but simply on the psychological need for certainty. In this sense Marxism performs the function of a religion, and its efficacy is of a religious character.[1]

Marxism once provided the image of a better future, and a prescription for getting there, to huge groups of people: workers, peasants, students. The failure of communism and the death of Marxism mean that in the new millennium there is only one saleable non-authoritarian political system – liberal (or not too obviously illiberal) democracy, and market (if regulated) capitalism. Far from wanting to overthrow the system and replace it with another, the excluded and the wretched of the earth now want to join it. Violent politics is unlikely to buy them entry.

There are of course the traditional recruiting areas of Marxism in developing countries, but leaders able and willing to exploit them have grown fewer since the fall of communism. The once-ubiquitous Marxist guerrillas and groupuscules have shrunk in number – but the number of fundamentalist parties, guerrillas and terrorist groups has grown; one religion has replaced another.

Sendero Luminoso, The Shining Path of Peru, was a curious survivor of traditional People's War, at least until its leader, Abimael Guzmán, the self-styled 'Fourth Sword of Marxism', was captured in 1992 after a Guevara-style blunder, and in 1993, from jail, called upon his followers to repent and return to conventional politics. Sendero started in the conventional way as a rebel faction of the Peruvian Communist Party, redefining Peru's Indians as peasants, and mobilising them in the traditional way by fire and sword. By 1990, from a standing start in 1980, Shining Path operations had resulted in one-third of Peru, containing half its population, being under military control in Emergency Zones. By 1992, bombs, murders and armed strikes had 'Beirutised' Lima itself. President Fujimori closed Congress and formed a government of national reconstruction. Then Guzmán was captured along with most of his staff in a meeting place they had used too frequently, which was under surveillance. After Guzmán's change of heart Sendero melted with remarkable speed, leaving the inevitable rump.[2] The fourth sword rusted through as those of Marx, Lenin and Mao had done, and nobody makes them nowadays.

The plot is familiar. Guzmán captured academic control of his own university, and at a time of huge expansion, turned it into a school for Marxism–Leninism. He was a prolific writer and speechmaker, whose writings became sacred texts: mystical, allegorical, millenarian, biblical: revolution, sacrifice and death; comradeship in adversity; the exaltation of a supreme leader; undivided loyalty to the *caudillo, führer, duce,* messiah; the infallibility of his doctrine; the historical inevitability of the movement and of victory; the necessity to suffer for redemption; things would never be the same again.

The society of 'great harmony', the radical and definitive new society towards which 15 thousand million years of matter in motion, which is the part that we know of eternal matter, have necessarily and irrepressibly set out towards ... The unique new society, for which there is no substitute, without exploited or exploiters, without oppressed or oppressors, without state, without parties, without democracy, without arms, without wars ... Let us uproot the poisonous weeds ... Let us cast out those sinister vipers... Poisons, purulence – they must be destroyed. The body is healthy, and if we don't destroy them it will lose its vigour ... armed actions confirm our preaching, that our blood merge with the blood of those who must spill it ... They in their old and bloody violence, in their peace of bayonets, in their accursed war which kills in the jails, in the schools, in the factories, in the fields, killing even children in their mothers' wombs. That sinister violence today has met its match.[3]

Sendero never had enough support to win power in conventional politics; only some 7 per cent even in Lima.[4] As a violent political party, however, it was a force to be reckoned with.

In Latin America, the military has become, as would be expected, the major player in violent politics, defending the incumbent regime from its enemies, and occasionally seizing power itself when dissatisfied with conventional politicians.

Meanwhile the successful Marxists in Cuba, Latin America and Africa have reaped the Martinez Paradox: transforming 'a world of plenty for the few into one of little for all ... from growth without redistribution to redistribution without growth'.[5]

Leninism

Lenin's Marxism was firmly voluntarist: his revolution was based on a strategy with an inherently low risk of failure, for the precondition he specified – the total breakdown of social order – made the strategy he advocated – a mass armed uprising of an allied proletariat and peasantry led by a monolithic vanguard party professionally prepared for revolution – almost certain to succeed. Lenin's achievement in seizing control of the Russian revolution and winning the civil war which followed it therefore lay, not in specifying the strategy, but in single-mindedly pursuing it and making it work.

Lenin's great contribution to Marxism was to show that jacqueries, riots, barricades, strikes, insurrections and other spontaneous violence by the oppressed against their oppressors did not make revolutions: for that, leaders were necessary, and a vanguard party of professional revolutionaries.

However, if the proletariat is the only class capable of overthrowing the bourgeoisie, and if to do so it must outmatch their military resources, very few countries would qualify as candidates for communist revolution; only during a national crisis which fulfilled Lenin's condition that it is only when the ruled do not want to live in the old way, and the rulers cannot carry on in the old way, can the revolution triumph.[6]

Nazism

The German revolution of 1918 fitted Lenin's dictum exactly. Though it was spontaneous in the sense that it was sparked by a small incident and spread extremely rapidly, with no predictable pattern and certainly without any conscious plan, the preconditions for it were clearly already present.[7]

The theory of the socialist assumption of power through revolution had been well publicised by socialist and even bourgeois politicians in Germany, and the recent example of the Russian revolution was fresh in everyone's mind. However, in Germany it did not work as it had in Russia. The workers' and soldiers' soviets were impatient with the bureaucracy of the government and of the trade unions, and started to take things into their own hands. However, they proved completely unable to manage complex activities such as food distribution, health, housing and the resettlement of the eight million returning troops.

The professional communist revolutionaries, the Spartacists, were in jail during the revolution, and had no party organisation worth speaking of; in any case they were mainly theorists, without a broad following among the workers. They had an image of the future, but they realised it attracted too little support for them to survive in an elected National Assembly. So they sought civil war instead, and lost.

Once the violent politics started, it was conducted by a process of political buccaneering, with rival leaders, released from the bounds of constitutional action, attempting to organise the base for success: willpower, manpower, skill, and materiel. Of these, skill eventually counted for most. The revolutionaries and counter-revolutionaries had equal access to the people, and indeed mass support swung from one to the other at different times. Both had almost equal access to what materiel there was: supplies were abandoned or plundered, and although the government succeeded in preventing the flow of money and food into the Bavarian Revolutionary Republic, that was a contributory factor rather than a decisive one.

The counter-revolutionaries won because they had two organisations with the skills to manage a country and to fight with modern heavy weapons: the ruling Socialist Party of Germany – the SPD – and the *freikorps*: a political party and a party army. Neither could have succeeded alone. The revolutionaries lost because they were outmatched: on the occasions, such as during the November Revolution, Spartacist Week and the Bavarian Republic, when they managed to mobilise more people and materiel than the counter-revolutionaries, their success was short-lived; they had not the political skill to beat the SPD nor the military skill to counter the *freikorps*. They lacked Lenin's talent for knowing what to do the day after, and the skill to carry it out.[8]

The civil war and the instability of the Weimar Republic, however, show how difficult it is to re-establish constitutional government once public confidence has been broken and private armies formed. Authority then yields to power, and consensual legitimacy to buccaneering. Might gains support from people who think it right, and if there are enough to do so, it will win. However, such might is not just democracy-under-arms, for the winner takes all. It is striking to see just how long a society can exist in a state of warlordism, or armed neutrality between its party armies once they have carved out their own sphere of influence, and yet how swiftly a single leader can gain popular support, utterly transform the institutions of the state to serve his party without more than token resistance, and restore stability – of a sort.

In the absence of a major national crisis the system could probably have continued. Weimar Germany was far from unique in suffering from weak governments, but though some governments elsewhere managed to survive the Depression, Weimar did not. The combination of huge unemployment, memory of the recent past, fear of the future, failed parliamentary democracy of both left and right, presidential rule, and almost constant electioneering had created the right climate for the rapid growth of the National Socialist German Workers' Party, NSDAP: the Nazis. As unemployment rose from two million in 1928 to six million in 1933, the votes cast for the NSDAP rose in parallel, from 3 per cent in the Reichstag elections of 1928 to more than 42 per cent in January 1933, and 44 per cent in March of the same year. After President Hindenburg's death in August 1934, Hitler was endorsed as head of state by 38 million votes to 4.5 million; less than 3 million eligible voters spoiled their papers or did not vote at all.[9] Interestingly, from the point of view of the analysis presented in this book, Leni Riefenstahl's famous film of Hitler was entitled *Triumph of the Will*.

'One could make a strong case for the thesis that Russian reactionaries invented fascism'.[10] One could also make a strong case for the thesis that Russian revolutionaries invented fascism, or at least the techniques which enabled fascism to succeed: the painstaking building of a disciplined, enthusiastic, professional vanguard party with its own institutions matching, infiltrating and subverting those of the state to form a dual power; catching the mood of the people and amplifying it by constant propaganda and by the charisma of the party leaders; ruthless 'co-ordination' into a one-party state once the party was in power.

There is a striking vein of intellectual and physical excitement running through contemporary documents on violent politics, whether they have been written by Marxist revolutionaries ranged against the Old Order or by fascists against revolutionary socialism. It is salutary to see how easily and rapidly, in conditions of such excitement, the civilised rules and customs of a society can be neutralised, destroyed or reversed; how easily violent politics trumps constitutional politics. Parliamentary opposition disappears if opposition members do, or are simply intimidated into silence or absence; constitutions are amended or ignored, laws suspended or countervailing powers granted; functionaries do as they are told (and even as they think they would be told) or pay with their jobs, their freedom or their lives.

Dissent thrives in civilised democracies because it is safe: once dissent means dismissal, arrest or death it ceases to be worthwhile, and many simply opt out of politics, living their real lives at their firesides with their families and friends, and taking a minimal part in public activities. They become what Eastern Europeans used to call 'radish communists': red on the outside and white within. People willingly or of necessity cleave to the group best able to protect them; small groups ally or are crushed; people move to areas where they feel safe, leaving no man's lands, perhaps fought over by the young men.

There never seems to be a shortage of people to do the dirty work. There is no doubt that violent politics can be deeply appealing, not only in the demagogic sense, but also in the emotional. It does not primarily appeal to the intellect, though there is no shortage of attempts to rationalise it intellectually. Action has its own rewards, especially for people whose everyday lives lack challenge and excitement. The New Messiah has his own charisma:

A non-Nazi who has not experienced the enormous elementary power of the idea of our Führer will never understand any of this. But let me tell these people as the deepest truth: whenever I worked for the movement and applied myself for our Führer, I always felt there was nothing higher or nobler I could do for Adolf Hitler and thereby for Germany, our people and fatherland ... When I say so little in the vita about my external life, my job, etc, this is only because my real life, the real content of my life, is my work for and commitment to Hitler and towards a national socialist Germany. Hitler is the purest embodiment of the German character, the purest embodiment of a national socialist Germany.[11]

The hard, painstaking work carried out by the NSDAP to serve the community and win its support by fair means as well as foul also tends to be forgotten, although it is as common, and indeed as essential, a technique for mobilising support in violent politics as in the conventional kind.[12]

Violent politics is not simpler and less demanding than non-violent politics but more subtle and complex. Necessarily so, for by its very nature it includes both kinds of politics: violent politics between protagonists, and non-violent politics to mobilise the base for success. Conventional politics of a high order within organisations – because the stakes are high – and violent politics between them.

Constitutional, institutional, non-violent politics requires a deliberate renunciation of the exercise of power, of force, in favour of conflict-resolution by argument and rules: rules which are certainly not arbitrary, but are not absolutely consistent, unarguably fair or infinitely reasonable either.[13] Once this consensus – the ready acceptance of an element of arbitrariness in the rules of a society – breaks down, violent politics begins.

Exported revolution

The Third International had been formed in March 1919 expressly to foment and aid the revolutions that were confidently expected to follow the Great War and the Russian Revolution.

However, by the time the Comintern's export manual *Armed Insurrection* was published in 1928,[14] the only successful communist revolution had been in Russia; infertile ground by Marx's standards. All the other attempted revolutions had failed, despite the existence of the objective pre-revolutionary conditions outlined by Marx.

The conquest of the Russian borderlands during the aftermath of the coup against Kerensky's provisional government was accomplished by the Bolshevik forces and not by insurrection. In none of the areas was the majority pro-communist, and the existing governments were uniformly anti-communist. The Red Army was sent into every area that attempted to exercise its independence.

Throughout its entire existence, from 1919 to 1943, the Comintern succeeded in spreading communism to only two countries, Outer Mongolia and its adjoining mini-state of Tannu Tavu, which was later incorporated into the Soviet Union.

The failure of exported revolution was clear, and from the introduction of Stalin's doctrine of 'socialism in one country' in 1924 until 1939, the Comintern made no serious attempt to spread communism abroad, with the one exception of China. None of the nine post-war communist governments in Europe,[15] and none of the seven in Asia,[16] came to power through a classical Marxist revolution of the proletariat against the bourgeoisie. Indeed, only two of the countries, East Germany and Czechoslovakia, were sufficiently industrialised for the proletariat to be a force to be reckoned with; the remainder were largely agrarian. Nor did any come to power through armed insurrection: both communist and anti-communist insurrections were defeated.

The two techniques of Communist violent politics which were most successful were straightforward military occupation (principally in Europe), and People's War (principally in Asia).[17]

People's War

Given Mao's emphasis on the need for specific strategies to fit specific circumstances, it is surprising that the principal changes he made to Marxist–Leninist orthodoxy – reliance on the peasants and other poverty-limited groups as potential revolutionaries, and basing the revolution on guerrilla warfare in the countryside rather than on insurrection in the towns – were accepted as Marxist, or as a contribution to any theory at all, for he warned time and again against the application of lessons learned in one place to another.[18] The Chinese revolution, the Sino–Japanese War and the civil war certainly resulted in the victory of communism of a peculiarly Chinese kind, but it owed little to Marx or Lenin.

To Mao and the other proponents of People's War, the guerrilla army and the civilian population were totally interdependent. The process of gaining power would necessarily be long drawn out, because the government was rich and powerful and the people poor, ill-organised and unarmed. The revolution would therefore have to proceed by stages, though not necessarily in the same way, nor at the same rate in different places. Small clandestine cells would carry out agitation, propaganda and isolated acts of terrorism and sabotage, while defending their village from interference by unpopular people such as policemen, tax collectors and landlords. As their strength and popularity grew, they could establish successively greater areas of control from which they could conduct large, co–ordinated guerrilla operations. Eventually the popular forces would create a regular force strong enough to outmatch the government forces, weakened by defections to the popular cause.[19]

The revolutionaries' strategy was based upon

- a belief in the justice of their cause;
- popular support for the cause, and popular willingness to suffer, perhaps grievously, for a better regime to come;
- co-ordination of political, military and social policies by a single organisation devoted to the cause.

Counter-revolutionary war

The Western strategy of counter-revolutionary war grew from the postwar conflicts in Asia. In French Indochina, for example, Giap's Vietminh had adopted techniques similar to those of Mao for mobilising the masses – winning people rather than territory. The efficacy of their techniques was beyond question: propaganda, the establishment of parallel hierarchies, and the destruction of the government hierarchy by systematic terrorism. Such techniques were by no means novel, but armies which had just finished fighting a conventional war were ill-trained to combat them, and governments still less so.

Many saw *la guerre moderne* as the communist answer to the nuclear stalemate: the replacement for conventional war, now made unthinkable by the advent of nuclear weapons, and the new mode of the international communist plan to dominate the world.[20]

The doctrine of counter-revolutionary war was simply that the government and its forces should apply the same techniques as the communists, resulting in their winning the hearts and minds of the people rather than the insurgents – a competition in good government, as it were. The government must present its case as superior to those of its opponents; it must compete with them for popular support, meeting the grievances of the people over land, taxes and unemployment; providing, from its superior resources, houses, schools, wells, electricity, roads and hospitals; using the mass communications media to promote the image, at home and abroad, of a good government confronting disruptive, selfish rebels, while building up sufficient intelligence about the rebels to eliminate them by killing them, jailing them, converting them to the government's side or driving them away, and forming self-defence militias to prevent their return. The government effort, too, had to be co-ordinated into a coherent yet flexible 'two wars strategy': one war to destroy the insurgents, the other to develop the political and economic infrastructure of the country, removing the causes of the insurgency.

The doctrine was simple to state but infinitely complex to put into practice. Native-born insurgents such as the Vietminh were obviously far better placed to understand the cultural and political milieu of the society they were attempting to dominate than outsiders such as the French. It followed that a method which was successful in the hands of one might well fail if used by the other. Furthermore, the 'causes' of insurgencies were by no means easy to identify, and still less so to solve. The opposing aims could well be politically irreconcilable or economically impossible to achieve.

The strategist of such a conflict must clearly know enough about the country in which he is operating to avoid using techniques which will be counterproductive, and themselves create more tensions than they relieve. For example, it is not sufficient to decide that if the peasants have no land, reallocation will solve the problem. The existing system of land tenure may be exceedingly complex, and meddling without an intimate knowledge of the system may well create more problems than it solves.

The methods by which communists successfully came to power in Asia were little different from the methods by which they attempted to seize power in Europe, and failed. In both cases they aimed to mobilise will, skill, men and materiel, and organise them so as to outmatch or undermine the institutions of the government, particularly its army. The explanation for the difference therefore lies not in the techniques used, but in the circumstances in which they were brought to bear.

In Europe the states which remained non-communist were well-established, their traditional forms of government enjoyed a high degree of legitimacy and popular support, the institutions of the state were strong, and their armies too united and powerful to be beaten by *ad hoc* or partisan forces.

In Asia, none of these factors applied. Few colonial powers could afford, either politically or economically, to retain a sufficiently strong government infrastructure and sufficient armed forces to resist popular forces which had been established, equipped and trained during the war; while the post-colonial governments were inherently unstable, and their power easily seized by those able to mobilise quite moderate opposition forces – and communists were adept at that.

There was nothing new about using military occupation to install a government, although that was not how Marxist–Leninists had envisaged its being done. Nor was there anything new in governments using their armed forces to defeat insurrection, though Marxist–Leninists might have expected the armed forces, or at least the huge proletarian element within them, to have joined their side, either through choice or as a result of the propaganda and revolutionary action within the armed forces which they advocated.

The Prodigal Son returns – revolution and the New Left

By the 1960s, it was apparent that Marxist revolution had fallen on stony ground in the industrialised states, where even the communist parties had become reformist, if indeed they had ever been anything else, and were taking part in conventional parliamentary politics, albeit with the occasional foray into direct action to bolster their arguments. In the Soviet Union and its satellite states, what communism had brought about was clearly more akin to state capitalism than to the stateless utopia of Marx and Engels. In the third world, the rulers had been corrupted by power, and had formed oligarchies of the left or right, scarcely distinguishable one from another.

So arose the student New Left, with a new–old vision of the world: in their eyes there was nothing to choose between western capitalism and state capitalism in the so-called socialist countries; nor between western imperialism and Soviet imperialism. The system corrupted everything it touched. If, against the odds, a poor man or a poor country made good, they would be the first to oppress their erstwhile neighbours. Students, unable to make their way in the world without passing the *rites de passage* of the system, were channelled by their parents, exploited by the academic bourgeoisie, tyrannised by examinations, their true consciousness of natural morality drained – and replaced by the false consciousness of the inevitability and correctness of the system. Then, the conditioning complete, they were set free to become exploiters in their turn. The proletariat had been corrupted too, on a lower plane of course and more insidiously, since they were not intellectuals and could not be expected to understand what was happening.

Fortunately, but inevitably, modern society had created such a complex and interdependent edifice that it could be brought down by a few people using the right lever at the right spot. The technological society would not work if even a few people were determined that it should not. A general strike would quickly bring society to a halt, allow workers to occupy factories, students universities and schoolchildren schools, and run them for the good of all in the brave new world.

The New Left's criticisms of society were valid, if overstated, but what they lacked was any concept of how things would be better after the Millennium, given the failure of trial and error over the previous millennia (and even they could not claim that there had been any shortage of that) to do any better than the admittedly imperfect, but hardly complacent, present.

Not only did they fail to provide an alternative model of the world, they explicitly denied that it was either possible or necessary to do so. Such obscurantism had a limited appeal, even to the lumpenyouth, while the New Left's insistence that nothing could be worse than the present system ran counter to experience. Even those who had not lived through wars and chiliastic revolutions before, knew that it most decidedly could.

The New Left's electoral appeal was too small for them to make any headway in parliamentary politics, while the technological society proved not nearly as vulnerable to violence as they had thought: after all, if it could cope with an immensely destructive world war, why should it collapse with a bomb in a police station or a barricade in a street? The practitioners of 'institutionalised violence', too, turned out to be rather better at their jobs than the amateurs, and unconvinced by the contention that it was they who should be in the dock.

The emotional appeal of the New Left reached its zenith with *les événements de mai* of 1968 and the similar demonstrations throughout the western world in the late 1960s, but without an intellectual or practical base it could not survive for long. The standard works, by Blackburn and Cohn-Bendit out of Fanon and Marcuse, became yellowing paperbacks on the bottom shelves; the students for a democratic society went back to their books.

It is only fair to note, however, that many leaders of the student New Left were acutely aware of the shortcomings of the movement:

It is non-political largely because of a lack of faith in the political process or in the established instrumentalities of change, but to these it offers no alternative beyond direct action ... There is no recognition that the various objects of protest are not *sui generis* but are symptomatic of institutional forces with which the movement must ultimately deal. We call for disarmament, but we say nothing of what to do with the manpower, resources, industrial plant and capital equipment that are tied up in the military machine. Problems of poverty, health care, wasted agricultural and natural resources, meaningless work – these issues arouse students neither to demonstration nor to discussion. Even in respect to civil rights, we do not speak to the essentials of social equality.[21]

The failure of the Student Revolution in the cities was foreshadowed by the failure of the students' folk hero Che Guevara. Both failures stemmed from the belief that revolution was a natural process, which only needed to be set in train to succeed.

Guevara and the *foco* theory

Violent politics might be regarded as the normal form of politics in Latin America in all but a few countries and for all but short periods. However, it was usually a minority interest: even the wars of liberation at the beginning of the nineteenth century were fought between a few thousand men, led not by natives but by rich *criollos*, South American born Spaniards such as Bolivar and San Martin.

Furthermore, topography, race, poverty and natural independence of spirit made the co-ordination of anything, for war or peace, difficult and unrewarding. In Bolivar's words:

There is no good faith in America, nor among the nations of America. Treaties are scraps of paper; constitutions, printed matter; elections, battles; freedom, anarchy; and life a torment ... America is ungovernable. He who serves a revolution ploughs the sea.[22]

Until recently, and even now in some states, government concerned the ordinary people little; effective power was in the hands of *caudillos*, local leaders, and central power often in the hands of the only body able to exercise it – the army. As in every situation but the most tranquil, justice was rough and ready: conspirators were shot 'while trying to escape', or simply disappeared; agitating students were rounded up and set to work on the roads; troublesome bandits hunted down by ex-bandits formed into quasi-official police forces; dissidents locked in jail for years (though their families were permitted to see them every day – as indeed they had to, to feed and clothe their relatives, for the prisons did not regard those as fair charges on their funds). Coalitions were formed by self-interest, bribery or threats: straightforward violent politics, in which the masses played walk-on parts.

However, Castro's revolution in Cuba brought in a new dimension by reaffirming the naturalness and spontaneity of revolution if the conditions were right. Or so it seemed at the time:

> What had happened? A heroic epic? The band of hunted men in the Sierra at the end of 1956 seemed to have turned, two years later, into an army large enough to beat the army of the nation, to expel the tyrant, to set the people free ... For a few weeks Castro was to Eisenhower's America what Lawrence of Arabia had been to England during the first world war. This popular success, national and international, helped Castro from the moment of victory to ignore his allies, to forget the 'pact of Caracas' and to let it be assumed that he alone had won the war ... But the defeat of Batista was not only due to the vanquishing of the army in the field, and the exploits of Castro's rebel army; indeed, the only serious battles fought in the civil war were those of Santa Clara and those which led to the defeat of the army's offensive in the summer of 1958. But even here the scale of combat was small – six rebels being killed in Guevara's army at Santa Clara, forty in the battles leading to the defeat of Batista's offensive in 1958. Such a dearth of pitched engagements is typical of guerrilla warfare, but in fact even the number of guerrilla engagements was small ... Castro operated as much as a politician seeking to influence opinion as he did a guerrilla leader seeking territory. [23]

On the model, or what was thought to be the model, of the Cuban revolution was built the *foco* theory of insurrection first expressed by Régis Debray, and first put into practice by Che Guevara in Bolivia.[24]

The new model should be a mobile strategic column, under a single commander responsible for both political and military affairs, reproducing itself like an amoeba as it grew, splitting into new columns of the same provenance as the old, and thus with identical aims and tactics. The tiny *foco* would grow into a mighty guerrilla army as a pair of locusts grows into a plague, and sweep throughout the continent, as the revolutions of 1848 had done. The guerrilla columns were not to move among the people like Mao's fish, because too much of their energy would be taken up by looking after the peasants and too little left for fighting. Nor would the *foco* rely for supplies on their supporters in the towns; the 'guerrillas of the plains' kept too much of the material they collected to themselves, squandered it on urban guerrilla activities which made no practical difference, and forgot the real fighters in the hills. The *foco* must be autarkic.

The theory was illustrated by seductive metaphors – the seed reproducing; the spark lighting the prairie fire; the small motor starting the large; the *foco* detonator in the TNT of dependent capitalism; the queen bee forming a swarm. But as Althusser pointed out, what was needed was a positive demonstration of its applicability outside Cuba.[25] Even there it was by no means certain, given the absence of reliable documents and objective historical analysis, that the *foco* theory adequately described what had happened.

While this debate was going on, Che Guevara, who had led one of Castro's columns in Cuba and had taken part in guerrilla actions on a similarly small scale in other countries, had returned from a proselytising mission to Africa, and was setting out to apply the theory to Bolivia, a country not unused to revolutionaries, having had more presidents than years of independence since 1825.[26]

> Mario has to understand that the struggle in Bolivia will be long because the enemy will concentrate all his forces against it. Bolivia will sacrifice itself so that conditions [for revolution] can be created in neighbouring countries. We have to make another Vietnam out of America, with its centre in Bolivia.[27]

Whether the Bolivian communist party would have been impressed by its role as the Forlorn Hope of the siege of America, had they ever received Guevara's message, is doubtful; it does not appear to have been favourably received by the 29 Bolivians in Guevara's group at any rate, since two of them deserted before the first engagement and three later, guiding the Bolivian army to the rest of the *foco*. Of the band of 51, small for its grand role but still four times the size of Castro's force that had survived the landing of the *Granma*,[28] only five survived.

As Althusser had pointed out, Guevara's analysis of Castro's 'campaigns' was *ex post facto,* and suspect without deeper examination of the mechanisms involved. Guevara had concluded that:

The Cuban revolution contributed 3 fundamental lessons to the conduct of revolutionary movements in America. They are
1. Popular forces can win a war against the army.
2. It is not necessary to wait until all conditions for making revolution exist; the insurrection can create them.
3. In under-developed America the countryside is the basic area for fighting.[29]

He was wrong on all three counts. His confidence led him into conducting a hopeless venture in a way so amateur that it would have earned a boy scout leader the sack. As Debray said: 'In order to destroy one army, another army is necessary, and this implies discipline, training and arms. Fraternity and bravery do not make an army. Witness Spain, and the Paris Commune'.[30]

Guevara, like others before and since, thought that he had found the magic ingredient which would allow violent politics to succeed without hard, painstaking, thoughtful and sustained work based on a thorough understanding of the political forces in the particular place at the particular time – especially those of the opposition.

During the 1960s and 1970s the largely rural guerrillas in Venezuela were defeated; the urban guerrillas in Brazil, Argentina and Uruguay were destroyed, the military arm of the Marxists in Guatemala hunted down by the army, and their once powerful political wing reduced to impotence. Allende rose and fell. Somosa's dynasty in Nicaragua was ended. Nothing new was added to the principles of violent politics. The weak and the unlucky lost, as they always had.

The base for success

The success of managed, voluntarist, strategies of violent politics compared with determinist theories is very clear. Indeed it is apparent that the greater the organisation and the more complex the infrastructure thus built up, the greater the chances of success.

There are four basic factors for success in violent politics – men, skill, materiel and will. Only a limited number of institutions in a country contain a sufficient number of the four key factors in sufficient strength to be important in high-level violent politics: the government bureaucracy, political parties, business, industrial trade unions, landowners, agricultural unions, the police and law enforcement system, the church, youth organisations (since young single males are the main fighters) and the military forces, particularly the army.

The spiritual is just as important a factor in violent politics as in religion, as Lenin, Hitler and Mao recognised. Indeed it is apparent that with enough will it is possible to win without having a material base capable of outmatching that of the opposition; but only if the opposition itself lacks will. Finding one man with will is reasonably easy. There is then no problem of co-ordination: *il duce ha sempre raggione*. But few leaders are great enough, and few issues simple enough, for them always to be right for long; then comes collapse, and the lamp post.

Since the bureaucracy of a state is the body through which government policy is executed, it certainly possesses adequate skills and manpower to form an alternative government itself. In practice bureaucracies do not do this: their organisation is geared for routine administration rather than for the upheavals of violent politics, while many of its agencies, for example hospitals, education, public building, social services and mail, are not important factors in violent politics. The hierarchical structure is strong within departments but poor across them, so unified action is difficult. Bureaucrats have families and secure jobs, and unless these are directly affected by the upheavals they have little incentive to join in. Bureaucrat–warriors and bureaucrat–revolutionaries are contradictions in terms; by training and long practice, by the distribution of age and authority, and possibly by disposition and self selection too, a bureaucracy is more inclined to pad along as best it can, layin' low like Brer Rabbit, and saying nuthin' like Tar Baby, rather than taking up the sword.

Bureaucracies thus tend to continue with business as usual during episodes of violent politics. Placemen are appointed to key positions, and officials who make a nuisance of themselves are exiled to harmless departments or dismissed on catch-all grounds: not being medically fit or properly qualified for promotion, refusing to accept transfer, being a security risk, or simply being redundant. Their *ex gratia* pensions then become hostages for their future good behaviour. However, winning authority over the bureaucracy is very important, because the state cannot function without it; but bureaucracies do not themselves become protagonists in violent politics.

The ordinary police and judiciary normally play a part in low levels of violent politics only, for reasons which will be explored more thoroughly in the chapters which follow. Police are easily neutralised by terrorist attacks on themselves or their families unless they adopt the gendarmerie technique of operating from barracks, and in an area other than their own. The Comintern's manual on armed insurrection recommends that if the police are organised as an internal security force based on secure barracks and equipped and trained on military lines, they should be treated as a regular army. If not, they are 'in reality nothing more or less than a stock of arms for the insurgents to take and use'.[31]

Organised labour is conventionally credited with the power to become a major actor in violent politics; but this has only been so in the modern world when the hammer and sickle have united under a vanguard party of left or right which has become sufficiently powerful to be autarkic: when it has gained skill and materiel to add to its organisation and manpower. Otherwise it depends too heavily on the existing infrastructure of a country to destroy it, or even to stop work for long. The proletariat can no longer afford to destroy the state with which it is in symbiosis – although it can afford to support its Allendes and Peróns; for a while.

Industrialists and landowners are equally conservative; they will put their influence and their money, overtly and covertly, where they believe it will do them most good; the more prudent in the less stable countries will also hedge their bets. But nowadays there are few industrial or feudal barons with private armies: they have materiel but no manpower; the converse of the unions.

In modern states the church has influence – sometimes great influence – but little power in violent politics; the church militant no longer exists. Youth groups have only one resource – young men willing to go anywhere and do anything – a key factor in violent politics, but only one of the four.

An army is conventionally regarded as important because of its weapons. For example:

> The armed forces play a key role in any revolutionary movement. The modern instruments of violence and coercion are increasingly sophisticated and are precisely those that armies monopolise. Revolutions can no longer be mounted by sword and shield alone; they demand modern weaponry and organisation, the very things that armies can provide.[32]

The unique strength of an army – or of a party army like the *freikorps* – in violent politics stems not from its weapons, however, but from its combining in one body men, skill, organisation and materiel on a scale which, provided it retains its will to win, only another army can hope to outmatch. Violent politics above a certain level thus always becomes a conflict of armies, but it is by no means inevitable that this stage is ever reached.

Armies may of course themselves become political actors if the circumstances are right.[33] They may, too, be politically inert even when they are directly and deeply affected – for example during Stalin's Great Terror, in which half of the officer corps of the Red Army perished, during the rise of the Nazi party in Germany, and during the Iranian Islamic Revolution.

It is essential, though, to re-emphasise the vital distinction between the language of politics and the alphabet of violence; between the form taken by the violence itself and its political substance; between the tactical success of violent means and the strategic success of political ends. A British army of 100 000 was apparently driven out of Palestine by a tiny handful of terrorists, another out of Cyprus, and yet another out of Aden; an American army of half a million, plus South Vietnamese forces four or five times as big, was defeated by men in black pyjamas; a French army of 150 000 was forced to relinquish a North African province of France, having earlier been driven from Indochina; Portugal was forced to give up its African colonies.

These apparent paradoxes arise both through false analogy, such as that between Vietnam and Malaya, and through our failure to distinguish between the efficacy of the *forms* of violent politics being pursued there and the *substance* of the political ends at home. In essence, though the forms were violent (and by and large effective against the rebels), the substance was political persuasion (or shame), and by and large also effective. The political and economic costs to the metropolitan power were escalated until they outweighed any possible benefit from retaining the territory, particularly as violent politics tended to swamp constitutional politics and make the territories ungovernable except by unified military-style governments which were effective in Malaya and the Philippines to name but two, and in the occupied enemy territories post-war (and, let it not be forgotten, in the vast areas occupied by both sides during the war as well) but were unacceptable in the post-war, decolonising, self-determining world.[34]

The 1919–21 rebellion in Ireland which ended with its partition into the Irish Free State and Northern Ireland also falls into this category. Ireland was not of course a colony in form, but the claim that it was a colony in substance would not be difficult to maintain. The IRA of the troubles later in the century certainly regarded Northern Ireland as a colony, and chose the colonial-liberation technique of operating through violence abroad on conventional politics at home:

A war of attrition against enemy personnel which is aimed at causing as many casualties and deaths as possible so as to create a demand from their people at home for their withdrawal. A bombing campaign aimed at making the enemy's financial interests in our country unprofitable while at the same time curbing long-term investment in our country. To make the Six Counties at present and for the past several years ungovernable except by colonial military rule. To sustain the war and gain support for its ends by National and International propaganda and publicity campaigns. By defending the war of liberation by punishing criminals, collaborators and informers.[35]

Conclusions

Determinist strategies of violent politics, relying on objective conditions of poverty, misrule or oppression to give birth to armed struggle and drive it on, have failed. There is nothing scientific about historical materialism. There is nothing inevitable about the defeat of capitalism – or its triumph. Successful campaigns are made, not born. They rely on the will of a leader, and on his ability to mobilise men, skill and materiel, and organise them to outmatch the political and military forces of his opponents.

Violent politicians require the skills of conventional politics to mobilise the base for success, and those of violence as well; one set of skills is not enough. They must fight a 'two wars strategy': one to defeat their opponents militarily, and the other to defeat them politically, which may well include providing better government. Spiritual factors are just as important in violent politics as in religion. They are necessary but not sufficient. They do not replace hard work based on a thorough understanding of indigenous political forces – particularly those of the opposition.

Armies are the backstops of violent politics because they combine will, skill, manpower and materiel in one organisation, on a scale that only other armies can hope to match. Provided an army remains intact, only a better army can defeat it. Provided it remains loyal to the government as well, it effectively prevents that government from being forced to do anything it is determined not to do.

The unfamiliarity of non-indigenous counter-insurgents with the language of indigenous politics has been a prime reason for their failure in violent politics, whatever their expertise in the alphabet of violence.

The efficacy of anti-colonial people's war and its derivatives was not due to the violent form of their tactics, but to their effects on the substance of metropolitan politics. Success resulted from operating *through* violent politics in the field *on* institutional politics at home.

Such a use of violent politics is not confined to anti-colonial movements operating on the metropolitan power. Violence can also be used by dissident factions within states to operate on its institutional politics in a similar way. The violence must be kept within bounds if the government is not to take to violent politics itself. None but the most powerful insurgent movements could then hope to win. Few have. Attempts at secession from an existing state have not met with the same success as anticolonial wars: Ireland is an interesting exception or, from another point of view, an interesting example. The economic and political costs of using force do not usually persuade governments to yield parts of their own territory.

The next steps

In theory, any violence is incompatible with institutional politics, not only because any state, however constituted, must necessarily claim priority for the interests of the whole over those of individuals, claim the ultimate right to determine disputes, and claim an absolute monopoly of force, but also because the modes of violent politics – prevention, fear and force – so easily override those of conventional politics.

In practice, of course, states do tolerate low levels of violence, for example during football matches, strikes and demonstrations, partly because of the impracticability of preventing them without disproportionate measures, and partly because they are taken as legitimate indicators of strength of feeling. So the more liberal the state the higher the level of tolerance. Such uses of violence themselves become institutionalised, part of conventional politics, with unwritten rules of their own. Minor violence may well be successful, since no government likes to have its disaffected citizens rioting in the streets. But how should the bounds of acceptable (or at least accepted) violence be set? And what can the government do to counter violence which breaches the bounds?

These problems become acute when killing starts. The next three chapters examine a typical example – the thirty-year campaign of violent politics in Northern Ireland between 1968 and 1998. The succeeding chapters then examine the options open to a state to counter violent political challenge.

4
Politics: Northern Ireland 1968–98

The story of the huge amount of political activity, overt and covert, national and international, bilateral and multilateral, republican and nationalist, conventional and paramilitary, which led to the Good Friday Agreement, via the Lynch/Wilson talks of 1968, Sunningdale, the Northern Ireland Assembly, the Anglo-Irish Agreement, the Mitchell Principles and the Downing Street Declaration has been told well and often.[1] So has the story of the social and political forces in Ireland which culminated in Partition in 1921: centuries-old wars of religion resulting in three times as many Catholics as Protestants in Ireland as a whole, and half as many in the North: a classic double minority which had defied resolution for several hundred years.[2] A short civil war between the pro-and anti-Treaty factions in the Free State from which the Irish Republic's present-day parties are descended; *de jure* claim to sovereignty over the whole island; *de facto* acceptance of the border; groups prepared to use violence to achieve a united Ireland when the time was ripe, and groups prepared to use violence to prevent them and maintain the union with Britain.[3]

This chapter summarises the political aims of the protagonists; the next, the violence used to pursue them. The succeeding one examines the countermeasures used: the strategy of treating terrorism as common crime. The final chapters examine other strategies: treating violent politics as an offence against the state; using emergency or martial law; treating it as internal war; and dealing with it outside the law.

Broadly speaking, there are about one million people in Northern Ireland who are more or less unionist/protestant, and 600 000 who are republican/catholic; the Republic contains over 3 million catholics and only about 100 000 protestants.[4] The inbuilt majority of the unionists in the north has always been reflected in their representation in local government, in the various Northern Ireland assemblies and power-sharing executives, and at Westminster.[5]

Devolution came unexpectedly to Northern Ireland following the 1921 partition – neither nationalists nor unionists had wanted it.[6] With hindsight, it becomes clear that it was a fundamental mistake. The monopolistic nature of the protestant government was there from the outset, built in by the very conditions which had created it, and reflected by the Irish Free State, later the Republic; a mirror-image catholic state.

Shortly after the troubles began, the Unionist parties' main rival in conventional politics became the Social Democratic and Labour Party (SDLP) founded in 1970 by Gerry Fitt and later led by his deputy, John Hume, who was awarded the Nobel Prize in 1998 with David Trimble, leader of the Ulster Unionist Party, for their leading roles in the peace process. The SDLP's rival for republican support was the IRA and its political arm, Sinn Fein.[7]

In 1982 the SDLP won 19 per cent of the vote in the elections for the new Northern Ireland Assembly, and Sinn Fein 10 per cent. In the 1983 General Election for the Westminster parliament the SDLP won 18 per cent and Sinn Fein 13 per cent. Those proportions were roughly maintained in subsequent elections.[8] In the elections for the 1998 Northern Ireland Assembly following the Good Friday Agreement, which were held by single transferable vote, the SDLP won 22 per cent of the 108 seats and Sinn Fein 17 per cent; their combined total of 39 per cent is close to the percentage of Catholics in Northern Ireland. The unionist parties won 51 per cent of the seats and other parties 10 per cent.

The IRA creed was very simple:[9]

- Ireland is a natural nation–state;
- Britain conquered it by force;
- Britain settled it to maintain its rule, and mistreated the Irish;
- Ireland freed 26 counties by an armed campaign of national liberation, but wrongly agreed to Partition;
- Britain made the six counties of Northern Ireland self-governing, permitting and encouraging protestant hegemony;
- Britain should withdraw, and return the six counties to Ireland;
- if the British do not, they should be compelled to do so by armed force;[10]
- the IRA is the lawful government of the Irish Republic; it has jurisdiction over the whole island;[11]
- it is a lawful army, and its war of liberation is morally justified;

- the united Ireland created by the IRA would be pluralist, non-sectarian, and socialist.

The British creed was equally simple:

- Ireland is indeed a geographical unit, as are the British Isles; but there are many such which have been divided by history;
- Britain did indeed conquer the island, at a time when conquest universally gave title; for that matter, the Irish Gaels conquered the west of Scotland, and we all live in harmony now;
- Britain did indeed settle Northern Ireland – with Huguenots fleeing religious persecution elsewhere in Europe centuries ago;
- It did indeed maintain hegemony – but who, including Ireland – did not? Recriminations about past mistreatment are two-sided, and only hinder the resolution of present problems;
- Britain has long acknowledged the Irish wish for the union of Northern Ireland with the Republic; the fundamental difficulty, then as now, is the wish of the majority in Northern Ireland for union with the United Kingdom;
- The UK and Ireland are both members of the EC, share a common history and language, and treat each other's citizens as their own: the only barriers between them are in people's minds. Force raises barriers rather than lowering them. The IRA cannot defeat the British Army. Armed force is a recipe for stalemate, not for resolution.

All of the Troubles have been variations on these few notes.

The single underlying problem is the constitutional position of Northern Ireland:

[1920] Although at the beginning there are to be two Parliaments and two Governments in Ireland, the Act contemplates and affords every facility for union between North and South, and empowers the two Parliaments by mutual agreement and joint action to terminate partition and set up one Parliament and one Government for the whole of Ireland ... there is created a bond of union in the meantime by means of a Council of Ireland ...[12]

[1937] The national territory consists of the whole island of Ireland, its islands and the territorial seas. Pending the re-integration of the national territory, and without prejudice to the right of the Parliament and Government established by this Constitution to exercise jurisdiction over the whole of that territory, the laws enacted by that Parliament shall have the like area and extent of application as the laws of Saorstat Eireann and the like territorial effect....[13]

[1972] Northern Ireland must and will remain part of the United Kingdom for so long as that is the wish of a majority of the people; but that status does not preclude the necessary taking into account of what has been described in this Paper as the 'Irish Dimension'.[14]

[1973] The Irish Government fully accepted and solemnly declared that there could be no change in the status of Northern Ireland until a majority of the people of Northern Ireland desired a change in that status. The British Government solemnly declared that it was, and would remain, its policy to support the wishes of the majority of the people of Northern Ireland.[15]

[1985] The Governments [of the United Kingdom and the Irish Republic] (a) affirm that any change in the status of Northern Ireland would only come about with the consent of a majority of the people of Northern Ireland; (b) recognise that the present wish of a majority of the people of Northern Ireland is for no change in the status of Northern Ireland; (c) declare that, if in the future a majority of the people of Northern Ireland clearly wish for and formally consent to the establishment of a united Ireland, they will introduce and support in the respective Parliaments legislation to give effect to that wish.[16]

[1993] The Prime Minister, on behalf of the British Government, reaffirms that they will uphold the democratic wish of a greater number of the people of Northern Ireland on the issue of whether they prefer to support the Union or a sovereign united Ireland ... he reiterates... that they have no selfish strategic or economic interest in Northern Ireland. ... The Taoiseach, on behalf of the Irish Government, considers that the lessons of Irish history, and especially of Northern Ireland, show that stability and well-being will not be found under any political system which is refused allegiance or rejected on grounds of identity by a significant minority of those governed by it. For this reason, it would be wrong to attempt to impose a united Ireland, in the absence of the freely given consent of a majority of the people of Northern Ireland.[17]

[1998] The two Governments [UK and Ireland] recognise the legitimacy of whatever choice is freely exercised by a majority of the people of Northern Ireland with regard to its status ... acknowledge that while a substantial section of the people of Northern Ireland share the legitimate wish of the people of the island of Ireland for a united

Ireland, the present wish of a majority of the people of Northern Ireland, freely exercised and legitimate, is to maintain the union and ... that it would be wrong to make any change in the status of Northern Ireland save with the consent of a majority of its people ... recognise the birthright of all the people of Northern Ireland to identify themselves and be accepted as Irish or British, or both.[18]

On 10 May 1998, a Sinn Fein conference in Dublin voted by a large majority to support the Good Friday Agreement, and to change Sinn Fein's constitution to allow its representatives to take their seats in the new Assembly. Symbolically, the conference was attended by the Balcombe Street gang, who added their support.[19] The president of Sinn Fein, Gerry Adams, sought to reassure his supporters that Sinn Fein still sought the end of British rule in Northern Ireland, and to reassure the unionists that that did not mean the end of them: 'we face the future seeking a good faith and genuine engagement with you. When we call for the end of the British presence in Ireland we do not mean our Unionist neighbours. You have as much right to a full and equal life on this island as any other section of our people'.[20]

In Northern Ireland, 71 per cent of the voters in a referendum in May 1998 approved the Good Friday Agreement; 94 per cent of those in the Republic agreed.

A unionist politician was quoted as saying that 'the Unionists have won, but are too thick to see it. The republicans have lost, but are too clever to say it'.[21] Their respective lumpensupporters soon proved him right; the Orange Order's determination to march through Catholic areas in July caused some 1000 disorders in one week, but were put to shame after the death of three small boys in a sectarian attack by militant loyalists.[22] In August, the Real IRA's Omagh bomb injured 220 and killed 28: the worst single atrocity in the whole of the troubles.[23]

For the student of violent politics, the slow and subtle changes in the constitutional documents over nearly eighty years, particularly during the intense political activity over the thirty years of the troubles which started in 1968, show that the devil is not in the detail, but in the minds of men. What could seem more absurd to a Martian than two liberal democracies being unable to rid themselves of violent groups akin to those in the Balkans, Africa and the Middle East – genuinely divided societies? France and Germany live happily together today despite the tremendous casualties of war.

There is no intellectually convincing reason why the Good Friday Agreement could not have been reached in 1968 or even 1948 rather than 1998: the strategic and economic interests of the UK and Ireland coincide; they have a common language, and for a long time had a common currency; their citizens could live and work freely in each other's countries even before they acceded to the European Union; they have similar taxes and laws (though not similar enough to prevent lucrative cross-border smuggling, and claiming farm subsidies on the same animals moved from one side to the other). Intellectually the conflict is absurd. It is only explicable emotionally and spiritually, as a clash of creeds; a lethal clash in which nearly four thousand were killed, ten times as many injured, and hundreds of buildings and businesses destroyed over thirty years, at a cost of billions of pounds: ancient battles being refought on modern ground; animosities held long after their analogues had died. No wonder that the Good Friday Agreement was nicknamed 'Sunningdale for slow learners', or that Sir Patrick Mayhew likened the political process to a slow bicycle race.

Unionist discrimination against republicans in housing, employment and local government was of course one of the sparks that ignited the troubles. The veto extreme unionists had over reforms proposed by the moderates was a compelling reason for the introduction of Direct Rule; and a good reason for never having devolved power in the first place. However, the problems raised by the civil rights marchers had been solved by the early 1970s, and such marches had ceased. Had such objective problems been the only ones there could have been a swift response to them, as there was to the poll tax riots in Britain for example. Everyone would have gone back to everyday life. But the tribal drums were beating the call to arms, and it was too late.

A complicating factor was the fear that a neutral 32-county Ireland would be a disadvantage, if not an actual danger, to NATO in the Cold War, as it had been a disadvantage to the UK in the Second World War. Chamberlain had given up the three ports in the South to which Britain retained rights under the 1921 treaty, expecting that the Irish Free State would join any war, but de Valera had refused to compromise Irish neutrality by giving them back. The southern sea route from the west coast of England via St George's Channel between Wales and the Republic was therefore not secure, and was not used. All ships had to go through the narrow North Channel between Scotland and Northern Ireland, and St George's Channel was closed by mines.[24]

It may be no coincidence that the first declaration that the British Government had no selfish strategic or economic interest in Northern Ireland, came not long after the end of the Cold War.[25] Only the state

papers will tell. The IRA had long contended that the UK/NATO strategic interest was paramount:

> Britain's continuing involvement in Ireland is based on strategic,
> economic and political interests. Strategic interests are now the
> most important consideration in Britain's interference in Ireland.
> Quite apart from the very real, if somewhat exaggerated, fear among
> the British establishment that an Ireland freed from British
> influence could be a European Cuba, even the prospect of a neutral
> Ireland is regarded as a serious threat to British, and NATO's, strate-
> gic interests.[26]

Given the strategic position of Ireland between Britain and the US it
would be strange if there were not some truth in this, although
whether even a Cuba-style Ireland would have had an adverse effect on
NATO in the event of a hot war must be very doubtful, and whether it
would have expected to survive such a breach of its neutrality even
more so.[27]

In the Cold War, of course, a Soviet-friendly Ireland could have
caused NATO a great deal of trouble, especially if it also controlled
Northern Ireland. A scenario-writer could have had a lot of fun imagin-
ing Soviet monitoring of the Trident fleet, intense intelligence-gathering activities, Soviet air and naval bases, ground-to-air missiles supplied
to Ireland for 'self-defence' – and making contingency plans for an
Irish Missile Crisis. Such things are the stuff of thrillers, but they do
not have to be nearly as dramatic to affect security – witness the effects
of political changes in Libya, Malta and Cyprus. It would be strange,
therefore, if absolutely no weight had been given to the geostrategic
position of Ireland and no thought to the possibility of its becoming
unfriendly or politically unstable. The end of the Cold War would of
course have allowed even these remote contingencies to have been
filed away.

Although the Republic maintained its constitutional claim to the
North, and although the IRA was able to support operations in the
North from the Republic despite the hostility of its government and
action by its police, there was actually very little popular support in the
Republic for the nationalist cause in the North. Sinn Fein regularly
polled less than two per cent of the vote in elections in the Republic.[28]
Sinn Fein itself complained about the lack of governmental interest:

> For the greater part of the 26 County state's existence, successive
> Dublin governments have adopted a negative attitude in regard to

the issue of national democracy. For most of that period the issue of the British-imposed border has been addressed largely for purposes of electoral gain. Since Hillsborough we now have a firm hands-on approach from Dublin in support of the partition of our country.[29]

The reality of a generation of violence has overwritten the myths and folk memories of bygone generations; few want to pay the price of entry into the museum, and fewer still want to risk the fire of loyalist terrorism to escape the IRA frying pan. No southern party wants to have the responsibility of ruling a hostile Northern Ireland, and no conventional political party of any complexion, north or south, now advocates uniting Ireland without the consent of the North.

What violent politics has achieved over a generation in Northern Ireland is a shared understanding by the mass of the polity on both sides that the old problems are as insoluble as they ever were, and that dreams of one Irish *volk* happily sharing one island under one rule, which could possibly have come about had there been no Troubles, are now fantasy. The new Sinn Fein generation of Adams and McGuinness, which replaced the old of O'Bradaigh and O'Conaill, changed the tactics of the IRA from the bullet to the ballot, but altered neither its creed nor its aim one whit.[30] Sinn Fein had always believed that Britain would give up Northern Ireland if it were bombed hard enough – witness the abandonment of the Irish Free State, Palestine, Cyprus, Aden, Kenya, Ian Smith and white Rhodesia. The unionists had always feared that it might; hence the strikes, reprisals and intransigent rhetoric. The main casualty of the IRA has been the dream of uniting Ireland by force. The main fruit of their campaign has been the acceptance, on both sides of the border, that there are worse things than diversity, and violence is one of them.

The vast majority of people, north and south, realised that in the first place. Conventional politics could have solved the problems in Northern Ireland had Britain and the Irish Republic taken rather more interest in them than they did before the troubles began. The determination of one small gang of violent politicians to unite Ireland by force, and the determination of another to stop them by force, trumped the conventional politics of everyone else, and continued to do so for thirty years, killing thousands, injuring tens of thousands, and destroying the political, social and economic life of one and a half million people. Only a few chose violence; but the many failed to prevent them: what a price to pay.

5
Violence: Northern Ireland 1968–1998

Defining events

The first defining event in the recent troubles in Northern Ireland was probably the celebration of the fiftieth anniversary of the Easter Rising in 1966. The next was certainly the cultural revolution of 1968: Martin Luther King, *les événements de mai*, protest marches about Vietnam, civil rights marches against discrimination in Ulster, in itself a product of previous Troubles. Ironically, they escalated in exactly the way that Debray had hoped his *foco* theory would work, but had not, from marches to attacks on marches, broken windows to bombed churches, burning flags to burning houses, bullets to bombs. The events recorded in the Scarman Report on the 1969 disturbances seem almost trivial today: marches, demonstrations, public burnings of unpopular Acts, sit-ins, damaged churches and post offices, wrecked electricity pylons, and burned-out buses.

Internment is often cited as another turning point.[1] The narratives about poor targeting match, the ones about torture do not. The Compton Report found that that no-one had suffered brutality, although the standard interrogation techniques did entail ill-treatment.[2] The predictable counter-narrative, initiated by allegations made in the press, is of beatings, cruelty and torture. It seems likely that the popular anger which it undoubtedly aroused among republicans stemmed partly from fear that they were being left defenceless, and partly from folk memories of previous uses of internment without trial, rather than from the faults in the way it had been carried out, numerous though they were. Internment was a traditional technique on both sides of the border, and folk memories last a long time in Ireland.[3]

If, therefore, one interprets Irish history in terms of a fundamental continuity, one has the impression that historical identity cards were handed out at some point in the seventeenth century, about the time of the plantation of Ulster, and that latter-day actors have no choice but to act out the roles assigned to them by history.[4]

Bew and Patterson go on to argue that the recidivist attribution quickly became out-of-date as important discontinuities appeared between the troubles of old and those which began in 1968, and the latter became essentially a tribal war between the working classes of the two communities.

They are clearly right in terms of substance: the similarities between the battle for Irish independence which climaxed in 1919–21 and the battle for a united Ireland which started in 1968 are superficial. In terms of form, however, folk memories of the first conflict clearly drove the second, republicans and nationalists vying for the parts of the heroes of independence: Redmond, de Valera, Collins, Griffith, Brugha, Cosgrave, Connolly; while their unionist and loyalist counterparts auditioned for Carson, Lord Randolph Churchill and the supporting cast.

We 'learned' that God and Irish nationalism marched hand in hand to a tune shrouded in mystery but which was always clear to the faithful. We were taught, over and over again, as part of our daily school routine, that Irish Catholics were special to God. The Virgin Mary was an Irish colleen. Padraig Pearse and the other rebel leaders executed by the British after the Easter Rising of 1916 were painstakingly interwoven with images of Christ and Catholic martyrs into a seamless mix of blood sacrifice for faith and fatherland.[5]

New myths were added to the old:

I felt I was looking at the military might of Protestantism, reinforced by the British government and now poised for victory. I felt that these Orange shock troops had to be fought and resisted: for the first time I thought about joining the IRA[6]...I regarded myself and my comrades as history's vengeful children, come to exact the price for a society built on injustice. I believed that in our actions we gave form to the stifled rage of our ancestors. I felt I was part of an organisation designed to make unionists feel the killing rage of generations past and present.[7]

New martyrs were added to the old:

> For me, to strike at Toombs was to strike at an ancient colonial system of élites. Killing Toombs would also be a symbol of our dogged resistance to inequality and injustice, a gesture of solidarity with the protesting prisoners in the H-Blocks who had just embarked on the first hunger strike. I was full of a heady mixture of anti-imperialism, anger, sympathy and self-importance.[8]

Modern Marxism was also added – or perhaps old-fashioned class hatred. Collins describes how an attack on a Catholic-owned hotel in Warrenpoint was planned:

> Middle-class Catholics and Protestants lived in harmony, united – as I would have put it from my Marxist perspective – by their class interests in maintaining a high standard of living ... I loathed the tranquillity of this little seaside town ... It was a safe haven for the Crown forces: a lot of policemen and soldiers lived there, enjoying a good relationship with their Catholic neighbours. The place had become the focus of all my anger. I was going to enjoy bringing Warrenpoint's fairytale existence to an end.[9]

Geopolitical analogies were also important drivers of the violent politics in Northern Ireland. Sinn Fein and the IRA regarded the province as Britain's last colony, and were well aware of its withdrawal from the others, and of the part violence had played – or was thought to have played. Their belief was reinforced in 1989 when the then Secretary of State for Northern Ireland, Peter Brooke, remarked during a broadcast interview:

> Let me remind you of the move towards independence in Cyprus, and a British Minister stood up in the House of Commons and used the word 'never' in a way which within two years there had been a retreat from that word. All I'm saying is that I would hope that the British government on a long-term basis would be sufficiently flexible, that if flexibility were required it could be used, but I am in no way predicting or predicting what those circumstances would be.[10]

He quickly backtracked, but Adams and McGuinness were not surprised by the original remark:

> Our attitude to the struggle for freedom is the same now as it ever was. We're here seventeen years on, [after the secret talks in London

in 1972] and we're still talking about Britain's disengagement from Ireland, and nothing Peter Brooke says about the republican movement not winning the struggle is going to convince us that we can't win. We're absolutely convinced that at some time in the future some British government will talk to the republican movement, that some British government will disengage from Ireland. We're absolutely confident about that.[11]

The pattern of the violence over the 30 years is striking. By the end of 1998, 3630 people had been killed. Nearly 60 per cent were killed by republican groups, nearly 30 per cent by loyalists, and 10 per cent by the security forces. The Provisional IRA alone accounted for almost half of all the deaths. More than one-third of the dead (34 percent) were catholic civilians; 19 per cent were protestant civilians. Fourteen per cent were members of the locally-recruited security forces: the Royal Ulster Constabulary and the Ulster Defence Regiment, later the Royal Irish Rifles. Another fourteen per cent were from the British armed forces, principally the Army. Eleven per cent of those killed were republican paramilitaries and four per cent were loyalist paramilitaries. Four per cent were prison officers, civilians killed outside Northern Ireland, or others. Of the total of 3630 dead, well over 90 percent were killed in Northern Ireland: 3370 people. Three per cent were killed in Britain (124 people), another three per cent in the Republic (118 people) and less than one per cent elsewhere in Europe (18 in Germany, the Netherlands and France).[12]

The number of people killed and injured in each year of the conflict is shown in Figure 5.1, and those responsible for the deaths in Figure 5.2. Since the aim of this chapter is to illustrate the pattern and scale of the violence over thirty years, it concentrates on deaths as the best measure of the misery caused by the troubles, but far from the only one. House-burning, robbery, intimidation, extortion, protection rackets and corruption cause no physical casualties, but are far from trivial.

Accompaniments of violent politics. So-called 'punishment beatings' have been common in Northern Ireland, and often unrecorded. 'There seems to be no shortage of baseball-bat wielders ready to cripple young men for the petty crimes of the poor.'[13]

Figure 5.3 illustrates the annual death toll during the thirty years of conflict. Four phases emerge: the four-year rise culminating in what became a straightforward battle of arms in 1972, followed by four years of tribal warfare; then eighteen years of stalemate before the peace process slowly emerged. It took another four years to achieve the Good

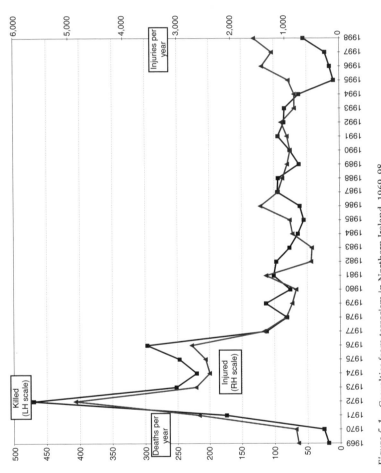

Figure 5.1 Casualties from terrorism in Northern Ireland, 1969–98
Source: Appendix: Table A.2.

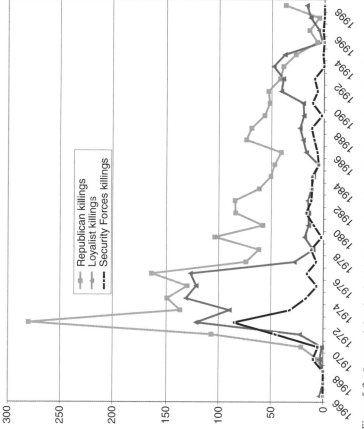

Figure 5.2 Responsibility for deaths from the troubles in Northern Ireland 1966–98
Source: McKittrick et al., *Lost Lives* (Edinburgh and London, Mainstream Publishing, 1999), table 2, p. 1475.

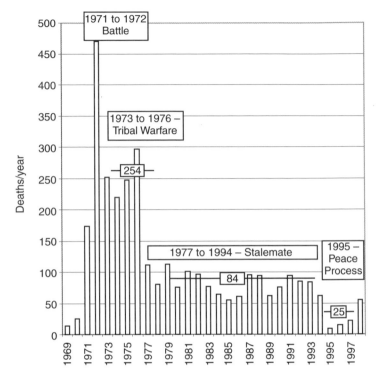

Figure 5.3   Pattern of deaths from the Troubles in Northern Ireland
Source: Appendix, Table A.1.

Friday Agreement of 1998, during which killings dropped to some 15 a year – a figure not seen since 1969 – but substantial property damage was still done.

Half of all the fatal casualties were killed during the six years of 1971 to 1976; the other half died over 24 years: four times as long.

Manpower, materiel and skill

Tiny numbers of people caused the casualties: perhaps three or four hundred members of the IRA, far fewer were active at any one time;[14] there were many more supporters of the loyalist paramilitaries, but fewer active terrorists. Whatever the headcount on either side, the number of people actually required to carry out and support the number of terrorist operations each year need only be a couple of hundred: only one person in every 7500 in Northern Ireland, for example.

Terrorist groups, from ETA and the IRA down to the Red Brigades and Red Army Faction, do not have difficulty finding the numbers they need. They may be short of materiel, including money, as the IRA was in the beginning; but they do not actually need much: arms and explosives are cheap, and dedicated people do not need financial reward; they may well live on the state they want to destroy.

O'Callaghan reports that in the early 1980s, Adams, then the IRA's adjutant-general, said it cost £2M a year to keep the IRA running. Belfast raised the bulk of the money, through IRA-controlled drinking clubs, the Falls Road's famous Black Taxis, which paid £15 a week each, and extortion, tax swindles and social security fraud.[15] Later it was to add the proceeds of cross-border smuggling, and frauds over EC grain and cattle subsidies. Money from the Irish diaspora flowed in, especially after pro-IRA fund-raising drives in the US.[16] Weapons and explosives were easy to find, even in the early days: 'they were coming from everywhere, mostly from old republicans who had buried gear in the twenties, thirties and forties ... We couldn't cope sometimes with the amount of gear coming in. It was unbelievable'.[17] In the 1970s some 2500 weapons and one million rounds of ammunition are estimated to have been smuggled in from America, despite FBI successes in interceptions.[18] In March 1973 the Irish Navy intercepted a shipment from Libya.[19] Another was intercepted by the French in 1986, when Colonel Gaddafi greatly increased arms supplies to the IRA in retaliation for the UK's support of US airstrikes designed to deter Libyan-backed international terrorism.[20] In October 1986 the *Villa* successfully landed 100 tons of Libyan weapons, including rocket launchers, surface-to-air missiles and a ton of Semtex explosive; there had been three earlier shipments.[21] 'All terrorist activity depends on funding, which in itself is a multi-million pound criminal conspiracy involving all the paramilitary organisations ... Further successes were achieved in the courts, bringing the total prosecutions so far to 400 and the sum of money involved to £49M'.[22] McGartland, IRA member and Special Branch agent, believes that $US10–12 million a year was flowing to the IRA in the late 1980s and early 1990s.[23]

Tracing and countering where money and materiel come from is an oft-cited counter-measure, but it may not be as useful as it seems. It is not difficult to find instances where violence has been ended by the capture of its leaders, but it is hard to find even one movement which has collapsed because it had insufficient materiel.[24]

The greatest death and destruction in Northern Ireland was caused, however, during the five years 1971 to 1976, long before the massive supplies from Libya, when the IRA killed 853 people, an average of 142 a year. In the five years which followed the Libyan supplies, 1986 to 1991, they killed 304, an average of 50; about a third of the figure before all the arms arrived.[25] There were 7828 bombings in the first period, and 2170 in the second.[26]

Mallie and McKittrick contend that before the arrival of the Libyan consignments the IRA's basic bottleneck was weaponry.[27] That may well be correct, but despite the relative scarcity of weapons in the early days they did an immense amount of damage. The amount of materiel required, even at the height of the troubles, was small.

Skill was a more critical factor. The IRA is conventionally portrayed as a highly skilled terrorist organisation. Sadly, however, most terrorist operations do not require much skill, so the paramilitaries of both sides were able to cause a lot of casualties and damage with the rough and ready people they had at their disposal. Many of the IRA's operations went wrong. According to Collins and O'Callaghan about half failed through muddle, disorganisation, or betrayal.[28] The other half was enough.

Despite apparent support for its aims, and despite the few people needed for a terrorist campaign, the IRA seems to have had difficulty recruiting members in the Republic. The problems Collins had in finding them illustrates the gap between the small number of those who are prepared to kill, and the large number of those prepared to protest. He describes his difficulties in getting information on potential targets, and his use of intimidation to overcome them.[29]

Nor are terrorists necessarily as hard as they seem. O'Callaghan describes how shocked he was by his IRA boss gloating that a police-woman killed by an IRA bomb might have been pregnant, and the IRA would have got two for the price of one,[30] how influenced he was by the reactions of his mother to IRA killings, by writers and columnists,[31] and by the IRA's bombing of Lord Mountbatten's yacht in 1979 in the Irish Republic itself.[32] Collins describes his growing disillusionment, *passim*.

The troubles were curiously isolated from everyday life; Irish butter did not lie unsold on British shelves when the Republic refused to extradite terrorists; Irish riverdancers were not booed off the stage after IRA atrocities; British tourists did not shun Ireland, or Irish workers England, although their governments disagreed, and their fellow-nationals were being killed.

The pattern of violence

The pattern of casualties over the thirty years was illustrated in Figure 5.1. About ten people have been injured for every one killed; a ratio not dissimilar to that in war. The relationship has been close enough over the period to use deaths as a proxy for injuries. There are differences, stemming from the particular weapons and tactics used at the time, but death remains the key measure. Many of the injured will get better; none of the dead will. On the other hand some of the injured will be maimed for life, and will be a permanent reminder of the atrocities which hurt them. Neither the dead nor the injured will be forgotten by their families or their community; nor will it be forgotten who did the killing and maiming.

The pattern of deaths from violence over the thirty years of the Troubles is striking: see Figure 5.3. The sharp drops in the number of killings in Northern Ireland clearly define four phases. There were nearly 500 killings in 1972; they dropped to half as many during each of the years 1973–6. From 1977 to 1994 killings averaged 84 a year, one-third as many as in the preceding four years. From 1994 to 1998 they averaged 25, less than one-third of the average over the preceding eighteen years.

These are quite dramatic changes by any account, and merit explanation. The narratives of the protagonists will of course conflict, as they always do in violent politics, especially over minute detail, and even more over grand conclusions. Reconciling their narratives is impossible and fortunately, from the point of view of this analysis, not necessary. The purpose here is simply to illustrate how quickly violent politics can grow to dominate a democracy, how long it can last, and how terrible its effects are. The next chapter analyses how it was dealt with through criminal and anti-terrorist law. The succeeding chapters outline other strategies.

Phase 1 – battle: 1969 to 1972

This is arguably the most important phase, for it is the only one in which things done differently might have nipped the whole conflict in the bud, or allowed it to wither on the vine. Once 1972 had happened, the battle lines had been drawn and the opposing forces deployed.

Starting dates are always arbitrary, and in Ireland, because of its long history of conflict, even more so than most. History – or what is passionately believed to be history – fuelled the flame from the most flickering match. The IRA border campaign of 1956–62 fizzled out under brisk action on both sides of the border and public revulsion, but nevertheless worsened Anglo-Irish relations and raised loyalist fears.[33] The 1966 commemoration of the fiftieth anniversary of the Easter Rising raised tension on both sides of the border. It sparked a counter-commemoration of the fiftieth anniversary of the Battle of the Somme – and the re-formation of the Ulster Volunteer Force, which then declared war on the IRA, and killed three people.

The Civil Rights marches in 1968 – against monopoly government, gerrymandering, discrimination in housing and jobs – led to counter-marches, confrontation, ambushes, street battles, riots, stones, petrol bombs, bans, curfews, deaths from RUC beatings, house-burnings. These may not have been taken as seriously as they deserved in mainland Britain because the UK government left Northern Ireland very much to Stormont and knew little about the province. Most people in Britain were familiar with sectarianism of the football team and pub brawl kind, but knew nothing of the two communities in Northern Ireland: living in different areas, going to different schools, practising different religions, playing different sports, reading different newspapers, giving their children different names, celebrating different festivals, drinking in different pubs, singing different songs, having different standards of living – some self-inflicted but others imposed by discrimination – and holding irreconcilable political beliefs. Nevertheless, the two communities lived, in reasonable amity, cheek-by-jowl, so the violence had all the greater effect when it came; houses on community boundaries became dangerous, and were abandoned and burned – or burned and abandoned.

It may also be that familiarity with the then-fashionable violent strikes and confrontations in the UK, student demonstrations and civil rights marches throughout 1968, and *les événements de mai*, raised thresholds so that the marches in Northern Ireland did not trigger alarms. Picture books on the Battle of the Bogside and the Paris student barricades appeared simultaneously.

During the battles between the RUC and the residents of the Bogside district of Londonderry in August 1969 the Irish government asked the British government to negotiate over the constitutional position of Northern Ireland, and to apply to the UN for a peacekeeping force because the RUC was no longer accepted as impartial and the Army would be unacceptable.[34] In the same month, republican paramilitaries shot two protestants during a huge number of street disturbances in Belfast and Londonderry, and loyalists shot one catholic; the RUC shot four catholics, and another died after being beaten with batons.

The events of August 1969 were undoubtedly defining. The republican narrative was of spontaneous and peaceful protests about social conditions being attacked by mobs of unionists and policemen who invaded their areas, burned their houses and shot at their people. The loyalist narrative was of republican opportunists taking control of the bandwagon of peaceful protests, converting them into riots and attacks on the state, and using the resulting mayhem to reactivate their campaign of armed force. The truth is no doubt far more complicated than either of these, as many have pointed out. It is likely to be further complicated as UK documents are released under the thirty-year rule.[35] For the purposes of this analysis, it does not matter where the objective truth, if any, lies; only how differing subjective truths were used to justify horrendous amounts of death and destruction over a generation or more.

There were only five more deaths in 1969, and none in 1970 until June. Twenty-six died in the rest of that year: fifteen killed by the IRA or other republican paramilitaries, eight by the Army and two by loyalist paramilitaries. One protestant was killed by a missile during a riot. In February 1971 the IRA killed nine people: two soldiers, two RUC, and five protestants in a civilian landrover mistaken for an Army one. The Northern Ireland Home Affairs Minister, John Taylor, told *The Times* that 'We are going to shoot it out with them, it is as simple as that'.[36] The IRA killed the first soldier since the 1920s, during huge riots in which the Army killed two, including one known IRA man. The Prime Minister of the province, Major James Chichester-Clark, announced that 'Northern Ireland is at war with the Irish Republican Army Provisionals'.[37] On 9 August, by which time the death toll had reached 76 and there had been 300 explosions and another 300 shooting incidents, internment was introduced. A series of gunbattles between the IRA and the Army followed. During the month, the Army killed twenty-three people and the IRA nine. The IRA chief of staff, Sean MacStiofain, declared all-out war.[38] Nobody actually waged war, of course, and if they had, there would have been a winner. Nevertheless a bloody battle took place. Nobody won.

Figure 5.4 shows those responsible for the deaths in each month during the three years before the outright battle of July 1972 in which nearly 100 people were killed, and for the year which followed.[39]

It is not as easy as it seems to associate the oft-quoted defining events during the period with the scale of violence. The initial gun battles after internment in August 1971 were followed by a drop in killings for the next three months, not the rise which is conventionally attributed to internment. Bloody Sunday at the end of January 1972

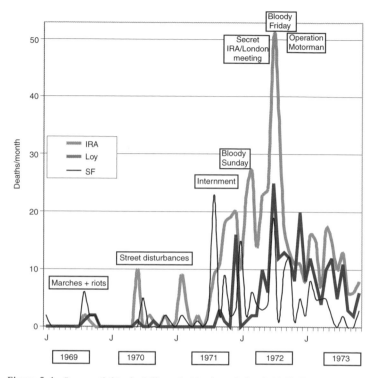

Figure 5.4   Responsibility for killings in Northern Ireland, 1969–73
Source: Sutton, Malcolm, *An Index of Deaths from the Conflict in Ireland 1969–1993*
(Belfast, Beyond the Pale Publications, 1994).

was another such defining moment.[40] Once again the name it was
quickly given harked back to history.[41] It is often blamed for increasing
killings, but if it did the effect was modest. Thirty-nine people were
killed in December 1971; 27 in January 1972, including the 13 of
Bloody Sunday, then 29, 37, 20, 39 and 35 from February to June.
Deaths dropped after the introduction of Direct Rule in March, but
only for a single month.

On 7 July 1972, the then Secretary of State for Northern Ireland,
William Whitelaw, secretly met MacStiofain, Adams and McGuinness
in London, ten days after the IRA had declared a ceasefire.[42] The IRA
probably saw the meeting as a historical parallel to the negotiations
between the British Government, the Provisional Government of the

Irish Republic and the IRA in 1921.[43] They demanded a general amnesty, the immediate withdrawal of British forces from 'sensitive areas', and complete withdrawal from Ireland by 1 January 1975.[44] They clearly did not like what they heard in reply.[45] On 21 July, Bloody Friday, the IRA exploded 26 bombs in Belfast in a single hour, killing eleven people and injuring 130. On 31 July the Army removed the no-go areas in Belfast and Londonderry in Operation Motorman, denying the IRA and loyalist paramilitaries the practical and political advantages of owning territory. Ninety-six people were killed in a single month.

The IRA killed 43 of the 96, including 18 members of the security forces; other republican groups killed eight. Loyalist paramilitaries, who had only started killing significant numbers after the IRA surge in late 1971, killed 25. The Army killed 19, eight of whom were known IRA. The killers of one man were unknown.[46] Such a flurry of figures is hard to follow: graphs may help. Figure 5.4 shows the close relationships between the actions of each of the protagonists, how late the killings of the loyalist paramilitaries began, and how quickly, once they had begun, they matched those of the IRA.

The graphs say nothing about cause and effect; from the protagonists' points of view, each was reacting to the activities of the other: returning the serve, as one of them put it.[47] There is little doubt, however, that strong action of any kind by one side or the other, whether deliberate or inadvertent, whether ostensibly defensive or obviously offensive, provoked a reaction. It is too easy to say that strong action is always, everywhere, and for ever counterproductive; only that it is likely to be so in its immediate aftermath, when reaction follows action; that the intended effect may take a long time to make itself felt; that there are likely to be unexpected, unintended, and unwelcome consequences; and that public opinion at home and abroad remembers only the act and its immediate consequences: it does not set them in context, or take a long-term view. The Army's shooting of 13 people on Bloody Sunday is remembered; its shooting 22 people in the two weeks of gunbattles following internment six months earlier is not. Interestingly, although Operation Motorman involved tanks and armoured engineer equipment clearing barricades which could have been regarded as necessary defences, and was a massive, though swiftly-conducted, operation, it provoked little reaction at the time and is consequently little discussed in analyses. It was arguably one of the most important reasons for the subsequent drop in violence.

Public opinion does not expect – rightly so – that the armed forces of the state will kill unarmed civilians; that is not what they are there to do. Sadly, however, it does accept that if terrorists kill unarmed civilians, that is exactly the sort of thing they would be expected to do. The killings are condemned, but there are no public inquiries, no investigative journalism, no documentaries and docu-dramas, not much exploration in depth of their meaning and consequences. Bloody Sunday (of which there never was another) had a much greater effect on public opinion than Bloody Friday (which was just one of many such) because the one was totally out of character and the other totally in character: another of the asymmetries in which violent politics abounds.

Bloody Friday was not the IRA's revenge for Bloody Sunday – that had come three weeks after Bloody Sunday, when the Official IRA had bombed the officers' mess of the Parachute Brigade headquarters in Aldershot, killing five women mess staff, a gardener and a Catholic chaplain. The Provisional IRA's target on Bloody Friday was not the British Army, but the British presence in Northern Ireland, and therefore the union.

A tragic mistake by the Army undoubtedly strengthened the resolve of the IRA, and legitimised its struggle. It is easy to see why deliberate attacks by the IRA would do the same, or even more, to strengthen the resolve of the loyalists and legitimise their counterattacks – but they were to continue for another quarter of a century before the message sank in:

> the most intense spate of loyalist killings – nine dead Catholics in seven days – came in the aftermath of 21 July 1972 when the Belfast Brigade of the Provisional IRA planted twenty-six car bombs in Belfast, slaughtering eleven people and injuring 130. That day became known as 'Bloody Friday' and was a watershed in the loyalists' response to IRA violence. Any inhibitions there may have been about targeting innocent Catholics were literally blown away.[48]

The pattern of the early years of the conflict can be simplified even more by treating the IRA and the other republican paramilitaries as having the common aim of creating a United Ireland, and the security forces and loyalists as having a common aim – to maintain the status quo of the United Kingdom of Great Britain and Northern Ireland – and plotting the killings of one against the other. That is emphatically not to say that the loyalist paramilitaries and the security forces fought on the same side, let alone in alliance; still less one under the command of the other. However, although that was manifestly untrue, it was often contended by the IRA, and understanding the mindset of the paramilitaries may help analysis.

Figure 5.5 omits killings by the security forces, and simply plots the killings by republican and loyalist paramilitaries against one another – what might be called the loyalist view of the battle. Republican killings far outnumber those by loyalists. Figure 5.6 represents what might be called the republican view of the battle: it plots killings by those fighting for a United Ireland against those fighting for a United Kingdom – loyalist and security forces combined. The reciprocity between the antagonists is striking. It is clear that the casualties caused by one side could readily be matched by the other. Whether the initiative was taken by those aiming to overthrow the status quo or by those whose aim was to maintain it does not matter. The paramilitaries clearly could not win the battle by force of arms, as if they were real armies.

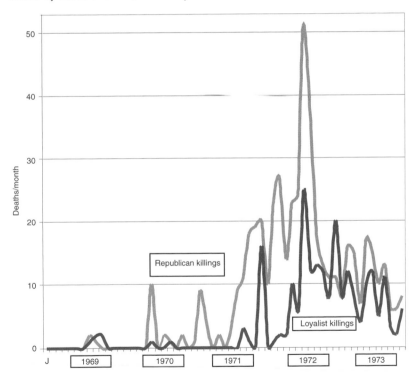

Figure 5.5   Sectarian battle, 1971–72
Source: Sutton, Malcolm, *An Index of Deaths from the Conflict in Ireland 1969–1993* (Belfast, Beyond the Pale Publications, 1994).

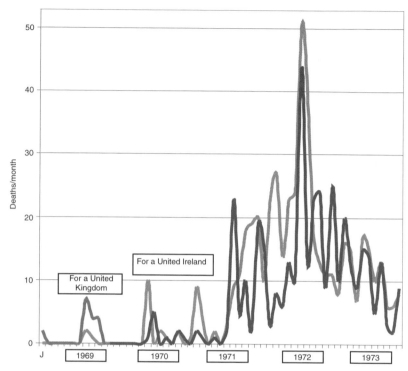

Figure 5.6   Battle for union, 1971–72
Source: Sutton, Malcolm, *An Index of Deaths from the Conflict in Ireland 1969–1993*
(Belfast, Beyond the Pale Publications, 1994).

Phase 2 – tribal warfare: 1973 to 1976

It is not difficult to see why there was such a sharp drop after 1972.
The violence simply could not have continued at that level: nearly 500
deaths and 5000 injuries in a year; 10 000 shootings and 2000 bombs;
2000 armed robberies; 19 tonnes of explosive and 1200 firearms found
by the security forces; all in a population of one and a half million:
that of a small city.[49] The equivalent for the UK's 55 million would
have been 18 000 killed and 180 000 injured in a single year. The
equivalent for the USA would have been 66 000 killed: more than in
the whole Vietnam campaign.

The 1972 scale of violence had shown the IRA that attacks on the
security forces could not weaken their resolve, nor that of the UK government, and that they exposed their own operations to successful

counter-attack. The paramilitaries of both sides had learnt that sectarian attacks were swiftly answered in kind by the paramilitaries of the other side, and thus damaged their own community as much as that of their opponents. By 1973, the security forces had rapidly replaced the unprotected accommodation and lightly protected observation posts thrown up in the early days, had adopted new methods of patrolling which made them hard targets, and had set up a rich network of observation posts equipped with newly-designed night vision equipment, large telescopes fitted with cameras, and swift communications.

Figure 5.7 shows the monthly death toll from 1973 to 1976, and those responsible for the killings. It is easy to attribute the peaks to specific attacks, but very hard to match the pattern to any political events. The first UK discussion paper on the future of Northern Ireland was published in October 1972.[50] It was followed by a White Paper proposing a Northern Ireland Assembly in March 1973, and by the first, stormy, meeting of the elected Assembly in July. The Sunningdale Conference on power-sharing took place in December 1973. The proposed power-sharing executive was duly elected and met. Power-sharing was anathema to militant unionists, all the more because of the events of the years before. The executive was brought down by a strike by the loyalist Ulster Workers' Council which paralysed the province. There were Constitutional Conventions in 1974 and 1975. The IRA extended its campaign to mainland Britain; a new Prevention of Terrorism Act followed immediately. The last detainees were released at the end of 1975.[51] By that time there was little fuss about detention, and the release, which had been intended as a reward for the reducing violence, arguably extended it by putting paramilitary leaders back on the streets. Special category status ended in the spring of 1976. 'Constitutionally speaking, the period 1974–94 was largely one of activity without movement.'[52] Indeed.

As Figure 5.7 illustrates, by far the biggest driver of the killing was tit-for-tat sectarianism, not political events. Killings by loyalist and republican paramilitaries rose and fell together. The IRA bombed an Army coach on the M6 in Britain in February 1974, killing nine soldiers and three civilians, and bombed pubs in Guildford and Birmingham in October and November, killing five off-duty soldiers and 20 civilians. The loyalists took their bombs to the Republic in May, killing 26 people in Dublin and seven in Monaghan.

The security forces killed very few during this period, which became one of straightforward tribal warfare. The security forces were rightly fully accountable for their actions, subject to strict rules of engage-

100

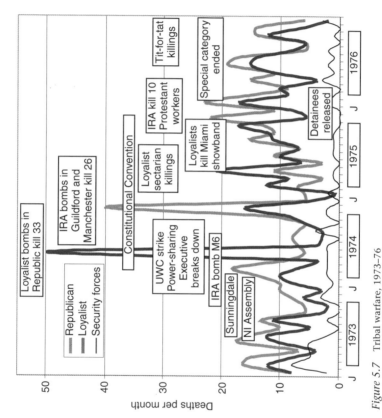

Figure 5.7 Tribal warfare, 1973–76

Source: Sutton, *An Index of Deaths from the Conflict in Ireland 1969–1993*
(Belfast, Beyond the Pale Publications, 1994).

ment, and to trial and punishment if they were broken. They were of course easily identifiable, and by now well trained to meet the unusual circumstances of Northern Ireland, which they certainly had not been in the beginning. The IRA and loyalist paramilitaries were none of these, except perhaps well-trained; but it does not take much training to be able to kill from the shadows and run away. They were accountable to nobody except their own side, and as long as the killings were roughly proportionate and roughly 'justifiable' as defence, retaliation or pre-emption, they would be rewarded rather than punished.

The IRA made much of the occasionally-discovered links between Protestant paramilitaries and the RUC, implying that these were systematic rather than rogue.[53] Public records will no doubt tell where the truth lies, but it would be contrary to the ethos of the RUC (much-maligned, but nevertheless well-maintained) for there to have been any systematic link, rather than leaks via rogue policemen or soldiers. Indeed, had there been any systematic links, few IRA would have survived loyalist targeting. Nothing more is necessary to explain the success of tit-for-tat paramilitary operations than the ease with which terrorists can move within a democracy, their small signal in space and time swamped by the noise of everyday activity.

The activities of unionist paramilitaries punished those of republican paramilitaries and *vice versa*, or rather punished the communities to which they belonged. The resulting check on their activities would not have been unwelcome to the authorities in Northern Ireland and in the Republic. It is highly unlikely to have been encouraged, let alone helped, by either, on grounds of both principle and practice: the difficulty of control after the wink had been tipped, and the consequences of discovery.

It is interesting to speculate on what the situation would have been had the paramilitaries of one side not been effectively neutralised by the other. The security of Northern Ireland would have relied purely upon the results of treating terrorists as criminals, which will be analysed in the next chapter.

Phase 3 – stalemate: 1977 to 1994

Thus began a period of stalemate which was to last for eighteen years. The IRA's search for a politico–military victory via the bomb and the bullet failed, together with the UK government's search for a political solution acceptable to all sides. Indeed the stalemate arose because the

IRA wanted only one thing – a united Ireland – and that was the one thing that the UK could not and would not deliver. If the UK had not abandoned the Falkland islanders on the other side of the world, it was hardly going to abandon its own countrymen twenty kilometres from the mainland. Nor, despite the rhetoric, would a thus-united Ireland have been acceptable to the South. If the IRA could do what it did in the North with a few hundred activists drawn from a more or less sympathetic population of half a million, it was obvious what the loyalists could do when they had a million to draw on, and controlled the entire infrastructure of the North – cities, ports, electricity, water, transport. Nor would the IRA, or Sinn Fein, have been a welcome addition to the politics of Ireland at any time – still less with success under their belts.

The years of battle and tribal warfare had shown that the IRA's campaign of violence had no positive effect. Its only effects were negative – to prevent any political accommodation other than a united Ireland, to poison relationships between the two communities and two countries, and to damage the social and economic infrastructure of the province which had been built up painstakingly by the UK government: new housing, new towns, new businesses, non-discrimination. The original civil rights issues had been successfully tackled; there were no more marches and riots on those grounds.[54]

By now, IRA activists could no longer move freely – or rather, they could, but they would be seen. The security forces took advantage of the same fact as paramilitaries and criminals – that it is very difficult to distinguish a small signal of clandestine activity among the huge noise of everyday life. Some of the Army's early intelligence activities were very bold: setting up a laundry in the heart of republican Belfast, for example, whose vehicles and building doubled as a clandestine observation posts. The story of the later covert surveillance organisations set up by the Army and RUC is just beginning to emerge into public view. The paramilitaries were of course always aware of their existence, and of the brake they put on their activities.[55] The Army moved freely, keeping its eyes and ears open, and producing a constant stream of detailed intelligence. Little about surveillance of the telephone network and airwaves is in the public domain, but it is not difficult to imagine how big a handicap the lack of secure telecommunications must have been to the paramilitaries.[56] Intelligence successes drove the IRA into a cell structure – more secure but less flexible and active.

The RUC took over from the Army as the co-ordinator of all anti-terrorist action: 'police primacy'. Their interrogation centres produced a steady stream of confessions, and conversions into 'supergrasses', without the excesses and backlash of the early days.[57] 'Special category' status for those convicted of terrorist crimes – called 'political status' by the IRA – was ended.[58] That led to the dirty protest, the hunger strikes, the election of Bobby Sands to the UK parliament[59] and of two other hunger strikers to the Irish Dàil. The strikes were intended to win recognition that the IRA was an army and its volunteers soldiers. It won support and sympathy, but not recognition. An unintended consequence was that the IRA entered conventional politics, in order to achieve concessions. Adams was elected to Westminster in 1983, and became president of Sinn Fein the same year. In 1986 Sinn Fein dropped its traditional policy of abstaining from the Dàil, and the traditionalists left.

By 1977 it had become difficult and dangerous to attack soldiers, policemen, judges and ministers, who were the only people who could be regarded in any way as 'legitimate' targets of the IRA's 'Brits out' campaign. Bombing shops and pubs caused horrendous casualties, public condemnation, and certain retaliation by the paramilitaries of the other side. Killing civilians could not be presented as in any way legitimate, or consistent with the IRA's stated aim. Nor, by that time, could apologists for the IRA present such killings as natural consequences of discrimination and repression by the loyalists and British, who were only getting what they deserved.

Figures 5.8 and 5.9 show the pattern of violence and major political events during the eighteen–year stalemate. There is no obvious relationship. There was of course a continuing search for a political solution, and continuing violence designed to push any solution in the direction desired by one set of paramilitaries or the other. There was also, of course, a continuous effort to find the authors of atrocities, and bring them to justice, to protect people and institutions from terrorism, and to develop the economic and social infrastructure of the province.

There were many courageous grassroots peace initiatives, which gained much international support, but not peace. Many praiseworthy, and equally brave, grassroots organisations were designed to bridge the gap between the two communities, particularly their children and young people. But the violence was driven by the paramilitaries; above a lower bound set by the need to demonstrate that they had not been defeated and were prepared to fight for as long as it took to get their way, but below an upper level set by the tolerance of their own community, the fear of triggering reprisals from their opponents, and the danger of being

104

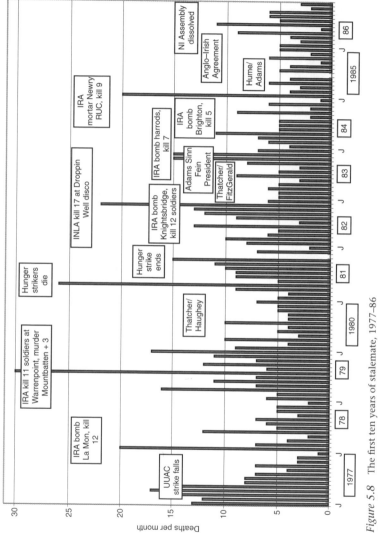

Figure 5.8   The first ten years of stalemate, 1977–86
Source: Sutton, *An Index of Deaths from the Conflict in Ireland 1969–1993* (Belfast, Beyond the Pale Publications, 1994).

105

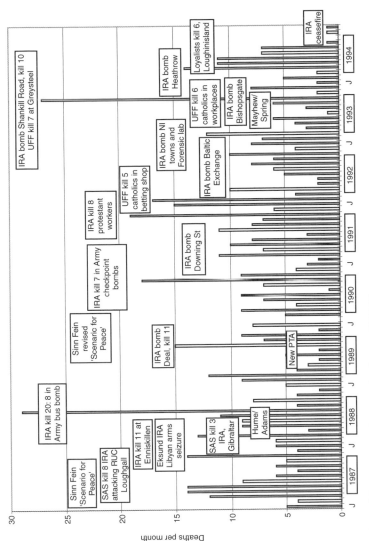

Figure 5.9 Another eight years of stalemate, 1987–94

Source: 1987–93 as Figure 5.7. 1994: RUC Central Statistics Unit.

caught by the security forces. The IRA had hundreds of tons of arms and ammunition by this time, from Libya and others, but used little.

If the upper level was breached, which happened from time to time, information began to flow to the security forces through the increasingly effective intelligence organisation. The system of violent and conventional politics was self-balancing, in stasis; but at an awful social and economic cost, which was of course the point of it all.[60] The IRA could not win, but it could stymie any political progress short of a united Ireland. It held the trump cards of violent politics: prevention, fear and force. Persuasion, shame and reward were not enough to counter them – though all were tried; and tried again.

The IRA's short war strategy had failed, so its only option was either no war or a long one. Nevertheless, the long war strategy is often attributed to Gerry Adams, who was released from the Maze in February 1977, and elected President of Sinn Fein in 1982.[61] In March 1984 he was wounded by loyalist paramilitaries in Belfast. O'Callaghan says that had he been killed there would have been no one to replace him. 'He and he alone was responsible for instigating the changes that were bringing the IRA out into the real political world.'[62]

Phase 4 – the peace process: 1995 to 1998

After eighteen years, the long war strategy had got nowhere. Adams and his associates changed tack again, and the 'peace process' began.

There was a new generation of politicians in Britain and Ireland: Hume, Adams, Trimble, Reynolds, Bruton, Ahern, Major, Blair, Mary Robinson, Mo Mowlem, Dick Spring, Peter Mandelson, John Reid. Leadership was a key factor, as would be expected from the analysis so far. ETA's campaign in Spain also lasted a generation; so had Al-Fatah and the PLO in the Middle East; so did the ANC in South Africa. Not until a complete generation had grown up with conflict and produced a new generation of political leaders was there any real change. On the other hand, most such groups cease to exist long before that. Action Directe in France, the Bader–Meinhoff/Red Army Faction in Germany and the Red Brigades in Italy all collapsed when their leaders were captured and imprisoned.[63] The loss of their leaders was also crucial in the collapse of the Tupamaros in Uruguay, the Montoneros in Argentina and the Sendero in Peru.

There was stalemate in the North, war-weariness, impatience with the old guard, and a realisation that the economic consequences of the violence bore at least as hard on nationalists as on unionists. Had the violence really arisen from the grassroots, or had it been an automatic consequence of repression and discrimination, it would have died out long before.

Sinn Fein had repeatedly been rejected by the electorate in the South, where there was growing sympathy for the unionists.[64] Under Adams and McGuinness it had reversed its policy of abstaining from political institutions and not taking its seats if it were elected, but the party got tiny shares of the vote when it advocated violence, and percentages in the teens when 'peace' was on its agenda, even while the IRA was active. The bullet had failed, and it was time to try the ballot. In January 1990 Danny Morrison, once the IRA's director of publicity, told O'Callaghan that the IRA Army Council had decided that they must be positive about peace; they were perceived to be anti everything, and their failure to make any political impact in the South was devastating. It was time to try to form a nationalist consensus involving the Irish government, the SDLP and Irish America. It could rely on the unionists to behave foolishly, and appear as an obstacle to progress; and on the UK government to be inflexible; the only sensible way forward would appear to be a unitary government of the island. American support was declining, the SDLP was winning seats and Sinn Fein was not; few in the South cared any more about the North; discrimination in the North had long since been overcome; the security forces were on top; the traditional remedy of violence had had thirty years to come up with a cure and had not; everyone was war-weary.[65]

The cold war had ended, and with it Britain's strategic interest in Northern Ireland.[66] The conflict in South Africa had ended. The Israeli–Arab peace process had begun. The thirty year ETA campaign in the Basque country seemed to be fizzling out.

Although the similarities between South Africa and Northern Ireland were more apparent than real, that did not prevent Sinn Fein seeking lessons from the one to apply to the other:

> In 1986, who could have foreseen Nelson Mandela as the South African President ... or the Palestine–Israel peace accord? [67]
>
> While there are obvious differences between Ireland and South Africa, there are also similarities. I hope to have the opportunity to learn from their experience of developing a peace process and to translate their efforts into the Irish peace process.[68]

The paradoxical effect of Sinn Fein's identification with the ANC in South Africa was that when the ANC successfully concluded a peace process, it put Sinn Fein under pressure to do the same.[69] And of course the ANC and its president won power.

The relevance of the Arab–Israeli peace process to the entirely different conditions in Northern Ireland was doubtful, though that did not stop comparisons being made. ETA's campaign for independence from Spain is a closer analogy; it lasted 30 years, claimed 800 lives, gained considerable autonomy, which satisfied the majority of Basques; but not independence, which satisfied the rest of Spain. Some 500 were in prison, roughly the population of the Maze prison in Northern Ireland. It was still difficult to gain convictions: in March 1997 a jury found a Basque radical not guilty of murder even after he confessed in court to shooting two people with a hunting rifle.[70] On the other hand, there were huge popular protests when ETA kidnapped and shot a local councillor. In December 1997 the entire 23-strong leadership of Herri Batasuna, the political wing of ETA,[71] was jailed for seven years for making a video glorifying ETA terrorists. Protest was very muted, both then and later, when a judge closed down the organisation's newspaper.[72] ETA declared an unlimited ceasefire on 16 September 1998.

Sinn Fein's first discussion paper, in May 1987, was entitled *Scenario for Peace:*

We offer them [the Unionists] a settlement based on their throwing in their lot with the rest of the Irish people and ending sectarianism. We offer them peace. We offer them equality. Britain must take the initiative and declare its intention to withdraw. That is the first step on the road to peace.[73]

The next steps to peace included the disbandment of the RUC and Ulster Defence Regiment, the unconditional release of all republican prisoners, a definite date for complete British withdrawal within the lifetime of a British government, and reparations in the form of British financial support for a united Ireland. Protestant rights would be respected, but anyone unwilling to accept life in a united Ireland would be offered grants to resettle in Britain.[74]

Scenario for Peace was followed in February 1992 by *Towards a Lasting Peace in Ireland.* It asked the Irish government to persuade the unionists and the British of the benefits of unity, and the British government to 'join the ranks of the persuaders in seeking to obtain the consent of a majority of people in the north ... for a united Ireland'.[75] There had to be a 'peaceful and orderly British political and military withdrawal from Ireland ... within a specified period', achieved 'either by continuing armed resistance or by an effective unarmed constitutional strategy'.[76]

Taylor and Mallie/McKittrick differ on whether the document meant that armed struggle was 'an option of last resort', or that it was likely to be sustained 'for the foreseeable future', because it actually said both. At any rate, two months later, on 10 April 1992, the day of the UK general election which saw John Major re-elected and Gerry Adams lose his seat to the SDLP,[77] two IRA bombs outside the Baltic Exchange in the City of London killed three people and caused damage of £700 million, more than the total paid in damage compensation in Northern Ireland up to that time.[78]

The IRA circulated its 'Totally Unarmed Strategy' (TUAS) document in the summer of 1993. 'Our goals have not changed. A united 32-county democratic socialist Republic.' However, it said, republicans were not strong enough to achieve that on their own. The strategy was therefore to build a consensus between the Dublin government, Sinn Fein, the SDLP, and governments in the US and EU, which would present the republican position as reasonable, expose the British government and the unionists as the intransigent parties, and develop a northern nationalist consensus for constitutional change.[79]

Even after adopting their totally unarmed strategy, TUAS,[80] and declaring a ceasefire in August 1994, the IRA continued to dominate the republican community through punishment beatings, and the loyalist paramilitaries theirs.[81] Killings dropped from an average of 84 a year during the eighteen years of stalemate, to 25 a year during the peace process; or to only 15 if Omagh is excluded. Figure 5.10 shows the pattern.

The Mitchell principles were published on 24 January 1996.[82] Two weeks later, the IRA showed that it was still prepared to bomb its way to peace, meaning British withdrawal. It detonated a huge bomb in Canary Wharf in the London docklands, killing two, injuring more than a hundred and causing £85 million of damage.[83]

> The cessation [ceasefire] presented a historic challenge for everyone, and Oglaigh na hEireann [the IRA] commends the leadership of Nationalist Ireland at home and abroad. They rose to the challenge. The British Prime Minister did not. Instead of embracing the peace process the British government acted in bad faith, with Mr Major and the unionist leaders squandering this unprecedented opportunity to resolve the conflict.[84]

Canary Wharf was aimed at overcoming British intransigence over impractical, unnecessary and politically impossible conditions such as IRA decommissioning and unionist consent to constitutional change. Its message was that there could be no peace while Northern Ireland was British; the message transmitted for many years.

110

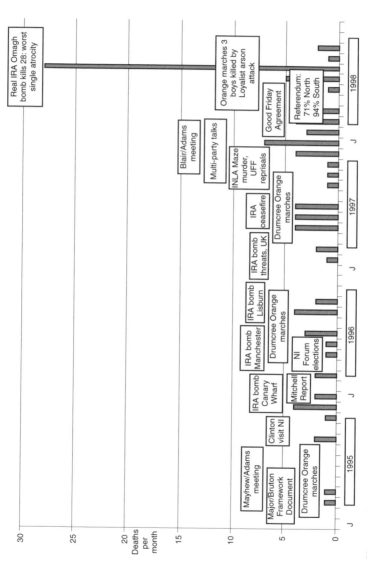

Figure 5.10 The peace process, 1995–98
Source: RUC Central Statistics Unit: NI only.

There are two key targets in countering violent politics: leaders and faiths. After a half-hearted attempt to intern the leaders, the UK made no attempt to remove them from the scene as it had done in countless other places. Instead, it relied on jailing terrorists only if they were convicted of criminal acts, which removed the easily-replaced footsoldiers one by one, and very slowly and uncertainly at that, leaving the leaders untouched.

Nor did the UK government seek to challenge the faiths and narratives of the militant republicans and unionists. Instead, it accepted them both, reinforced their acceptability by negotiating with both sides, and attempted to find a compromise between them. The militants' faiths were intellectually and emotionally incompatible; there was no possible compromise between them.

> Sinn Fein's political objective is a united Ireland free of British interference. Everything we do is intended to advance that entirely legitimate and realisable goal. We see a 32-county republic as the best way to eradicate the range of political, social, economic and other inequalities which affect the people of this island.[85]

Thirty years' experience of armed conflict, death and destruction eventually brought together the narratives of the conventional politicians in Britain and Ireland, North and South. The form looked like splitting the difference; the substance, however, was sharing the narrative. The proof is that splitting the difference could have been done at any time, but it was not. Only when the narratives had been reconciled could it be made to happen. That is not a trivial distinction; confuse form and substance, and the wrong one will be targeted, uselessly.

Once Sinn Fein had ended abstentionism, as it did in 1986, and had accepted the Mitchell Principles, as it did in May 1996, and the Good Friday Agreement of 1998, it was only distinguished from the SDLP by its link with the IRA. If the IRA disarmed that would be the end of it, and of Sinn Fein too as likely as not. Even if the IRA surrendered some arms, which it could well afford to do – even tons of them[86] – it would be a proof that it was not independent of Sinn Fein, that it accepted the principle of Northern consent, and of eventual disarmament. Decommissioning would remove its only bargaining counter, and show that the IRA trusted, and recognised, the British and Irish governments it had been fighting for decades. In its own eyes, the IRA is the lawfully-constituted army of the legitimate government of Ireland: why should it disarm, any more than the British or Irish armies? To Sinn Fein, it is the RUC which ought to be disarmed and disbanded, not the IRA. The fact that the Agreement had been overwhelmingly endorsed by the whole population, North and South, was irrelevant. The IRA had stolen the unionists' clothes: No Surrender.

The Real IRA's Omagh slaughter was a message that Sinn Fein had betrayed the republican community by signing up to the principle of consent. Furthermore, if the aptly-named Provisional IRA had accepted the Good Friday Agreement through Sinn Fein, then it too had surrendered. If it was not prepared to fight any longer, the Real IRA would do it instead. Sinn Fein had maintained for the best part of a century that it had the right to fight for a united Ireland, free from the British. How could it now deny that right to others? What monopoly did it have of the one true faith?

A year after the signature of the Good Friday Agreement in 1998 four dilemmas remained. The first might be called the Adams Dilemma: Sinn Fein was at the negotiating table because it was believed to have the power to deliver the decommissioning of the IRA to which it had signed up. If it could not, there was no point in its being there. The second was that if the IRA did not disarm and disband, the protestant paramilitaries would not do so either, and any move towards a united Ireland, even by consent, would almost certainly trigger a dirty war between them; the McGuinness Dilemma was therefore that Sinn Fein could not possibly deliver its aim of a peaceful united Ireland while the IRA remained. The third was the Erin Dilemma: Sinn Fein regards itself as the legitimate successor of the first Provisional Government of the Republic, and the IRA as its lawful army; unless the IRA disarms and disbands it remains a threat to constitutional politics in the Republic. The fourth was the Britannia Dilemma: while the paramilitaries remained, Britain would have to have contingency plans to deal with a restart of the Troubles. Its government could not simply rewind the 1969–98 tape and replay it for another thirty years. It would have to do things differently. But there are not many options open, as the succeeding chapters will demonstrate.

To earn their place in history as more than a footnote, to achieve their aim of joining de Valera, Griffith and Brugha in the Pantheon,[87] Sinn Fein and its leaders would have to deliver two things: no more violence – peace as most people understand it – and a united Ireland – peace as they understand it. Delivering non-violence alone would earn them no credit: the IRA started, it killed two thousand people, it stopped; big deal, no prize. Delivering a united Ireland – keeping the faith – is the only real measure of their success. Short of a Damascene conversion, it could be a long, long, war.[88]

6
Crime: Northern Ireland 1968–78

Violent politics and the law

The law plays a key part in violent politics, because it defines the rules of engagement between the protagonists. Insurgents do not of course regard themselves as being bound by the law, but the law nevertheless sets the boundaries of acceptable action, and defines the measures which the constitutional political process has authorised the government to take if these boundaries are crossed: making clear the circumstances in which the state will operate in the modes of prevention, fear and force in order to counter opponents operating similarly; setting the bounds of legitimacy, in one sense at least.

Great care must be taken to distinguish between the three senses in which the powerful word 'legitimacy' is used. Legitimacy-as-legality and legitimacy-as-consensus are straightforward, and though it would be possible to argue whether they applied in one instance or another, in many such cases the argument is reducible to the third category: legitimacy as a dissenter's right of direct action.

Legitimacy as a right to violent dissent is constitutionally confined to the extreme case of the right to overthrow a government which has ceased to be legitimate in the consensual sense. In effect it is not a separate case: the dissenters are simply claiming the mantle of consensual legitimacy. Indeed Jefferson and his co-authors took great pains to make this clear:

> He [George III] has abolished government here, by declaring us out of his Protection and waging war against us ... our repeated Petitions have been answered only by repeated injury. A Prince whose character is thus marked by every act which may define a tyrant, is unfit to be the ruler of a free people.[1]

A few years later, the French Declaration of the Rights of Man and the Citizen also included the right of rebellion against tyranny:

> The final end of every political institution is the preservation of the natural and imprescriptable rights of man. These rights are those of liberty, property, security and resistance to oppression.[2]

The present-day constitution of the Federal Republic of Germany also includes the right of resistance, albeit in an (understandably) somewhat different form: 'All Germans shall have the right to resist any person or persons seeking to abolish that constitutional order, should no other remedy be possible.'[3] Achieving consensus-legitimacy and translating it into legal-legitimacy is the stuff of conventional, institutional, non-violent politics. Legitimacy as an independent right of direct action is incompatible with such politics and indeed forms the conceptual base of violent politics.

The reason lies in the nature of states and their relations with their subjects. Fundamental to any conflict between the state and the individual is the state's claim to primacy; its rights must necessarily take precedence over those of individual subjects. That is not to say that individuals do not have rights against the state, even powerful ones, nor that individuals cannot challenge the state, but they are required to do so within the bounds of law and custom. In this context it matters not whether the state's claim to primacy is based upon the divine right of the sovereign or a vanguard party, the *führerprinzip* of a dictator, or the common good as represented by an elected assembly or dictatorship of the proletariat; it matters not whether the king is law or the law is king – the common good necessarily takes precedence over private interests. It follows that where there is a conflict of interest, the state must also claim the right to decide the matter. There can be no other courts but the state's, and no other way of deciding disputes that cannot be resolved by private agreement. Furthermore, if the individual does not willingly obey the rulings of the courts, the state must be able to compel him to do so. The state's monopoly of force may have a utilitarian element in it – force being inherently undesirable – but it stems from the nature of states, and not from moral principle.

The difficulty in knowing what 'cures' violent politics is much the same as with crime. American crime rates in many places fell substantially in the 1990s, and the fear of crime with it.[4] The putative reasons included zero-tolerance policing; police reorganisation; community policing policies; an increase in police numbers; computerised intelligence; more being sent to prison; a demographic fall in the number of young men; lower unemployment; the moderation of drug-taking and the stabilisation of the drug market; easier divorce leading to fewer family murders; less alcohol; stronger locks, more garages and burglar alarms; stolen TVs and car radios becoming unsaleable because everyone had them; more people working at home and keeping an eye out; less cash and more fraud-resistant cards. The demographic factors will reverse with time; so may others. The crime rate may follow; or it may not. All the putative reasons are plausible, and all are therefore worth reinforcing, even if it is too difficult to disentangle which of them are important and which incidental.

The state already possesses institutions for enforcing the criminal law and punishing offenders, so it makes practical sense to use these, particularly when the level of common crime committed with a political motive is low enough not to overburden the existing institutions. Treating all offenders as common criminals also avoids difficult problems of interpretation: for example, is a bank robbery committed to fund a political organisation a political crime? It avoids difficult decisions on how to treat political prisoners vis-à-vis common ones: should they be treated more harshly because they have offended against the common good rather than against a single individual, or less harshly because their motives, if illegal, are at least altruistic? If they were treated more leniently, might this not encourage more political dissenters to take the law into their own hands, and more criminals to claim political motives? The reasons for treating political offenders as common criminals are therefore perfectly understandable; and intellectually justifiable with just the merest hint of sophistry.

If increasing political dissent expresses itself in increasing terrorist crime, there will clearly be a point at which the existing institutions for enforcing the criminal law reach capacity, even if they are not themselves the object of attack. The existing institutions, particularly police, courts and prisons, take time, money and expertise to expand, and their practicable rate of growth may well be lower than the rate of growth of terrorist crime. Furthermore, terrorist crimes may, by their amount or seriousness, preoccupy the law enforcement system, displacing common crime. It is easy to list these disadvantages in principle, but to determine their scale in practice we must look at an actual example: the violence in Northern Ireland which began in 1969.

The level of violence

The Troubles are well-documented; or at least there is no shortage of writing about them and no shortage of statistics of a reliability unusual in such a campaign. The political issues and the pattern of violence have been discussed in the two previous chapters: this one simply concentrates on the practical problems of implementing the criminal law during episodes of violent politics.

Despite the attention drawn to Northern Ireland by the violence there, or perhaps because of it, the popular impression is of a high level of political violence. However, this has only been true for a few short periods and in a few circumscribed places, although many of Northern Ireland's extended families have had casualties, and all have suffered from the by-products of the troubles.[5] However, compared with campaigns of violent politics elsewhere in the world, the level of violence in Northern Ireland has been low. The homicide rate in Northern Ireland, which averaged seven murders per 100 000 over thirty years, is not unusual by international standards. For all but five of the years the rate in Northern Ireland has been below the comparable US rate of some nine murders per 100 000 of population each year, although much higher than the British rate of about one.[6] In only one year, 1972, did it exceed the rate in many major cities of the United States of 20 per 100 000 per year, when it reached 30, a rate comparable with some Latin American countries.[7]

In Turkey, by contrast, there were 1361 political murders in the first six months of Mr Demirel's administration in 1979.[8] The total for 1980 was widely reported as having reached 2000, and was running at 20 murders a day when the Army took power in September and ended the killing.[9] The election campaign in Jamaica, a state little larger than Northern Ireland (2 million against $1^{1}/_{2}$) cost 500 lives between January and October 1980.[10] Eight thousand were reported killed in El Salvador, whose population is three times Northern Ireland's, between January and November 1980.[11] By 1998, 30 000 had been killed in Turkey during the fifteen years of battling with Kurdish separatists: taken in proportion to the Kurdish population in Turkey, the rate is about twice that of Northern Ireland.[12]

Those living in Northern Ireland, as in other parts of the world where political violence is endemic, adapt with remarkable skill and go about their ordinary business. Many fewer die by the gun in Northern Ireland than by the motor car and the cigarette. However, the political, social and economic effects stemming even from this level of violence should not be underestimated.[13]

Terrorist murder

The pattern of violence in Northern Ireland was described in the last chapter. Figure 6.1 shows the deaths, murders, and convictions in each year of the Troubles. In 1969 four of the five murders in Northern Ireland were cleared,[14] and four people were convicted of murder.[15] That is analogous to the figures for England and Wales.[16]

The civil rights campaign which began in 1968 caused some damage and a number of casualties. Neither of these appear to have been systematically recorded, though much detail is given in the Cameron Report.[17] On 6 May 1969 the Northern Ireland government announced an amnesty for all offences connected with the disturbances, so they are not reflected in the crime figures. However, when terrorist murders started, the effect on the crime statistics of the province was dramatic.

In everyday life most murders result in a charge, and most charges result in a conviction. However, as life in Northern Ireland was overlaid by violent politics, that ceased to be the case. Only five of the 14 murders in 1970 were reported as cleared, and one person was convicted. In the worst year of violence 470 people were killed, of which 376 were regarded by the police as murder; 32 cases were reported as cleared, (8.5 per cent), and 9 people were convicted: one person for every 42 murders. The clearance rate and the number of charges then rose rapidly: there were 82 murders in 1978, and 40 murders cleared.

The clearance rate includes murders committed in past years, so the truest picture is given by comparing the total number of murders reported in the 29 years of the Troubles for which detailed figures are available (3199 from 1969–97 inclusive), with the total number of murderers actually convicted by the courts during the same period (732): a rate of 23 per cent. That is about one-quarter of the rate for ordinary criminal murders.[18]

There are five reasons why this might be so: that the police in Northern Ireland were not as competent as the police on the mainland; that they were overloaded by the sheer number of crimes; that there were not enough police to cope; that there were not enough funds; or that it is much more difficult to secure convictions for terrorist murders, because they differ from ordinary homicides.

Police competence

In England and Wales there were 14 116 indictments for homicide from 1969–94, securing 10 874 convictions;[19] one conviction for every

118

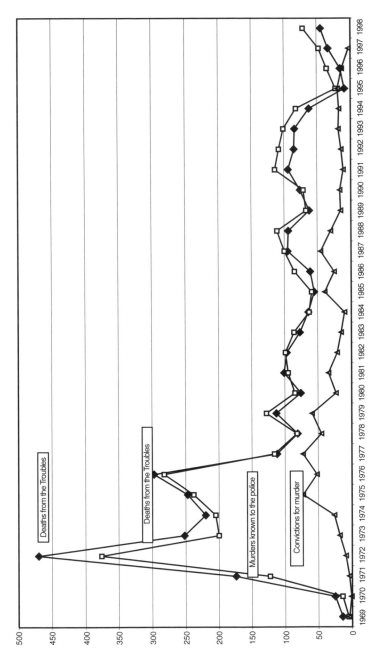

Figure 6.1 Deaths from the Troubles in Northern Ireland, murders and convictions, 1969–98

Source: Appendix: Table A.1 (The figures are for Northern Ireland only. Murder convictions in 1998 not yet known.)

1.3 indictments, compared with the Northern Ireland equivalent of one for every 4.6. That is not a very useful figure by itself, quite apart from the differences in the content of the statistics, because it takes no account of time.

Figure 6.2 therefore plots the number of murders per conviction in both places over time.[20] Although the performance of the police and judicial system in Northern Ireland in bringing murderers to book in times of peace was similar to that in England and Wales, the chances of a terrorist murderer being convicted in Northern Ireland have been many times lower than those of a criminal murder. The chances of getting away with political murder were much greater when violence was high: during the worst year only one murder in every twelve was cleared.[21]

During the worst of the violence, the battle from 1969 to 1972 described in the last chapter, ten per cent of the murders were reported cleared. During the tribal warfare of 1973–6, 36 per cent. During the stalemate of 1977–94, 54 per cent.[22] Even allowing for the lag between offences and clearances, these are very significant differences. The higher the level of killings, the more difficult it was to identify the perpetrators; even during the years of moderate violence, it was not possible to bring a lot of killers to book. Of the 2788 murders recorded up to the start of November 1998, charges were brought in respect of 947, roughly one-third.[23]

Acts of terrorism only account for a small percentage of the crime in Northern Ireland; the rest is committed by what are known there as ODCs: ordinary decent criminals. Three-quarters of recorded crimes are thefts and burglaries; ten per cent are offences against the person (murder, attempted murder, criminal injury and robbery, whether terrorist or not), seven per cent fraud, five per cent criminal damage, and one per cent offences against the state, such as firearms and public order offences.[24] The performance of the police against ODCs could therefore be expected to reflect their overall competence at dealing with crime.

Figure 6.3 therefore plots the indictable (serious) crimes per conviction in Northern Ireland, Scotland, and England and Wales, from peace in 1968, up to the peak of terrorist killings in 1972, and down to the tribal warfare which followed. The RUC's performance was clearly in the same zone as that of the mainland police forces, except for the three most violent years.

It is clear that the performance of the RUC against crime dropped when the level of terrorist crime was high. The reason might have been

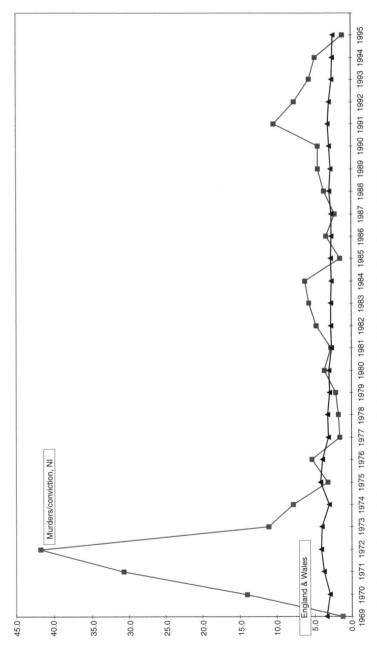

Figure 6.2 Comparative conviction rates for murder in England and Wales and Northern Ireland, 1969–95
Source: Appendix, Table A.1

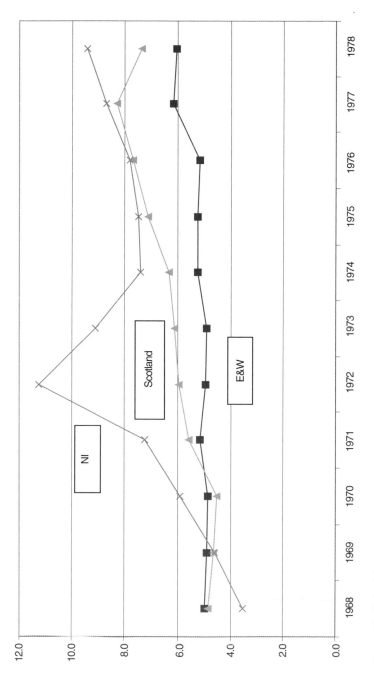

Figure 6.3   Indictable crimes per conviction, 1968–78

that the sheer volume of crime was too high for them to cope. Figure 6.4 therefore examines the comparative rates of indictable crime in the three countries over the same period.

Crime volume

The number of indictable offences known to the police in Northern Ireland multiplied threefold in the first decade of the troubles, from 16 000 in 1968 to 45 000 in 1978.[25] Some of the rise may be explained by the parallel rise in terrorist crime over the period, although terrorism only accounts for a small percentage of total crime. However, even taking this into account, it is clear that common crime grew sharply, even as terrorist crime was falling. Common criminals were taking advantage of the disorders, as the Chief Constable reported:

> In 1971 the total number of robberies was 640, while in 1972 it had increased to 2310. The continuing civil unrest and terrorist activity undoubtedly contributed much to the increase, but it is evident that the ordinary criminal fraternity took advantage of the situation.[26]

Interestingly enough, the level of known indictable crime relative to population was lower in Northern Ireland than in Great Britain throughout the decade. Indeed, by the end of the decade, although the rate in Northern Ireland had multiplied threefold, it had barely reached the levels in Great Britain at the beginning of it. The crime rate more than doubled in Britain during the same decade.

The rise in common crime in Northern Ireland was obviously linked to the civil disorders, though the link is not as strong as it is often thought to be, as the parallel rise in the rest of the UK demonstrates. Furthermore, the crime level does not appear to have been high enough of itself to degrade the law enforcement system, since higher rates were present in Britain throughout the decade. Yet it is clear that such a degradation did take place.

Police strength

Nor is the degradation of performance explicable by the number of police in Northern Ireland being proportionately lower than in Britain. In 1969, there were some 200 policemen and women for every 100 000 people in the province, much the same as in the rest of the UK and throughout the USA. Ulster's police then grew much faster than

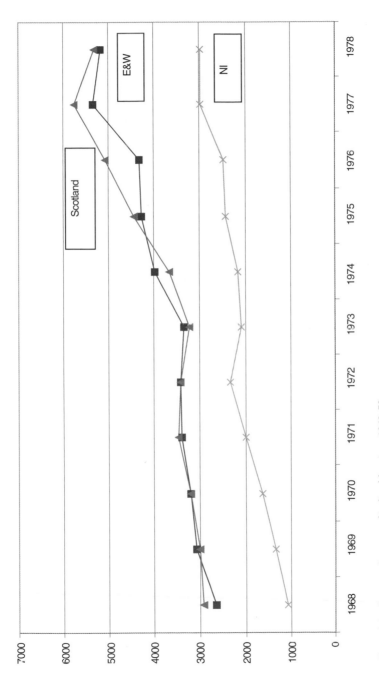

Figure 6.4 Comparative rates of indictable crime, 1968–78

Britain's, especially during the most disturbed years, and by 1995 there were over 500 police per 100 000 in Northern Ireland, almost double the number in Britain: Figure 6.5.

Funding

Resources were poured into Northern Ireland on a scale they could not have been had it not been a small part of the UK. It is difficult to arrive at an unchallengeable figure for the total, because the figures are widely scattered and their bases ill-defined. In 1990, the Bank of Ireland estimated that the annual cost of the troubles to the British and Irish governments was £410 million.[27] The official handbook on Britain says that 'the British government makes a contribution of over £3 billion a year to maintain social services in Northern at the level of those on the mainland, to meet the cost of security measures, and to compensate for the natural disadvantages of the province.'[28] It is not clear whether that includes the cost of the Army presence, and other mainland-based support; probably not. The Maze prison for convicted terrorists costs £52 million a year for some 500 prisoners: £100 000 each. The other prisons house 1100 prisoners at a cost of £78 million.[29] The Royal Ulster Constabulary costs some £650 million a year.[30] Over the thirty years of the Troubles, compensation for the 41 000 people killed and injured by terrorism, and for criminal damage, has cost £1300 million (Figure 6.6).[31] Compensation for security forces operations has cost another £20 million.[32]

Shortage of funds clearly did not put a brake on law enforcement.

The nature of terrorist crime

The low conviction rate for terrorist crime was not caused by lack of police competence or numbers, nor to their being swamped by the growth of terrorist and common crime *per se*, nor because there were insufficient funds. The reason was that terrorist crime is inherently more difficult to investigate and control. It is not the actual number of political killings which makes a difference to law enforcement, but their difference in kind from criminal murders. Most criminal murders are committed in the heat of the moment; the victim and the killer are often related or at least known to each other, and the killer often makes no attempt to conceal the offence, gives himself up voluntarily, or commits suicide.[33]

125

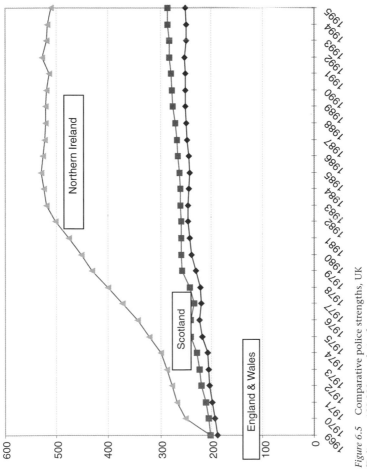

Figure 6.5 Comparative police strengths, UK
[Police per 100 000 population]
Sources: GB: Office of National Statistics, *Annual Abstract of Statistics*. (London, HMSO) series.
NI: Northern Ireland Office, *Northern Ireland Annual Abstract of Statistics*. (Belfast, HMSO) series.

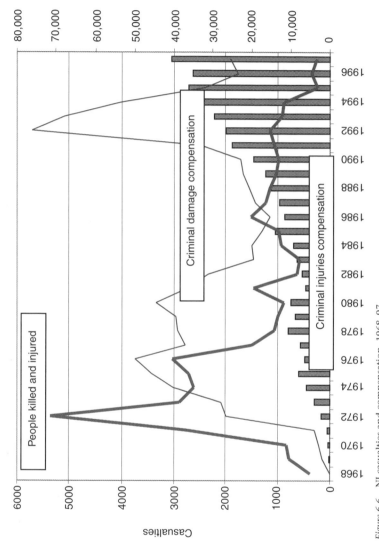

Figure 6.6 NI casualties and compensation, 1968–97
Casualties in calendar year (eg 1968); compensation in FY (1968/69)
Source: Appendix: Table A.4.

Terrorist targets are chosen more or less at random. The killings are directed at an opposing community rather than an individual, and thus affect a large number of people, not just family and friends. They are committed in cold blood, and are random in time and place, so taking precautions against them is very difficult. Their effect on public confidence and morale is immeasurably greater than that of a criminal murder. Multiple killings by the same criminal are rare, but they are not uncommon in violent politics. Political killings therefore have a greater adverse effect on the community than criminal killings, and, as was shown earlier, the criminals are harder to convict. Figure 6.7 demonstrates how much harder it was to gain convictions for terrorist crimes overall, not just for murder. The effect is even more marked.

Terrorist offences are not separated from common crimes in the official statistics of total indictable crimes known to the police.[34] It is possible, however, to construct a rough measure of terrorist crime by adding together murders, attempted murders, injuries, shooting incidents, bombings, weapon finds, armed robberies and other incidents which are *prima facie* terrorist crimes.[35] The totals are very approximate, because more than one charge could be expected to arise from any one incident, and because it leaves out crimes such as intimidation and riot. It is clear therefore that Figure 6.7 greatly underreports terrorist crimes, especially those not involving death or serious injury, and especially in the more violent years.

On this rough basis, however, serious terrorist offences rose from 1500 or so in 1970 to a peak of over 21 000 in 1972, then declined to 3000 in 1979. The numbers charged with serious terrorist crime, on the other hand, remained remarkably constant between 1973 and 1977 at 1200 to 1400 a year, so the chances of getting away with terrorist crime were greatest when the disturbances were at their height: a not unexpected effect.[36] However, the scale of the differences was remarkable, especially as the figure for incidents grossly underestimates the number of people involved in crime during them.

Comparing the rising number of murder charges with the constant rate of charges for all terrorist-type crime, it is evident that law enforcement resources were diverted, as would be expected, from less serious terrorist crimes to more serious ones. When this is allied to the inherent difficulty of proving any crime, it is clear that 'minor' terrorist crimes could not be allotted sufficient resources to achieve any useful percentage of convictions. For example, in July and August 1969 the police received 431 complaints of intimidation for which 20 people were prosecuted: less than five per cent.[37] In 1977 only 63 of the 3039

128

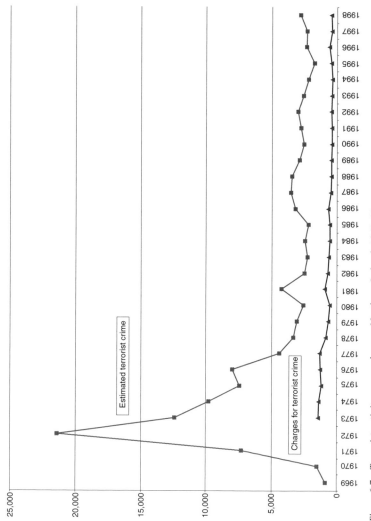

Figure 6.7 Terrorist activity versus charges, Northern Ireland, 1969–98
Source: Appendix: Table A.2

incidents of intimidation were cleared, some two per cent.[38] Intimidation is not a trivial crime: according to the Scarman tribunal, over 1800 families (accounting for 1.6 per cent of the population) moved house in Belfast during July, August and September 1969 alone.[39] While only 128 of the moves were associated with complaints to the police of intimidation, Scarman concluded that it was likely that the root causes of this exodus were direct violence, intimidation or general fear from the disturbances, and isolation from co-religionists.[40]

Common crime

Conviction rates for crime are low in any case: see Figure 6.8. Over 19 representative years in Northern Ireland, someone was charged in 21 per cent of the recorded cases of crime (terrorist and ordinary); in nearly 80 per cent of cases there was no charge, so there could be no

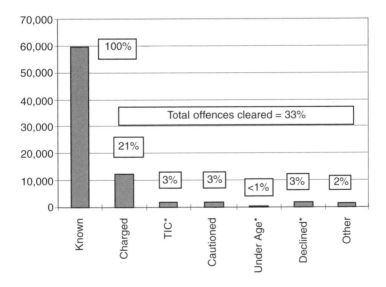

Figure 6.8 Outcome of notifiable offences, Northern Ireland
*TIC = taken into consideration. Under age = *bl10
Declined = victim declined to prosecute. Other includes unfit to plead.
Sources: Reports of the Chief Constable of the RUC, 1971 to 1995. Data before 1975 and for 1976 and 1983 is not given in the reports. The chart shows averages for the 19 years for which data is reported.

conviction either.[41] One-third of all crimes were cleared; the other two-thirds were not. However this takes no account of the so-called 'dark figure of crime': those that are not reported for one reason or another.

A Home Office crime survey in England and Wales found that only half of all offences were reported, only about one-quarter were recorded, and only five per cent were cleared up by identifying those responsible. That in turn resulted in a caution or conviction for only three per cent of all the crimes committed.[42] If the same applied in Northern Ireland the charge rate would only be five percent of all offences, and the clearance rate eight or nine per cent.

Conclusions

It is evident from this survey of the data from Northern Ireland during its first, and worst, decade of civil disturbances that:

- The overall crime rate in Northern Ireland was markedly below the rates in the rest of the United Kingdom throughout the decade, even when the content of terrorist crime was very high by UK standards.
- Common criminals took advantage of the disorders: the number of common crimes rose sharply even as terrorist crimes were declining. Crime rates in Britain and the US also rose over this period, so the growth attributable to the disorders themselves may be less than might otherwise be thought.
- The murder rate, though high by British standards, was no higher than the US rate throughout much of the decade and only in one year was it higher than the rates common in US cities.
- Accidental deaths in the home and on the roads together far exceeded deaths in the civil disturbances, even in the worst year. Injuries from the troubles were far less numerous than those on the roads or at work.[43] But death and injury caused by terrorists was, unsurprisingly, far more disturbing socially and politically.
- The number of full-time police in Ulster was substantially greater than the number in Britain or the US relative to both population and crime rate.
- There was no shortage of funds for the Province.
- The situation in Northern Ireland was thus not markedly abnormal by British or US criminal law enforcement standards if terrorist and ordinary crimes of the same kind are considered as one. They clearly cannot be. They are completely different in substance, however similar they may be in form.

- Because of this, terrorist crime clearance rates in Northern Ireland been have low compared with common crime clearance rates in Britain and the US, and conviction rates even lower. Throughout the three decades of the troubles, committing terrorist crime in Northern Ireland has been a low-risk occupation, and the chances of getting away with terrorist murder and other serious crimes have been high.
- The throughput of the system for dealing with indictable crime remained practically constant throughout the first decade, despite the huge rise in civil disorder, a trebling of the recorded crime rate and a doubling of the number of full time police. In the worst years for terrorist crime, the throughput actually fell.
- High rates of increase and, more significantly, high levels of terrorist crime were associated with sharply-depressed conviction rates for both terrorist and common crime.
- The inescapable conclusion is that the poor performance of the law enforcement system was due solely to the growth and quantity of terrorist crime, which is inherently more difficult to investigate and control.

The most significant indicator of the success of the strategy in Ulster throughout the Troubles was that the vast majority of the community only briefly and sporadically resorted to violent politics on any scale. The most significant indicator of its failure was that paramilitary violence lasted thirty years, cost nearly four thousand lives, ten times as many injuries and billions of pounds, had a huge impact on the family and economic life of the province, resulted in terrorist-dominated organised crime, and had a negative impact on Britain's international reputation. Terrorism in Northern Ireland became a high-status, low-risk, money-spinning occupation; violent politicians are unlikely to seek solutions when the problems pay so well.

Common crime is not eliminated by the ordinary processes of criminal law enforcement, nor even prevented from growing, so there is no reason to suppose that it will fare any better against terrorist crime. On the contrary, terrorist crime is very much more difficult to counter than common crime. The next chapter will demonstrate why.

If the violent politics had increased to an intolerable level (a frequent fear throughout the early 1970s), what could have been done? The succeeding chapters explore other options for dealing with internal conflict.

7
Countermeasures: Criminal Law

Low levels of violent politics can be dealt with by the criminal law. The data presented in Chapter 6, however, showed that that was ineffective: the conviction rate for terrorist crime in Northern Ireland was far below the comparable rate for ordinary crime, not because of incompetence, shortage of resources, or factors peculiar to the province, but because of the inherent differences between terrorist and ordinary crime.

Those differences set quite low limits on the level of political violence that can sensibly be countered by the criminal law. Only a small percentage of terrorist crimes will be solved, and only a few people will be convicted for them – and rather slowly and expensively at that. Once that matters, or the law enforcement system is swamped by the sheer volume of crime, neutralised by fear, or broken down by direct violence, it will no longer work either technically or, which is far more important, politically.

> People everywhere demand from governments security against the worst evils: war and civil disorder, criminal violence, and lack of the means of decent subsistence. How a state performs this protective role is the core test of its legitimacy. Unless it is discharged competently no other criterion can come into play. Thus it is not whether a state is a liberal democracy that most fundamentally determines its legitimacy; it is how well it secures its citizens against the worst evils. This is a universal requirement, rooted in human needs that are universal; but how it is met depends on many and varying circumstances. No one regime is always and everywhere the best.[1]

Another option is to make use of the body of law dealing with offences against the state such as treason and sedition – political crimes. No liberal state takes that step lightly, for cogent political reasons; but there are technical reasons too for its limited value as a strategic countermeasure, as we will see in the next chapter.

A third option is to declare martial law, or, as a fourth option which is really a variant of the third, to enact a body of emergency law. A fifth is to treat the armed opponents of the state as combatants in an internal war. The international laws of war cover such a contingency, but if a state wishes to create a body of domestic law dealing with internal war it can clearly do so.

These five options exhaust the strategies for dealing with violent politics within the law. Insurgents do not of course regard themselves as being bound by the law of the state they are trying to overthrow. That is one rationale for international law, to put humanitarian constraints on their methods, if only through international opinion. Only recently have there been any international bodies to bring them to book. Another reason is that some states do not regard themselves as being bound by law when dealing with armed dissidents, and the resulting conflicts outdo traditional war in inhumanity.

Violent politics as common crime

Chapter 6 showed that terrorist crime and common crime differ in nature. Because the one is so different in substance from the other, despite the similarity of its forms, many emergency provisions had to be written into United Kingdom law, and measures had to be taken in Northern Ireland which were not part of the normal law enforcement machinery. In August 1969 the Army was called in to assist the civil power, and stayed for more than thirty years. Internment, detention without trial, was introduced in August 1971 and phased out by the end of 1975. Courts without juries were introduced in 1973.[2] These measures were introduced to counter terrorist crime rather than common crime, and the fact that the government felt it necessary to take such politically unpleasant steps is further evidence of the difference between the two types of crime, and of the inherent difficulty of dealing with terrorist crime through the normal system of law enforcement.

The dip in the number of convictions for terrorist crime was at its most marked during 1972 and 1973 when internment was in full swing, so it could be argued from the figures that internment was being used as a substitute for trial. However, internment was not introduced as a means of short-circuiting trial, but in order to detain people who were known to support terrorism or to have taken part in it, in circumstances where the evidence was inadmissible or could not be given without compromising intelligence sources, or endangering the lives of witnesses. It was there simply to take terrorists out of play, not to punish them. As the then Prime Minister of Northern Ireland, Brian Faulkner, said in announcing the decision to introduce internment in August 1971:

> Every means has been tried to make terrorists amenable to the law. Nor have such methods been without success, because a substantial number of the most prominent members of the IRA are now serving prison sentences. But the terrorist campaign continues at an unacceptable level, and I have had to conclude that the ordinary law cannot deal comprehensively or quickly enough with such ruthless viciousness.[3]

Broadly speaking, three types of crime committed with a political motive – 'complex crime' in legal terminology – arise during episodes of violent politics:[4]

* Offences against public order, such as rioting, barricade building, looting, marching in paramilitary uniform or after a ban; offences which are committed by people in the mass, where individual responsibility is shared and diffused. Although such things are standard techniques in violent politics, and may be initiated or exploited by terrorist organisations, they are not of themselves terrorist acts.
* Crimes such as theft, fraud or extortion, which only differ from their purely criminal analogues because their motive is to benefit an organisation rather than an individual. In essence, they are forms of organised crime. They are just as difficult to deal with as any other type of organised crime, but the techniques are the same.
* Shooting, bombing, firebombing, assassination, kidnapping: acts by armed individuals or groups aiming to overthrow the state from within: terrorist acts.

Mass complex crime

Mass demonstrations have come to be tacitly recognised as a valid form of political protest: direct action against a government or a policy when individual action through the established political institutions is unsuccessful, inappropriate to the scale of the grievance, or too slow. In short, they have become legitimate in the consensual sense, *de facto* but not *de jure*. In law every rioter or illegal marcher is guilty of an offence. In practice only a handful of people are arrested. The government pays compensation for the injuries and damage done by the crowd, as a kind of fine upon itself for enraging so many people, or accepts public punishment in the form of its surrogates, policemen and soldiers, being stoned. In practice too, it is very difficult to make mass arrests, and equally difficult and time-consuming to prove the offences in court. In any case, courts are understandably reluctant to hand down heavy penalties to a rioter who was no more responsible than many who did not have the misfortune to get caught. Whatever the letter of the law may be, therefore, the conventional maxim that the law takes no account of trifles – *de minimis non curat lex* – is matched by one at the other end of the scale – *de maximis non curat lex*.

Mass offences against public order also require massive numbers to contain them – numbers which the police in Northern Ireland could not provide, not having the mainland's capacity for swift reinforcement across a police authority boundary:

> overall, the RUC struggled manfully to do their duty in a situation which they could no longer control. Their courage, as casualties and long hours of stress and strain took their toll, was beyond praise; their ultimate failure to maintain order arose not from their mistakes, nor from any lack of professional skill, but from exhaustion and shortage of numbers. Once large scale communal disturbances occur they are not susceptible to control by police. Either they must be suppressed by overwhelming force, which, save in the last resort, is not acceptable in our society, and was not within the control of the Northern Ireland Government; or a political solution must be devised.[5]

In Northern Ireland therefore, especially during the early stages, the responsibility of the security forces was to maintain public order as best might be; keeping the opposing communities from each other's throats and minimising the damage to people and property. The law served as the ropes of the ring – defining the area in which the fight could go on. The referee – the courts – played little part. As Lord Justice Scarman said at the conclusion of the paragraph just quoted: 'There are limits to the efficiency of the police and the criminal law: confronted with such disturbances the police and the ordinary processes of the criminal law are of no avail.'

Terrorist crime

With one type of complex crime – mass offences against public order – thus removed from its ambit, the 'ordinary processes of the criminal law' still had the other to deal with: individual acts of killing, wounding, bombing, hijacking, theft and so on, which differed from common crimes only in their motive. However, the ordinary processes of criminal law, and even the various emergency amendments to it which were introduced from time to time, actually played only a small part in countering individual complex crime as well, as we have seen.

This is also true to some extent of common crime. A vast amount of common crime is not reported, a lot of reported cases are not solved; some that are solved cannot be brought to trial; some people who are tried are found not guilty; and some who are found guilty are released on appeal. These shortcomings do not matter as much in common crime as in complex crime. Common murder is usually a private affair: people killing their spouses, lovers, children or rivals. Political killings are affronts to a community, or open challenges to the state. Complex theft is carried out to fund, and thus increase, other complex crimes, rather than for individual gain. The key difference of course is that complex crime is not committed for the immediate reward given by the crime itself; its meaning lies in its long term and indirect effects. This gives the complex criminal far greater flexibility in choosing targets for his operations. A common criminal may change his targets to a degree, but since to the complex criminal the effect is all and the target incidental, he can change his target in kind without failing in his aim. In everyday life, most crimes are detected and reported by ordinary individuals.[6] Few dare to do that in conditions of violent politics.

There was little change in the attrition of complex criminals as measured by the numbers convicted each year, despite the huge number of people in the security forces. Even in 1977, by which time the stalemate phase had begun, the security forces consisted of 14 000 soldiers, 8000 part-time members of the Ulster Defence Regiment, 5700 full-time police and 4680 part-time: a total of more than 32 000: one member of the security forces for every fifty men, women and children in Northern Ireland. Crime nearly trebled during the first decade of the Troubles: convictions rose by only 14 per cent at the peak. Order had returned to Northern Ireland before the end of the first decade. Law had not.

There were four reasons for this:

- the difficulty of detecting complex crime;
- the problem of gaining convictions in the courts;
- the meaninglessness of punishment and deterrence in complex crime;
- the difference in status of complex and common criminals convicted of the same offences.

Problems of detection

It is totally impracticable to create a network of surveillance with a mesh fine enough to detect everything that goes on. Even in a totalitarian society in which enormous resources are devoted to surveillance, such as the former Soviet Union and Eastern Europe, it is possible for people to act inside the interstices, meeting, publishing, robbing. The bigger the mesh of the intelligence net the larger the groups can become without being detectable, and the greater the range of their activities.

In democratic societies, poor ones, and ones with weak governments, the intelligence net is very coarse, and the interstices huge. In practice such societies attempt to provide a fine network in critical areas – particularly crime and internal security – but even so, much illegal activity will escape direct detection. The *de jure* liberty of plural democracies and the *de facto* liberty of loosely governed states results in a substantial amount of freedom for any purpose – good or bad.

It is a practical impossibility for a government to stop theft, prostitution and drug smuggling for example, without increasing the resolution of the intelligence network to the point of oppression. Moderate levels of illegal activities of any sort, including sedition and terrorism, can go on in all societies. The tolerable, or rather tolerated, levels will also be determined by public opinion, which creates, in effect, cultural Black Holes in which the centripetal forces of the community are so strong that information cannot get out, and outsiders cannot get in – or escape if they do.

It is impossible to gain much information without inside access. Most munitions for IRA operations in Northern Ireland came via the Republic. Its level of operations during the late 1970s required only some 20 tons of munitions a year to cross any one of the 297 crossings on the 303 mile long border, among some 20 million tons of ordinary cargo. The chance of detecting one ton in a million is not very good in the first place, and it becomes much worse if the terrorists take simple precautions. Detection of such a small signal in such a large noise is just not practicable without good intelligence. However, most intelligence is strategic: command structures, policies, internal quarrels, external links. Few people know about the movement of weapons, or the planning of terrorist operations, and by the time information leaks out it is often too late for an interception. However, like ordinary criminals, terrorists are slaves of habit, so it is not always impossible to detect their operations. Nevertheless, the problem of convicting them remains.

Problems of conviction

Achieving a conviction in a criminal court requires a high-fidelity playback of the events which gave rise to the charge. There are strict rules about the sorts of evidence which can be given, and about the standard of proof required for conviction. There are only three acceptable sources: witness evidence, where someone other than the criminal tells the story; forensic or circumstantial evidence, where things tell the story; and confession, where the criminal himself tells the story.

Even in everyday life, witness evidence may be difficult to come by. In some societies and sub-cultures it is regarded as dishonourable and unmanly to appeal to the police to solve violent conflict. The *omerta* of the Mafia is based on the conviction that the victim or his friends and relations should avenge the wrong he has suffered, not the state. A Chicago poll revealed that between one-third and one-half of all assaults in the city went unreported, usually because the fight was regarded as a private matter, or the victim did not want to get the aggressor into trouble.[7] Such acceptance of everyday violence is by no means confined to Chicago or Sicily of course. In conditions of violent politics, witness evidence is understandably even more difficult to get.

Even when many witnesses are available, their testimony may be conflicting or worthless. Thousands of people, with hundreds of police and tens of Secret Servicemen were all on the spot in Dallas when President Kennedy was assassinated. Even so, it took many months of investigation to attribute responsibility for his killing, and the attribution that was finally arrived at officially was by no means universally accepted.

Forensic evidence requires the criminal himself to leave traces. Experienced criminals have read the same detective stories as everyone else and will take good care they leave no evidence. In practice, that leaves confession as the prime, indeed almost the sole, method of achieving a conviction through the criminal courts in conditions of violent politics.[8] In fact, it is a prime source of convictions even in 'ordinary decent crime'.[9]

In Northern Ireland, the IRA has therefore organised a campaign to destroy the credibility of confessions and to restrict the ability of the police to conduct interrogations. It trains its members in the well-established techniques of resistance to interrogation.[10]

Furthermore, the process of gaining evidence may be horrendously expensive in resources – far too expensive to be used to counter violent politics on anything but the smallest scale.[11] Cost, and the practical difficulties of obtaining a high-fidelity replay in the courts, rule out a strategy of dealing with violent politics as common crime except when its level is low, and it occurs in an area small enough to be swamped by overt and covert security forces.

Problems of punishment and deterrence

If it is impracticable to convict terrorists for more than a small proportion of the crimes they commit, would it not be practicable to deter them by imposing condign punishment on those who were convicted?

The concepts of punishment and deterrence that are implicit in the treatment of common crime have different meanings for the terrorist. The fear of capture and punishment, of public humiliation and private shame, of being condemned, literally and metaphorically, by society, may act as a powerful deterrent upon individuals tempted to commit common crimes. The psychological deterrents on a complex criminal are however completely absent: he is fighting for a society he considers more moral, more just, more right, than the society which punishes him; or if he cannot claim such a grand aim, he at least sees his ends as justifying his means. The physical unpleasantness of punishment on the terrorist and his family are mitigated by the support of the organisation to which he belongs. His position is akin to that of a prisoner of war; he has fallen into the hands of his enemies, whom he must perforce obey meanwhile. He may be angry with himself for being captured, or with his organisation for getting him into that situation, but he feels no guilt for what he has done to the enemy. He knows his family and friends will be well looked after. When he returns to his own group his status will be enhanced by the punishment he has undergone, not diminished. The success of the H-block hunger strikers of 1981 in gaining public support, despite the appalling crimes for which they had been convicted by due process of law, is a good example.

This failure of punishment to deter is also true of a criminal subculture, and of organised crime. What these have in common with terrorism is that they seek to create groups with enough cohesion, resources and mutual support to make what the state may do to any individual of little importance to the group as a whole, and to minimise its ill effects on the individual himself. Such a group immunises itself against any action against individuals which falls short of exhausting the resources of the group.

The group will hamper investigations, provide wanted men with shelter, and carry out reconnaissance with unknown men who can be accused of nothing more serious than loitering with intent if they are caught. Early warning can be provided by members of the group who may well not know what it is that they are covering, while services such as finance, transport, medical treatment, legal advice, couriers and accommodation, can all be provided by group supporters whose acts have an inherently low probability of being detected, whose offences would be very difficult to prove in court, and even if proved would only be lightly punished – unless special steps were to be taken to stiffen them. Even so, it is doubtful that condign punishment would act as a deterrent, since it is apparent that even capital punishment does not.

The evidence for capital punishment acting as a deterrent to ordinary murder is equivocal, so there is a *prima facie* case for not extending capital punishment to terrorist offences on that ground alone. Furthermore, a terrorist who risks his life directly when he carries out his operations is unlikely to be deterred by the remote possibility of his being captured alive, convicted and hanged. Once the murderer is in custody he can do no more harm, so killing him adds nothing to the nation's security.

Conversely, his death sentence will encourage his friends at large to campaign for his release, and provide a fine opportunity for propaganda. If the prisoner has the sympathy of a large body of people, martyrdom provides a stronger focus for their feelings than incarceration. Furthermore, live prisoners are hostages for the good behaviour of their side. US policy in Vietnam was severely constrained by the need to secure good treatment and eventual release of the American prisoners of war in North Vietnam, few though they were. Such constraints operate in every war, and *a fortiori* in every smaller conflict.

Capital punishment also affords direct opportunities for revenge. The execution of four terrorists who had attacked Acre gaol and a police armoury in Raman Gat, was matched by the Irgun hanging two kidnapped British sergeants.[12] Although the reprisal created public outrage in Britain, the message was not lost on the government: no more executions were carried out.

It was shown earlier that because of the circumstances in which political murder is committed, only a small proportion of those who are in law guilty of such crimes can ever be brought before a court, and even fewer convicted. Capital punishment would not make conviction easier (indeed it would be expected to have the reverse effect), and since the number convicted is already low, it makes no practical difference to the conflict how they are dealt with.

The effect of capital punishment on the general public is also important, and was the key issue in the arguments over the reform of capital punishment in Britain in the nineteenth century. Dickens held no brief for the criminal, who was already being treated more mercifully than he deserved by being (usually) cleanly hanged. He was much more concerned by the effect on the public:

> I believe it to have a horrible fascination for many of those persons who render themselves liable to it, impelling them onward to the acquisition of a frightful notoriety; and (setting aside the strong confirmation of this idea afforded in individual instances) I presume this to be the case in very badly regulated minds, when I observe the strange fascination which everything connected with this punishment, or the object of it, possesses for tens of thousands of decent, virtuous, well-conducted people who are quite unable to resist the published portraits, letters, anecdotes, smilings, snuff-takings of the bloodiest and most unnatural scoundrel with the gallows before him. I observe that this strange interest does not prevail to anything like the same degree where death is not the penalty. Therefore, I connect it with the dread and mystery surrounding death in any shape, but especially in the avenging form, and am disposed to come to the conclusion that it produces crime in the criminally disposed, and engenders a diseased sympathy – morbid and bad, but natural and often irresistible – among the well conducted and gentle.[13]

That the emotional ferment caused by executions created more crime than it solved is amply attested by contemporary writers.[14] Murders following executions were common, while crime flourished in the crowds attending executions, which were held in public until 1868; pressure to stop such spectacles was strongly resisted on the grounds that private execution was no deterrent. Public executions gave the accused an opportunity to leave life with a flourish, exciting public sympathy. The condemned man's last words, genuine or made-up, were avidly bought. The authorities were well aware of the psychological impact of a last speech:

> Level with the tumbrils were detachments of drummers beating a muffled roll. Their task was to counter any attempt on the part of the prisoners to address the crowd; they had instructions to beat loud enough to drown the voices if the prisoners began to speak.[15]

Executions are no longer carried out in public view, save in a very few countries, but whether this makes them any the less public nowadays is doubtful. Whatever the underlying psychological reasons, killing in the heat of combat is publicly regarded as just, equitable, and even honourable. Execution in cold blood is quite different: on *a priori* grounds it would not be expected to deter politically motivated men, and such evidence as there is shows that it does not. The effect on the public appears to be almost wholly bad, creating emotional excitement and increasing polarisation.

Throughout the thirty years of violence in Northern Ireland there has in effect been capital punishment, of a particularly arbitrary and summary kind: the killing by paramilitaries of soldiers, policemen, and civilians of the opposite confession, and of their own. It has not been without effect, but it could not be said to have deterred more than a small proportion of the groups which became targets.

Problems of status

A soldier who kills does not change status, even temporarily; he may have killed, but he is not a killer. He has risked his own death in the service of his country and, provided he has not violated the laws and usages of war, his countrymen will be grateful, and his conscience clear. A criminal conviction changes the status of an individual for ever: he will be a convicted criminal to the day he dies.

A terrorist murders unlawfully in cold blood, and though he takes the lives of others, he rarely puts his own at risk. That clearly distinguishes him from a soldier, and clearly makes him a criminal. He should bear that stigma for life, and if his conscience does not trouble him for ever, it ought. But no terrorist, especially one from an organisation claiming to be a legitimate military force fighting a just war, is willing to accept that stigma: hence the blanket, the dirty protest and the hunger strikes in Northern Ireland. Nor will a dead terrorist be buried like a common murderer; there will be flags and wreaths, high-ranking bearers, great processions, even balaclava-clad, uniformed and armed men to fire a military salute. Nor yet will he be treated as a criminal on release from prison, but as a hero, a soldier returning from captivity.

Negotiations, amnesties, grants of immunity, and changes of policy such as varying the profile of the security forces, draw the executive into the functions of the judiciary, weakening its real and perceived independence. Unless one side has been utterly defeated, the end of an episode of violent politics will be followed by the release of those who have been imprisoned for taking part in it, and an amnesty in nature if not in name. If they have been convicted as common criminals, that raises questions about the treatment of common criminals who may well have committed far less terrible crimes. When the law is flexibly and unevenly applied, and the executive overrules the judiciary whenever it is expedient, how can the law be said to rule?

Another problem of status arises from the policy of treating terrorists as common criminals. Paramilitary leaders are not held accountable for the actions of their men, as the commanders of conventional armies are: no *superior*, no *respondat*. The leaders need only keep their own hands clean to keep their freedom; and if terrorism is to be countered effectively they must not be free.

Conclusions – criminal law

A state can no more stop low levels of violent politics than it can stop drug smuggling, prostitution, pornography, gambling or theft.

The detection and conviction of complex criminals is much more difficult than of common criminals. There are only three ways of achieving the high-fidelity playback of the events giving rise to a criminal charge which is required by the courts: witness evidence, which virtually disappears during violent politics, for understandable reasons; forensic evidence, which a few elementary precautions will prevent; and confessions, which are therefore brought under strong attack by those who might be affected by them – often successfully. Under conditions of violent politics it is not possible to convict more than a small proportion of those guilty of murder, or indeed any other offence. Even if terrorists are convicted, punishment and deterrence do not work.

Using the criminal law to deal with crimes committed with a political motive means that the law is unevenly applied, that the independence of the judiciary is called into question, that difficult questions arise over equity of treatment for common criminals, and that it muddies the status of the men of violence themselves.

States treating terrorists as common criminals therefore lose all of the apparent advantages of treating them thus, and gain none of the real ones. They cannot make the leaders accountable; the followers are soldiers *de facto* whatever they may be *de jure*; and the status of ordinary criminals becomes blurred.

A strategy for dealing with violent politics through the ordinary criminal law cannot succeed unless the opposition is weak. It was not weak enough in Northern Ireland. The conflict killed thousands, and deeply affected the lives of one and a half million people for thirty years.

8
Countermeasures: Political Crime

Dissenters who cannot achieve their political objectives through the institutions and customs of conventional politics must either give way, or continue their political battle by taking direct action which breaks the law. They may set out deliberately to break a law which they regard as unjust, or they may choose ways of pursuing their campaign which inevitably bring them into conflict with the law. In either case they commit crime. What sort of crime?

There is clearly a distinction between crimes which are committed for individual gain and immediate reward, which do not challenge the law itself but simply hope to avoid it, and those in which the motive is the benefit of a group which is not just a gang of organised criminals, in which the act is done not for its own sake and for its immediate reward, but for its political effect elsewhere and in the long term. Such acts are regarded, certainly by their perpetrators, as political. They are often not so regarded by states: English and American law, for example, is often said to have no concept of political crime, a statement which is true only if political crime is so narrowly defined that it ceases to correspond to the common-sense meaning.

There are three senses in which political crimes exist even in states which claim they do not: crimes which national law defines as offences against the state; offences against national criminal law committed for political reasons rather than criminal ones; and crimes committed abroad for political reasons, for which extradition may be refused under international law.

Offences against the state

To begin with, offences against the state are obviously political crimes; treason, sedition, espionage and rebellion simply do not make sense as common crimes. It is therefore very difficult for a state to try someone for offences of such a character without being forced into recognising them as political, and therefore into facing the difficult problem of how to treat them *vis-à-vis* criminal offences.

English law defines crimes against the state as treason, treason felony, misprision of treason, and sedition. Treason consists of killing the sovereign, levying war against him in his realm, endangering the purity of his blood line, or aiding his enemies.[1] War is levied:

[w]hen an insurrection is raised to reform some national grievance, to alter the established law or religion, to punish magistrates, to introduce innovations of public concern, to obstruct the execution of some general law by an armed force, or for any other purpose which usurps the government in matters of a public and general nature.[2]

Enlistment and marching are sufficient overt acts to constitute levying war. Treason was a capital offence in Britain until 1998: the only one apart from war crimes, and mutiny in the armed forces.

Treason felony includes such things as deposing the sovereign, encouraging foreign invasion, and levying war against Her Majesty within any part of the United Kingdom:

In order by force or constraint to compel her to change her measures or counsels, or in order to intimidate or overawe both houses or either house of parliament.[3]

Misprision of treason is the common law offence of concealing treason, and carries the splendidly archaic penalty of forfeiture of all the offender's goods and profits from his lands during his life.

Sedition is a common law misdemeanour:

an intention to bring into hatred or contempt, or to excite disaffection against the person of Her Majesty, her heirs or successors, or the government and constitution of the United Kingdom as by law established, or either house of parliament, or the administration of justice, or to excite HM subjects to attempt, otherwise than by lawful means, the alteration of any matter in church or state by law established, or either house of parliament, or to raise discontent and disaffection amongst HM subjects, or to promote feelings of ill-will and hostility between different classes of such subjects.[4]

However, despite the existence of a powerful body of fine-sounding law, and the frequency of acts which clearly fall within the definitions of treason felony, sedition and other crimes against the state – *prima facie* political crimes – UK trials for such offences have been exceedingly rare in the twentieth century, except in times of war.

Non-extraditable political crime

There is a second sense in which states recognise the existence of political crime, at least in states other than their own, since by international law they may refuse to extradite anyone accused of a 'criminal offence of a political character'.[5] It is clearly inconsistent for a state to safeguard the right of an alien political criminal whose extradition is demanded by the country of which he is a subject, while denying the existence of a concept of political crime in its own country; nevertheless it is done.

English law on the non-extradition of political offenders stems from the principles established in the Castioni case (Castioni had killed a man in the heat of an attack on government buildings in Lugano and fled to England).[6]

To make a case political and thus non-extraditable it must have a political motive, *and* be committed during a political disturbance. However, political motives, even during war, do not of themselves excuse war crimes or crimes against humanity. The Hague and Geneva Conventions prohibit even invaders from killing non-belligerents or robbing them. The same principle must apply to self-appointed belligerents. Anything less would allow any individual to murder his opponents – in effect creating outlaws of them – while claiming the protection of the law for himself.[7]

Political considerations may also make governments unwilling to try, or to extradite international offenders.[8] The British released the PLO terrorist Leila Khaled without trial, and the French released Abu Daoud, who was wanted for 14 terrorist acts, including the massacre at the Munich Olympics. He was arrested by the French security service, but released after protests by Algeria, Egypt, Saudi Arabia and Syria. President Giscard was about to fly to Saudi Arabia to negotiate for oil.[9]

Domestic political crime

Here the state finds itself in the greatest difficulty: it can give political asylum to an offender from another state, in effect admitting the right of the offender to use violence to change the foreign state and denying the latter the right of redress. It cannot do the same in its own country without creating a right of armed opposition to itself. Even if the Castioni principle were invoked internally, only permitting crimes to be qualified as political if they had been committed during a political disturbance, it would be easy enough for dissidents to engineer such a disturbance. They would then have *carte blanche*.

Indeed, if governments were to recognise crimes as political, it would entail political trials, political judges and juries, and the creation of political prisoners – all hard things for democracies to justify, and unfashionable even in totalitarian states.

Memories of the use of political trials by Hitler and Stalin – to name only two representative tyrants – as the principal means for dealing with political opponents, while being further evidence of their technical efficacy, has meant that liberal democracies have been very reluctant to try people for political crime. Indeed, although incitement to racial hatred is clearly sedition in English law, it was specifically included in the Race Relations Act instead.

Conclusions – political crime

Although at least three classes of political crime exist: offences against the state, non-extraditable 'criminal offences of a political character' committed abroad, and similar crimes committed at home, it is not surprising that many states deny having a concept of political crime in their domestic law, and treat anyone accused of it as a common criminal, ignoring his motive.

However, invoking the law of offences against the state could be a valuable technique for dealing with some practitioners of violent politics: printers, publishers and speakers could be tried for sedition, for example, without the need for introducing emergency legislation on censorship – itself politically undesirable. Anyone taken in arms, marching, or supporting an armed group could be tried for treason felony.

Nevertheless, political crimes must be proved in court in the same way as other crimes, and achieving conviction is technically just as difficult as for a common crime. The trial itself may give a public platform to the dissenters which the state would rather avoid: it was, for example, Hitler's trial for his part in the Munich putsch that first gave him the opportunity to proselytise the army. In any case it may be impracticable to capture sufficiently important people to warrant a trial for crimes against the state: they may be too well protected, or given sanctuary in a neighbouring state, for example.

Such a strategy is therefore politically unattractive at low levels of violent politics, and technically impracticable when the insurgents possess secure territory or substantial armed forces. It clearly has its uses between these two limits. Many states with an active extra-parliamentary opposition and limited resources to devote to law and order could not hope to maintain political stability and reasonable freedom from violence without dealing briskly, if often moderately, with political crime. Witness Singapore, for example.

However, to use the law of offences against the state invites accusations of tyranny (or indeed tyranny itself if the circumstances are right); not to use it leaves many options open to dissenters (including the overthrow of the state if the circumstances are right). Since a monopoly of armed force is an essential of any state, it would seem sensible, on the face of it, to resolve this difficulty in a country like the United Kingdom by using the law of treason to deal with the use of armed force against the state – and for no lesser offence. However, anyone taken in arms can be tried under the criminal law, and even if treason could be punished by death and carrying arms could not, we have seen that this is unlikely to be of value. If it were thought necessary, it would of course be simple to amend the law to provide for the death penalty for carrying arms too.

The previous two chapters have demonstrated the fundamental disadvantages of treating violent politics as crime of any sort – common or political – and how this has led to liberal democracies making little use of the law of offences against the state.

However, no state can afford to allow armed opposition to build up unchecked, and if violent politics exceeds the quite moderate level which renders the law enforcement system ineffective, the next strategic step is towards a state of internal war, as it were. However, if the conflict is not to degenerate into anarchical civil war, both sets of belligerents must remain bound by a body of law.

9
Countermeasures: Internal War

Martial law and emergency law

A third option for countering violent politics is to take special powers to deal with dissenters who take up arms against a state, rather than treating them as common criminals or as political offenders.

Medieval monarchs not unnaturally claimed the prerogative of dispensing summary justice to rebels caught waging war against them in their realm. The conventional way of indicating that such a state of insurrection had been declared was for the king to suspend the operation of his courts and to display his battle banner. Indeed the red flag owes its existence as a symbol of revolution to this use. It had been France's royal flag from the eleventh to the fifteenth centuries, when it was replaced by white (and later joined with the red and blue of Paris to form the revolutionary tricolour). In August 1792 it was adopted by the revolutionaries in order to proclaim 'the martial law of the people against rebels to their power':

> it is we, the people, who are now the law ... We are not rebels. The rebels are in the Tuileries, and it is against the factions of the court and the party of the constitutional monarchy that we raise, in the name of the country and of liberty, the flag of legal repression.[1]

In Britain, the royal prerogative of summary justice in time of war and insurrection was delegated to the sovereign's lords lieutenant, who were responsible for levying and leading men to defend the realm. Each lord lieutenant had a provost marshal, corresponding to the king's earl-marshal, responsible not only for the execution of summary justice against rebels, but against those unfortunate enough to be levied as soldiers to fight on the king's side. The 'marshal's law', brisk, cheap, convenient (and no doubt effective) was extended by the Tudors to a wide range of offences of a mildly rebellious nature, but certainly far from 'waging war against the king in his realm': breaking down enclosures, possessing heretical books, or creating disorders in the Scottish and Welsh marches. Martial law was also applied to troublesome people who were not (or at least not then) soldiers, such as rogues, vagrants, and discharged soldiers inconveniently agitating for their back pay.[2]

Law stemming from the royal prerogative instead of from the common or statute law was understandably unpopular with parliament, but it seems to have been self-interest rather than constitutional form which led to the Tudors taking less advantage of it than they might have done. A rebel convicted under martial law forfeited his goods and his life, but if he were convicted by judicial process, he forfeited his lands to the crown as well.[3]

In Britain, martial law thus stemmed directly from the royal prerogative: it was neither part of the common law, which nevertheless requires every citizen to preserve the peace and come to the aid of the civil power if necessary, nor of statute law. It was not a form of military law; still less a form of military rule. The martial law administrator had enormous powers, but they were delegated to him by the government, which could dismiss him at will.

The British army's rules of engagement for dealing with episodes of violent politics changed markedly during the second half of the twentieth century. The early manuals covered two distinct contingencies – the use of military force in support of the civil power, to deal with isolated cases of civil disorder such as strikes and riots; and 'imperial policing', in which the army took the lead:

> Once outbreaks of this nature [civil disorders] have assumed serious proportions, they can as a rule no longer be dealt with by a series of isolated actions in support of the civil power, and their suppression consequently demands a concerted military plan of operations, the execution of which may extend over a considerable period.[4]

All of the military manuals (or pamphlets, rather, since none of them amounted to more than a few pages) emphasised the army's obligation to come to the aid of the civil power on request, or if necessary on its commander's own initiative, to fulfil the common law obligation of every citizen to help keep the peace.

Regulations clearly defined the civil power in various places:

In such event troops may have been asked for by the civil authority, and sent to a locality where trouble is expected, accompanied
by a magistrate, who is the competent civil authority for the
purpose[5]... a Magistrate, Sheriff or Sub-Sheriff having jurisdiction
in the place where the services of the troops are required; or of
Resident Magistrates, the Chief or Assistant Commissioner of the
Dublin Metropolitan Police and Officers of the Royal Irish
Constabulary.[6]

These rules remained much the same until 1971, after the army's
involvement in Northern Ireland had begun. From then no longer was
a police officer or magistrate able to call for troops in his own right,
except in 'grave and sudden emergencies ... which in the opinion of
the commander demand his immediate intervention to protect life and
property'. Instead the request had to be made by the chief officer of
police in person, and to the Ministry of Defence.[7] The use of troops
against their own people is always fraught with political danger. It
makes sense for ministers to control their use, and modern communication makes that practicable.

Until the second half of the twentieth century, martial law was the
principal instrument for dealing with more serious outbreaks of violence, such as armed insurrection. It suspended the civil administration
and courts, and replaced them by unified military command. *Notes on
Imperial Policing, 1934* devoted more than half of its 50-odd small pages
to the principles and practice of martial law, and made the point that
there was no British equivalent of the statutory 'state of siege' which in
other countries transfers administrative and legal powers to the armed
forces in circumstances in which the civil power can no longer operate.
The justification for the imposition of martial law is evident necessity. It
need not even be proclaimed, but 'it is, however, usual for the civil government or the military commander-in-chief to issue a proclamation.'[8]

When martial law was in force, the military commander became
responsible for administration, which was still exercised by the normal
civil staff wherever possible, although they were responsible to him.
The military commander also became responsible for justice, which he
might exercise in any way he wished. Once the state of martial law was
over, however, the civil courts could examine the actions of the military. It was therefore usual to pass an act of indemnity:

the object of which is to make legal transactions which, when they
took place, were illegal, and to free the individuals to whom it

applies from liability for having broken the law. [For] However careful a soldier may have been in the conduct of martial law, there are bound to be some actions which are not strictly legal. But this protection will be afforded only to those whose acts were done *bona fide* and in the honest belief that they were doing their duty.[9]

Martial law was imposed to ensure unity of control, and to enable justice to be dispensed swiftly. It was not always necessary. For example during the 1929 inter-communal fighting in Palestine, then ruled by Britain under a mandate of the League of Nations, unity of control had been achieved by mutual agreement between the government, the police and the armed forces. The more subtle crimes such as espionage and sabotage had not appeared, and the crimes which were being committed – rioting and murderous attacks – were such that the troops could exercise their powers under common law. Administering martial law would have overwhelmed the tiny military staff. Military courts would have found it very difficult to determine which killings had been committed in self defence, and which were murders.[10]

During the second world war, the powers of civil government in an emergency were greatly increased, and by the end there were 342 Defence (General) regulations and 345 other regulations in force – all with many subsidiary orders.[11] The government had in effect created statutory powers for the declaration of a state of siege, thus producing:

a state of affairs where, in the whole territory, or in any particular part or parts thereof, there will exist a large degree of military control ... In an emergency, however grave, except in an occupied country ... it is probable that military control will be preferable to Martial Law.[12]

Paragraphs on the imposition and withdrawal of martial law, and on acts of indemnity, remained in the manuals. In 1957, however, martial law was dismissed in a single sentence: 'Military participation under emergency legislation does not constitute 'martial law' and it is extremely unlikely that a proclamation of martial law will ever be made.'[13] Five years after that, martial law had disappeared entirely from the military pamphlets, except for an oblique reference to the Manual of Military Law.[14]

Later doctrine went further, implicitly ruling out the imposition of martial law through 'evident necessity':

The existing law in the area of operations may be inadequate to meet the needs of counter-revolutionary operations, and in such circumstances, governments may confer some additional powers upon the security forces by emergency legislation.[15]

In the United Kingdom, statutory emergency legislation gradually replaced martial law based on evident necessity, allowing for a graduated response to disorder rather than all-or-nothing: a clear advantage, and right in both political and humanitarian terms. But the advantages are not all on one side – the insurgent profits from the self-imposed restriction of the powers of the government and its forces, and also benefits by exploiting the vulnerabilities of a civil administration operating in conditions of disorder.

The experience of the partial imposition of martial law during the 1916–21 campaign in Ireland had been unhappy both for the politicians and the soldiers. The nationalist leader Redmond had warned Prime Minister Asquith that General Maxwell's executions following the Easter Rising, (which the Prime Minister had found, somewhat to his surprise, he had no authority to stop since martial law was in force) would create martyrs and rally ordinary men to a previously unpopular cause, and so it proved. The army warned the government that the partial martial law which was proclaimed in 1920 would not work, and so it turned out: 'it caused endless complications and rendered the administration of it ineffective'.[16]

The Malayan Emergency of 1948–1960 was dealt with by what amounted to statutory martial law, in which the martial law commander was either a soldier or a civilian but in either case had absolute power. Sir Henry Gurney, High Commissioner until he was assassinated in 1951, is reported to have said that the huge volume of Emergency Regulations could be summarised in a single sentence: 'the High Commissioner can do anything, and he can delegate his power to do anything to anybody'.[17] The campaign was indeed conducted under the rule of law – but the law was very far from being everyday criminal law.[18]

In substance, emergency law is statutory martial law: parliament now exercises the power of the king and his earl marshal. That is absolutely right in constitutional terms, and it has practical advantages too. The government and its forces of law and order must be of one mind if violent politics is to be countered effectively, because both the violence and the politics are crucial. Violent politics will trump constitutional politics if it is given the chance. Handing over absolute power to the armed forces and then wringing hands when things go wrong, or not handing over enough power and being blamed for tying hands behind backs, are both recipes for failure. If a campaign is proving ineffective because the forces of law and order have insufficient powers, it is the government's responsibility to change them, or to accept the political consequences of not changing them. In form, the forces of law and order win or lose; in substance, governments do. Dissent between them may prove fatal to success. If it does, the responsibility lies where it ought: on the constitutional government of a country, and not on the agencies under its command.

In 1995, the UK government set up an inquiry:

> To consider the future need for specific counter-terrorism legislation in the United Kingdom if the cessation of terrorism connected with the affairs of Northern Ireland leads to a lasting peace, taking into account the continuing threat from other kinds of terrorism and the United Kingdom's obligations under international law; and to make recommendations.[19]

Northern Ireland was to be 'assumed to be enjoying the same state of lasting peace as Great Britain'. The inquiry therefore concerned itself with the standing powers that should be written into statute law, leaving the question of emergency law until an emergency actually arose. It therefore assumed that there would be no need for non-jury courts, detention without trial (internment), or exclusion orders: (internal exile). It recommended powers to proscribe terrorist organisations, to make it an offence to be a director or member of a terrorist organisation, whether it was proscribed or not, to prepare for terrorist operations, to fundraise, launder money, gather intelligence or publicly support terrorism. It recommended reduced sentences for terrorists who gave evidence against others, which had been successful in Italy.[20] The inquiry rejected a standing body of emergency law, since it would require legislation for the unforeseen, and would have to be so broadly drawn that it would almost certainly be struck down by the European Court. It therefore did not recommend legislation-in-advance for the sort of conflict that had been taking place in Northern Ireland, and for the use of the armed forces in it, although it did recommend contingency planning.[21]

It recognised that the conflict in Northern Ireland had been too severe to be dealt with by standing counter-terrorist legislation. The question of what should be done in future conflicts on a similar scale therefore remains open.

The laws and usages of war

Governments can choose whether to treat those who take up arms against them as common criminals, as political criminals, or as participants in an internal conflict governed by national emergency legislation or martial law. Another option is to treat them as combatants in an internal war governed by the laws and usages of war (now called humanitarian law), rather than by domestic emergency legislation; or indeed to write international humanitarian law into domestic emergency legislation.

The humanitarian need for laws of war is self-evident, but there are prudential considerations too. It does not make sense to wage a conflict in ways which expose the protagonists to contumely and lose them support, which make reconciliation impossible, which render prisoners or civilians in occupied territory vulnerable to reprisal, or which lay the losers of the conflict open to unlimited revenge.

In the light of the experience of the Second World War, the four 1949 Geneva Conventions revised the laws of war previously codified by the thirteen conventions of 1907 agreed by the Hague Peace Conference. The first and second of the 1949 Conventions deal with wounded on land and sea, the third with prisoners of war and the fourth with civilians. The bulk of the 1949 Conventions deal with conventional warfare between states, although they contain a common Article 3 setting out the basic rules which bind all parties in 'armed conflicts not of an international character' occurring in the territory of any of the states bound by the Conventions:

> Persons taking no active part in the hostilities, including members of armed forces who have laid down their arms and those placed *hors de combat* ... shall in all circumstances be treated humanely ...To this end, the following acts are and shall remain prohibited at any time and in any place whatsoever with respect to the above-mentioned persons: violence to life and person, in particular murder of all kinds, mutilation, cruel treatment and torture; taking of hostages; outrages upon personal dignity, in particular humiliating and degrading treatment; the passing of sentences and the carrying out of executions without previous judgement pronounced by a regularly constituted court, affording all the judicial guarantees which are recognised as indispensable by civilised peoples.
>
> The Parties to the conflict should further endeavour to bring into force, by means of special agreements, all or part of the other provisions of the present Convention.[22]

The Hague and Geneva Conventions divide the population into combatants and non-combatants; no individual can claim the privileges of both. People such as doctors, nurses, priests, war correspondents and sutlers are unarmed combatants, and are protected in defined ways.

Irregular combatants such as resistance fighters must be commanded by someone responsible for their actions, bear a fixed sign recognisable at a distance, carry their arms openly, and conduct their operations in accordance with the laws and usages of war.[23] Captured combatants must be treated as prisoners of war; they cannot be killed, nor tried for operations conducted within the laws of war, though this does not debar a lawful government from trying captured insurgents for treason.[24]

Both combatants and civilians can be tried for war crimes – grave breaches of international humanitarian law. In the context of violent politics these include attacking civilians, taking hostages, killing prisoners, maltreating the wounded or dead, assassination, firing on undefended localities or on non-military objectives, trying individuals in improperly constituted courts, combatants engaged in battle wearing civilian clothes or enemy uniform (though they may do elsewhere, for example on reconnaissance), or civilians taking part in hostilities.

An order to commit a war crime is not a lawful order, so no combatant can offer a plea of superior orders in his defence. Nevertheless, junior individuals cannot be expected to make fine judgements about the law, nor to pause for long before obeying orders, so this provision could only be invoked against them if the order were manifestly unlawful. That concession does not apply to their commanders, who are subject to the principle of *respondat superior;* the commander must answer for the deeds of his subordinates. He is granted the authority to give orders to them, and to enforce their obedience, and he is expected to know what goes on in his command. If he fails to enforce the laws of war, the presumption is that he has authorised the crimes, acquiesced in them, or turned a blind eye.[25]

International humanitarian law therefore binds the belligerents of both sides in any form of armed conflict, even in an insurgency which does not amount to civil war. All war crimes are capital offences, and all may be tried by tribunals convened for the purpose.

Immediately after the second world war, however, states were unwilling to surrender any part of their sovereign right to deal with internal affairs, or to give the appearance of legitimising insurgents by recognising them as belligerents. None built up a code of law on internal belligerency. It was not clear how Article 3 applied in the many post-war internal conflicts, and its provisions were too sketchy to be put into practice. The International Commission of the Red Cross therefore organised the drafting of two protocols to the 1949 conventions; Protocol I was intended to extend the protection afforded to civilians during international conflict, and Protocol II to codify laws of internal armed conflict.

All parties to a conflict regard their cause as just, and if they all claimed the right to use unlimited means to pursue their just ends there could be no law. Hence the preamble to Protocol I:

> Reaffirming that the provisions of the Geneva Conventions ... and of this Protocol must be fully applied in all circumstances to all persons who are protected by these instruments without any adverse distinction based on the nature or origin of the armed conflict, or the causes espoused by, or attributed to, the parties to that conflict.[26]

Nevertheless, during the Conference which was convened by the Swiss Federal Council in Geneva in the mid-1970s to discuss the draft protocols, the third world countries succeeded in removing national liberation movements from the scope of Protocol II and bringing them into Protocol I, in effect treating them as non-state nations, as the UN had also done in granting observer status to the national liberation movements in Portuguese Africa and Palestine for example.[27] This created in effect a right to rebel in the cause of national self-determination, and hence paradoxically imposed a duty on the affected state not to resist by force.[28] Internal conflicts were defined in a way that would allow national liberation movements to fight 'illegitimate' incumbent governments, and 'legitimate' incumbent governments to fight their opponents. There were no definitions of legitimacy.

By 1977 the debate about the laws of war had become thoroughly politicised:

> a majority of members of the United Nations by the sixties shared the view that wars against imperialist, colonialist and racist regimes were fought in causes just as good as any for which armies of imperialist and colonialist powers had ever fought, and that the laws of war ought not to be allowed to make things more difficult for them.[29]

National liberation movements are not automatically governed by the Geneva Conventions, since they are not states, but Article 96 (3) of Protocol I provides a way for them to declare that they accept the obligations and protection of the Conventions. Since, if they do not make this declaration, liberation movements would not be bound by the conventions while their enemy states would, it is not surprising that none ever did.

Protocol II was originally intended to codify the laws of all internal conflict. However, once national liberation movements had been removed from it, its draft provisions ceased to command much support, since states feared it would inhibit their dealing with rebellion or counter-revolution.

Its original 48 articles were pruned to 28, and its scope limited to conflict approaching the scale of civil war:

1. This Protocol, which develops and supplements Article 3 common to the Geneva Conventions of 12 August 1949 without modifying its existing conditions or application, shall apply to all armed conflicts not covered by Article 1 [of Protocol I] and which take place in the territory of a High Contracting Party between its armed forces and dissident armed forces or other organised armed groups which, under responsible command, exercise such control over a part of its territory as to enable them to carry out sustained and concerted military operations and to implement this Protocol.

2. This Protocol shall not apply to situations of internal disturbances and tensions, such as riots, isolated and sporadic acts of violence and other acts of a similar nature, as not being armed conflicts.[30]

Article 4 (2) (d) of the protocol prohibits acts of terrorism. It does not define them, although Article 13 (2) is slightly more explicit: 'The civilian population as such, as well as individual civilians, shall not be the object of attack. Acts or threats of violence the primary purpose of which is to spread terror among the civilian population are prohibited.'[31] Again, because of their removal from the ambit of Protocol II, this prohibition does not apply to national liberation movements. Nor could it apply to groups such as the Red Army Faction, ETA or the IRA while the states in which they are operating do not recognise them as being in a state of armed conflict, and while they do not control territory. Protocol I weakened the distinction between combatants and non-combatants by permitting combatants (except regular armed forces) to disguise themselves as civilians except when actually taking part in an operation and sometimes even then.[32] It resurrected the concept of a just war. It prohibited indiscriminate attacks in which the damage to civilians was 'excessive in relation to the concrete and direct military advantage expected':[33] a prohibition before and since ignored or rationalised by terrorists and warring governments alike. Its provisions were so weak, said the representative of the Vatican, that it had restricted itself to a statement of good intentions which in terms of humanitarian law came down to a 'legal ectoplasm', for the text would be devoid of any real humanitarian substance and of any mandatory character. Yet its creators were daring to claim that it would serve to control internal conflicts, a euphemism for civil wars which, as everybody was aware, were the cruellest and most pitiless of all conflicts.[34]

The participants in domestic violence on a lesser scale than that defined in Protocol 2 are nevertheless bound by Article 3 of the 1949 Conventions willy-nilly.[35] However, the legal powers and obligations of the government forces in all states are already compatible with the provisions of Article 3, so although it would greatly limit the activities of many dissidents if they could be forced to obey Article 3, it is not surprising that neither states nor dissidents appear to have invoked it at any time since the Conventions came into force in 1950. It was clear that governments had decided that national trials for breaches of the international laws of war in anything else than the aftermath of a major war were not worthwhile.

There are many reasons for this. War crimes, like other crimes, are inherently difficult to prove – in the nature of things, even more difficult to prove than domestic and political crimes. The trials are costly. Furthermore, since the war-criminals to be tried must already be in custody they are no longer a danger to their captors. The primary objective of the trial is thus not to punish them, but to deter further crimes – *pour encourager les autres*. That is pointless if it is done when the conflict is over, and it may revive political tensions that would best be left to die. If it is done during the conflict, it invites counter-accusations and counter-trials of prisoners, or straightforward (if forbidden) reprisals. Material for such counter-accusations would not be hard to find, given the nature of war, and few governments would shrink from exaggeration or plain fabrication in time of need. Neither can governments try their own nationals for war crimes without giving comfort to the enemy and weakening the morale of their own forces; they may well prefer the blind eye to blindfold justice, the more so since military *omerta* and rank-closing may well prevent conviction in any case.

War crimes trials are a slow and inefficient way of achieving control over an enemy's behaviour when there are more direct methods available, and usually ample public support for them. For example, the prisoners of war held by one side are *de facto* hostages for the good behaviour of the other. Attacks may well be answered by attacks in kind, whatever the law may say – witness the prompt Israeli reprisals on what the PLO claimed to be refugee camps and the Israelis claimed to be training bases, following PLO raids. Governments, or would-be governments, can be accused of war crimes, but they obviously cannot be convicted of them.

Furthermore, the requirements of the laws of armed conflict may conflict with national and international law. Articles 48/50/129/146 of the four Geneva Conventions of 1949 require states either to try war crimes themselves or to extradite an accused war criminal to another state, but the constitutions of many states prohibit the extradition of their own nationals, and international law permits any state to refuse extradition for 'criminal offences of a political character'. Perhaps most important of all, no government can be compelled to try a war criminal, or to extradite him, if it does not wish to do so. Article 3 of the 1949 Conventions has been in force since 1951, and Protocols I and II since 1979. Despite the frequent and flagrant breaches of their provisions since then, including a million dead in the killing fields of Cambodia, not until the mid 1990s was anyone brought to trial in any state for breaching any of the provisions of any of the Geneva Conventions, let alone article 3, although some such breaches, for example the My Lai massacre in Vietnam, were tried under domestic law.[36] While the international laws of war set reasonably civilised standards for what is otherwise an unreasonable, uncivilised activity, in the absence of an effective means of enforcing them they are no more than that. 'Quand je vais dans un pays, je n'examine pas s'il y a des bonnes lois, mais si on exécute celles qui y sont, car il y a des bonnes lois partout.' [37]

By the 1990s, most national liberation movements had succeeded in their aims, were on their way to an acceptable compromise, or had faded away. They were no longer a problem – but genocide during tribal warfare had become so. In 1993, 'ethnic cleansing' during the re-balkanisation of Yugoslavia prompted the UN to set up an international tribunal to prosecute individuals for such crimes.[38] In 1994, a similar *ad hoc* tribunal for Rwanda was set up.[39] Disputes among member states about the jurisdiction of a standing international court prevented progress until 1998, when the International Criminal Court was finally set up.[40]

The International Court of Justice at the Hague deals only with cases between states, and the European Court of Human Rights mostly with individuals challenging their treatment by states.[41] The International Criminal Court aims to complete the spectrum, by holding individual people accountable for crimes against humanity, including systematic murder, extermination, persecution and disappearances,[42] and for war crimes, including: "Intentionally directing attacks against the civilian population as such or against individual civilians not taking direct part in hostilities ... Taking of hostages ...The passing of sentences and the carrying out of executions.'.[43] Riots and sporadic acts of violence are excluded, as they are from Protocols I and II. The definition of war crimes expressly applies to 'armed conflicts that take place in the territory of a State when there is protracted armed conflict between governmental authorities and organized armed groups or between such groups.' [44] Those who aid and abet war crimes and crimes against humanity are included: 'Orders, solicits or induces the commission of such a crime ... aids, abets or otherwise assists in its commission, including providing the means for its commission [or] in any other way contributes to the commission or attempted commission of such a crime by persons acting with a common purpose.'[45]

Action lies in the first instance with national courts, which should normally try individuals within their jurisdiction; the International Court would be needed only when national institutions have collapsed (as in Rwanda) or states prove unwilling to try their own people (as in the former Yugoslavia). The Statute makes it clear that 'Nothing ... shall affect the responsibility of a Government to maintain or re-establish law and order in the State or to defend the unity and territorial integrity of the State, by all legitimate means.'[46]

The UN has also drafted an international convention for the suppression of terrorist bombings, defined as exploding bombs or other lethal devices intending to cause death, injury or economic loss. It does not apply within states, but it does require states to extradite wanted terrorists, and to ensure that terrorist acts 'are under no circumstances justifiable by considerations of a political, philosophical, ideological, racial, ethnic, religious or similar nature and are punished by penalties consistent with their grave nature.'[47]

The wheel of international humanitarian law has rolled on; no longer are terrorists to be indulged by not being required to obey humanitarian law, or excused if they are fighting for national liberation. Terrorists violating the human rights of their victims are to be held to account, just as states and their agencies have always been. Organisations which are in protracted armed combat with governments or each other are combatants subject to the laws and usages of armed conflict, whether or not they claim to be belligerents or are recognised as such.

The change in international opinion is the important thing, not the setting-up of the international enforcement bodies. The prime right and obligation to take action lies with states themselves; only when they cannot or do not act, will the international bodies take over. Protecting the citizens of a state requires governments to counter the infrastructure of violent political organisations, their leaders, and the faith which drives them. The criminal law has a place in removing manpower, but it has severe limitations, as we have seen. Emergency law plays an essential part in giving security forces and judges additional powers, eroding materiel by reducing the flow of arms and funds, and facilitating intelligence-gathering, but the difficulties of law-enforcement remain. Ultimately, it may become necessary to treat organisations which take up arms as waging war against democracy, and require them to do that within the internationally-recognised laws and usages of armed conflict, or pay the consequences.

Conclusions – internal war

The creation of a body of emergency law setting rules of engagement between a government's security forces and a violent opposition is one strategy for dealing with violent politics within the law. It matters not whether the emergency regulations are produced by a martial law commander, a parliament sitting in emergency session, a head of state ruling by decree, or a government bringing into force dormant legislation. What is important is that the regulations are effective – which means of course being effective in both modes: violence and politics – for if they are not effective, only one option is left. That is to conduct violent politics outside the law, either as a deliberate strategy, or because the conflict has become uncontrollable. In either case, the opposing sides in effect outlaw one another.

10
Countermeasures Outside the Law

It could be argued that individuals who did not accept their duties towards the state and opposed the decisions of its government by force, *ipso facto* forfeited the rights guaranteed them by the constitution and law of the state, and could be declared outlaws, enemies of all mankind, like pirates of old: their persons and property denied the protection of the law, and made fair game for all. This would, however, be a disproportionate way to deal with all but the most extreme forms of illegality. It would be impracticable to draw sufficiently sharp boundaries between offences which merited outlawry and those which did not, and between political and criminal lawbreaking. It would permit private violence against the outlaws, because they were no longer protected by the law, and would thus breach the state monopoly of force; it would be an invitation to tyranny; the lack of clear rules of engagement understood by both sides would invite barbarism. Privateering, banditry and warlordism would be encouraged.

Although insurgents are always operating outside the law, in practice they often conduct their operations within a code of practice familiar to both sides, either because they obey the customary rules of violent conflict within that society (and there is a rich array of such customs in all societies), or because they dare not provoke the opposing force too far. They may fear political consequences such as desertion by their friends and allies, or increasing the will of the opposing side, and its popular support. Violent politicians always have to be careful not to legitimise (in the consensual sense) counter-action which could overwhelm them.

Indeed, one could define terrorism as violence which breaches the customary rules of a society for the use of violence. Gang fights do not amount to terrorism, nor punches traded in hot blood (nor even knives and bullets in some societies), nor pickets battering strike-breakers, nor

164

police battering pickets, nor even British police being battered with stones and petrol bombs on occasion. If the rules are understood and tacitly accepted, there will be fear from time to time, but pervasive arbitrariness and uncertainty are necessary for terrorism, and a sustained campaign.

Nevertheless, if insurgents use terrorism because it works, the same must be true for forces operating against them.

For less scrupulous governments, 'disappearance' is a more attractive technique than overt arrest, because of the complications caused by political trials and the difficulty of getting convictions in criminal trials. It also avoids providing a platform for the accused during the trial, and for their supporters. Since governments do not admit to holding the *desaparecidos*, they cannot be levered into releasing them by further kidnappings or crimes. Conversely, terrorist organisations may well be deterred by the suspicion that their comrades may disappear for ever if they persist.

The freedom of movement conferred on insurgents by the small signal they make in the great noise of everyday activity, the difficulty and cost of surveillance, and the difficulty of convicting them even if they are caught, may also be exploited by governments, operating clandestine counter-terrorist forces of their own – death squads: even countries such as Israel, which formed a group to track down and kill all those involved in the Munich massacre. Others used to operate in the Basque country, spectacularly assassinating ETA members using their own methods (the killers of Admiral Carrero Blanco were blown up in their car exactly as he was), and in Latin America. Death squads may be official (but denied), or formed by freelancing police or soldiers; or they may simply be vigilantes. All make use of the practical impossibility of stopping low levels of any activity, slipping through the interstices of their opponents' surveillance nets. Many are protected and actively fed with information and materiel by overt legal organisations; they are privateers carrying secret letters of marque, which they need never reveal unless they are accidentally captured by their own side, when, after a decent interval, they escape in mysterious circumstances or are released 'through lack of evidence'. The penetration of the opposing side may simply yield information instead of action: a codeword given by telephone, or information passed swiftly in a clandestine encounter, yields both excitement and untaxed earnings.

Observers who mistook the tactical success of violence for strategic, political, success – mistook the letters for words – characteristically overestimated the power of urban guerrillas and underestimated the efficacy of the counter-terror which would be used against them:

There remains little doubt in the minds of experts that little Uruguay, with a population no more than 2.5 million, has become the home of a well-disciplined and potentially effective guerrilla movement of about 1,000 men that includes members of the nation's elite. It appears to have extensive ties in other Latin American countries including Cuba. Furthermore, there are strong indications that the Tupamaros represent a new approach to guerrilla warfare in Latin America – an emphasis on urban guerrilla activity that its advocates hope will work better than the pattern followed by Ernesto Che Guevara .... The Tupamaros have dealt Uruguay's Democratic Government a series of massive shocks during the last year – and the repercussions have been felt in Washington. They have blown up radio stations, carried out a series of bank robberies, stolen weapons and dynamite, and organised a variety of strikes and riots.[1]

Both the Tupamaros and Carlos Marighela in Brazil tried to adapt the foco theory of Guevara and Debray to urban conditions. Marighela was killed in 1969, but in 1972, five years after the death of Guevara in Bolivia, the Tupamaros were still firmly established as a key element in the political future of Latin America. In spite of a fierce counter attack, their staying power seems inexhaustible.[2]

A year after the publication of the English translation, there was nothing left of the Tupamaros. They appeared to be about to topple the government, until they tried to expand from their middle-class base areas and mobilise the working class in the shanty towns. In doing so they exposed themselves to the informers of the intelligence services, and once their operations had expanded to the point at which the army intervened they were swiftly destroyed – no doubt along with a number of non-Tupamaros too.

The Montoneros of Argentina grew from a small utopian group to several thousand, and by 1975 they were causing such disruption to the everyday life of the country that their actions had in themselves provided a justification for all-out war against the guerrillas.[3] Argentines had become prepared to tolerate any government action to get rid of the Montoneros: when people disappeared 'there must have been a reason'.[4] There were contemporary reports that the captured guerrillas were too numerous to imprison, so they were drugged, flown out over the Atlantic, and dropped in – a technique nicknamed *Sol Tours* after the name of a Buenos Aires travel agency, and one reportedly criticised by the Uruguayan security experts for 'destroying the archives'.[5]

In several Latin American countries would-be revolutionaries were inspired by Castro, Guevara and Allende:

> The overthrow of Chile's brief venture into revolution by parliamentary means left the field to Marxism-based theoreticians and publicists of every stripe, 'scientifically' diagnosing the myriad defects of the existing regime and preaching the gospel that structures so awful could not stand up to a good revolutionary push. Bank raids, barrack-bombings, urban kidnappings, and so on, advertised as 'urban guerrilla warfare' by its aficionados and sometimes justly denounced as terrorism by its victims, became the hallmarks of the most active pushers, with crime and banditry, as always, not far behind them. But all that their confident revolutionism and political romanticism achieved (in the short term anyway) was to provoke the forces of the existing regimes to counter-revolutionary action of terrible efficacy and extraordinary illegality. Its hallmarks were indiscriminate attacks on everyone labelled 'subversive', detention without trial, torture, murder, and – giving a new grim word to the language – 'disappearances', which all too often included the other three as well. It was a regional adaptation of Nazi Germany's 'Nacht und Nebel' technique of terrorising occupied populations in the Second World War.[6]

Chile's then head of state, General Pinochet, was amnestied in his own country and made a senator for life, but was arrested in London in 1998 on a Spanish warrant to answer for the disappearance of several Spanish citizens. Ironically, he had been entertained by Baroness Thatcher on the same visit, thanking him for his support in the Falklands War of 1982. By an even greater irony, the President of Argentina, Carlos Menem, was on a state visit to the UK at the same time. Argentina had had a similar 'dirty war' from about 1976 to 1980, after which similar amnesties had been granted. Then came the Falklands war of 1982, the overthrow of General Galtieri, the investigation of the juntas and the dirty war, and the imprisonment of many of the principals. The Chinese head of state made a similar official visit in the following year, despite accusations of many human rights violations; General Pinochet was still under arrest in Britain. Shortly afterwards, the Spanish judge who had requested his extradition also issued extradition requests for 98 Argentines, including former presidents

Videla and Galtieri. President Menem instructed the foreign ministry not to co-operate.[7]

The initial media reaction supported Pinochet's arrest; some doubted the wisdom of its time and place, and some its legality; few set his dictatorship in historical context, and fewer still invoked *realpolitik* of the sort which had led Menem to pardon all those jailed for the dirty war in Argentina – and the surviving Montoneros.

The Economist was criticised by several letter-writers after it supported Pinochet's arrest. The points they made are worth quoting because they hint at the opposite side of the coin. States may not be able to afford enough resources to deal with violent politics within the law, which is undeniably costly. They may not be able to afford the time: courts are undeniably slow. They may need to neutralise a set of leaders: the law is undeniably ineffective there. Savage measures on one side may therefore be used to justify savage measures on the other:

> You say arresting General Pinochet was right. Not so. This is a matter for the Chileans. Some years ago they made a pact with the devil; an inelegant pact, repugnant to those who love justice. But because of it Chileans now have peace, democracy and hope for a better future. That peace is fragile. It may be that the arrest of General Pinochet is justifiable in international law. But there are some laws which the wise magistrate hesitates to impose. In London or Madrid it is too easy to say: 'Let justice be done, though the heavens fall'. Especially when the heavens will fall on people on the other side of the world.[8]

> Chile has successfully embarked on a peace process. This has its moral ambiguities. Does the return of democracy justify immunity for those suspected of atrocities? Britain has taken a decision in Northern Ireland. Would it be grateful if another country were to jeopardise the process by arresting Gerry Adams? The arguments you raise are for Chileans to decide. It is breathtaking arrogance for outsiders to take upon themselves the right to upset Chile's constitutional settlement.[9]

> None of the Europeans that want General Pinochet in jail experienced the Allende government that he overthrew in 1973: no food in the shops, 900% inflation, Cuban army brigades in the country, a clear move towards a communist government. The Pinochet government probably has 'violated plenty of international laws'. But if you did not

help us in the early 1970s, we do not need your help in the late 1990s.[10]

Despite the legal absolutism which obtains in societies which are free from large-scale violence, it is, sadly, not easy to see how a dirty war fought by one side can always be countered by a clean war fought by the other. Would that it were so.

It has become customary to conduct more or less impartial inquests on major 'dirty wars' as part of peace-making and reconciliation. Four 'Never Again' reports were commissioned by the successor governments in Brazil, Argentina, Uruguay and Chile. One was established by the UN as part of the peace process it had brokered in El Salvador.

Alexandra Brito's assessment of them was:

This 'truth-telling' exercise combined elements of political retribution, moral cleansing of society and assertion of the dignity of the victims ... It is in this pure 'truth-telling' capacity that the reports were most successful ... For these people [victims and relatives] and a great proportion of the population in all four countries ... the books became surrogates for legal justice.[11]

A similar cathartic exercise was carried out in South Africa, to fulfil the concluding sentence of the 1993 Constitution: 'There is a need for understanding but not for vengeance, a need for reparation but not for retaliation'.[12]

After the fall of communism, the former Iron Curtain countries faced the same dilemma, to punish or forgive, and solved it in similar ways. It was impossible to punish every inhuman act, and arguably unfair to punish some but not others. Nevertheless, they all decided to put only the worst offenders on trial, setting the thresholds higher in some countries than others, and with differing levels of punishment. The effect was to draw a line under the past as a start line for the future; and by and large it worked. Timothy Garton Ash's tentative conclusion after studying this process, and his own Stasi file, was that it serves as a barrier against the grosser kinds of political denial and myth; that opening the files helps to close them.[13]

Only two options remain open, therefore, as violent politics rises above the critical level at which the law enforcement system breaks down, either because of direct attack or because it is simply overwhelmed: either to apply the laws of armed conflict internally, by writing them into emergency legislation for example, or to accept that the conflict will be conducted outside the rule of law.

11
Conclusions and Consequences

War is one way of resolving conflicts of interest; politics is another. Violent politics, lying in the zone between peace and war, is a third. Conventional politics uses the modes of persuasion, shame and reward; violent politics adds prevention, fear and force. The belief that societies are naturally peaceful and that violence is a perversion, is utopian. When people consider their vital interests threatened – and it is impossible in practice to avoid this entirely – they do not voluntarily eschew the powerful modes of violent political change and limit themselves to constitutional modes, since the modes of violent politics trump those of conventional politics. Conventional politics is a subset of violent politics, not the reverse. Violent politics is universal; it is of no value to argue that it is unnatural. Violent politics is more demanding than constitutional politics, since it encompasses both forms: conventional politics of a high order within a community, to mobilise the base for success, and violent politics of equal skill between factions, in order to outmatch the opposition.

It is comforting to believe that violence never achieves anything, or anything long-term, or anything worthwhile, or anything that could not be achieved without it; but these are illusions. History is full of examples where violence in politics has worked. It is, however, easy to mistake success in violence – or counter-violence – for political success. The political substance of an act is primary. Its violent form is secondary, so speaking of 'political violence' puts the noun and adjective the wrong way round. Speaking of 'terrorism', although the word is unavoidable, also puts violent form before political substance. Violence is not a language but an alphabet: the meaning of its acts – its letters – varies with the circumstances.

The base for success in violent politics has four elements: will, skill, manpower and materiel. By far the most important factor, both for violent politicians and for the states they oppose, is will. Violent politicians need little skill, manpower or materiel to cause much death and destruction; even so, countermeasures must be aimed at their infrastructure as well as their will. States usually have ample skill, manpower and materiel; the only sensible target for the violent politician is their will. The successes of insurgents in anti-colonial campaigns and in the wars of the colonial succession stemmed from their operating *through* violent politics in the field *on* institutional politics at home, escalating the political and economic costs of the conflict beyond the benefits to the metropolitan power: breaking its will. Attempts at secession from a geographically integral state have, however, met with little success. Although the forms of conflict were the same, their political substance was different.

The belief that political violence is caused by inequity, by relative deprivation, by the suppression of natural rights; and that societies therefore deserve the violence they get, is wrong. There is no causal connection between the problems and the associated violence in scale, scope or timing. Huge injustices can coexist with domestic peace; trifling ones with dreadful violence. A peaceful society is not necessarily a just one, nor a violent one unjust.

The genesis of violent politics lies in the minds of men. The key factors in mobilising fighters are psychological and spiritual, as Mao, Hitler, Giap and Perón realised, and not material and determined, as Marx argued. The lack of intellectual coherence in the writings of successful leaders in violent politics may not be due to intellectual poverty, as is often thought, but simply to the realisation that what matters far more in violent politics is emotional coherence. Intellectual purity, logic and truth are not ingredients of success in violent politics. Faith is.

Faith need not be true, or even reasonable, to be an effective driver of violent politics; it is not the truth which matters, but what is passionately believed to be the truth. Conventional politics works by reconciling faiths; violent politics aims at victory alone. Violence polarises, and makes reconciliation more difficult, so campaigns of violent politics tend to be long and bitter. Faith is very resistant to change; the faith of a community, particularly of its leaders, may only change when a new generation replaces the old, so once violent politics begins, it may take a generation to end. Unchecked, violence can drive politics for many years, be very costly, and make many people's lives a misery.

Violence has its own attractions and its own excitements, particularly for the young and the disaffected. While the pool of such manpower remains small, the political temperature low, and the balance of power between the protagonists even, institutional politics can continue. Once the balance is upset it is striking to see how swiftly violence can grow, and how easily it stops institutional politics from working. The determination of one small gang of violent politicians to unite Ireland by force, and the determination of another to stop them, trumped the conventional politics of everyone else, and continued to do so for thirty years, killing thousands, injuring tens of thousands, costing billions, and wrecking the political, social and economic life of one and a half million people. Only a few chose violence; yet it proved very difficult, expensive and time-consuming to counter them.

There are six broad strategies for dealing with violent politics: treating it as common crime; treating it as political crime; declaring martial law; using emergency law; dealing with it outside the law; or treating it as an internal war. They are not mutually exclusive, and are often mixed. Different strategies or different combinations are often used at different stages of a conflict. Whatever the strategy, countering violent politics effectively requires sound political leadership, appropriate emergency legislation, good intelligence, professional police work, skilful military support, an effective judicial system, good co-ordination, an efficient civil service, a press office which is trusted by the media – and lots of money. The processes and pitfalls have been described in many analyses – in Britain particularly in the work of the St Andrews and Exeter schools, led by Paul Wilkinson and Richard Clutterbuck. Their emphasis on the sensitive, intelligent, all-encompassing, multi-disciplinary, multi-agency nature of successful campaigns is entirely right.

All of that is easier said than done, however, and the law of unintended consequences plays an even greater part in violent politics than it does in the conventional sort. Soldiers and policemen may well see exactly what has to be done to reduce the violence: usually by raising the stakes sufficiently to discourage all but its most daring practitioners. However, few policemen and soldiers have the skill to get the politics right too (though it is far from true that none of them ever do). Conversely, skilled politicians may over-value the power of the pen as a weapon against the sword: if the epigram were true of course, violent politics would have died out long ago. In any case, they are unlikely to be skilled swordsmen. Neither politicians nor their security forces are likely to be expert in the multifarious skills of administering a country. Hence the great emphasis placed in counterinsurgency doctrine on the importance of unified political, military and administrative command. It requires great skill to achieve that. Insurgents must also achieve such unity if they are to have any hope of success.

Anti-terrorist security measures overlap with those against organised crime, drug trafficking, espionage, subversion and single-issue fanaticism: things in which police and intelligence agencies have indispensable expertise. Soldiers take a long time to learn techniques such as maintaining the continuity of evidence which are second nature to policemen and women; they may over-react, as if their opponents were enemy soldiers rather than fellow-citizens, causing problems rather than solving them. They need to be specially-trained and tightly-controlled. This is true for everyone involved in internal security, of course, but it is less easy to achieve with soldiers, who have action-man mindsets and are here today, gone tomorrow. On the other hand, soldiers can operate in any terrain, however inhospitable and violence-ridden, and prevent its becoming a base or no-go area; they are robust and flexible; they are less likely to be *parti pris*, and they carry their baggage with them when they go. They too are indispensable once violence rises above a certain nature and level.

Violent politics in Northern Ireland during the troubles of 1968–98 was countered in just such a multi-agency way. Security policy relied on a two-pronged strategy: treating terrorist acts as common crimes, and using emergency legislation to aid the control, detection and conviction of the men of violence. It was, however, only partly successful. During the first decade of the troubles, the amount of crime rose three-fold but the throughput of the courts remained flat. Throughout the thirty years, terrorism continued to be a high-status, low-risk, money-spinning occupation, with the paramilitaries increasingly dominating organised crime and drug-running. They are unlikely to seek solutions when the problems pay so well.

The poor performance of the law-enforcement system during the Northern Ireland troubles was not attributable to overload caused by the sheer number of crimes or their rate of increase, nor to a lack of police manpower or expertise; nor yet to any shortage of money. The ordinary processes of law enforcement do not eliminate common crime; there is no reason to suppose that they will fare any better against terrorism. On the contrary, terrorist crime is very much more difficult to counter than common crime.

This is because there are only three ways of achieving the high-fidelity playback of the events giving rise to a criminal charge which is required by the courts: witness evidence, which, for understandable reasons, virtually disappears during violent politics; forensic evidence, which a few precautions will prevent; and confessions, which are therefore brought under strong attack by those who might be affected by them – often successfully. Under conditions of violent politics, it is not possible to convict more than a small proportion of those guilty of murder, or indeed of any other offence.

Even if terrorists are convicted, punishment and deterrence do not work: convicts are treated as heroes by their own community, which is the only one which matters to them. Paramilitary leaders are not held accountable for the actions of their men. They need only keep their own hands clean to keep their freedom. But if terrorism is to be countered effectively, its leaders must not be free.

Furthermore, even if a state troubled by violence treats its violent politicians as criminals, others may not. Governments and individuals are easily able to justify helping conflicts within other states. Even when there is obvious sophistry in their case, nothing much can be done about it: people are perfectly capable of saying one thing and doing another, while others will purport to believe them. Violent politics is not a game for the honest – or the naïve.

Another problem with treating violent politics as common crime arises as the conflict approaches resolution. It is important in violent politics, as in war, that the end is accompanied by reconciliation. Catharsis must not be allowed to become recrimination, nor start a new campaign. Reconciliation may well require amnesty, and the drawing of a line under the past. However, if the policy has been to convict terrorists as criminals, the rule of law is weakened by such amnesties, grants of immunity, prisoner releases, and changes of policy. Using the criminal law to deal with crimes committed with a political motive means that the law is unevenly applied, that the independence of the judiciary is called into question, that difficult questions arise over equity of treatment for common criminals, and that it muddies the status of the men of violence themselves. States treating terrorists as common criminals therefore lose all of the apparent advantages of treating them thus, and gain none of the real ones. They cannot make the leaders accountable; the followers are soldiers *de facto* whatever they may be *de jure*; and the status of ordinary criminals becomes blurred. A strategy for dealing with violent politics through the ordinary criminal law cannot succeed unless the opposition is weak. It was not weak enough in Northern Ireland. It is not weak enough in many other countries.

The second strategy, treating terrorist offences as crimes against the state, suffers from the same technical disadvantages, and introduces the concept of political crime, and therefore political trials, judges and juries: unpopular even in totalitarian states, let alone democracies.

The third strategy, to declare martial law, suffers from a more serious disadvantage. It is always open to states to suspend their legislature and judiciary, especially when violent politics has stopped their normal operation, as it can readily do; to invoke the ancient power of the head of state to rule by decree or by martial law during disturbances of the peace; and to dispense summary justice. Even leaving human rights and natural justice out of consideration – and no democracy can afford to do that – prudence and a sense of history would prevent wise governments taking that course except *in extremis*. In practice, martial law has been replaced by statutory emergency law in many countries.

Yet another option is to operate outside the bounds of law and custom, with no regard for human rights or even common humanity. Insurgents use terrorism because it gets results. The same must be true for forces operating against them, and so it proves. Sadly, counter-terror is a remarkably effective way of defeating violent politics, however much we may wish it were not. In the absence of an effective legal framework for conducting violent politics, or a tacitly understood body of traditional forms and customs which amounts to the same thing, violent politics will be conducted willy-nilly outside the law. In this mode it is technically very effective: the strongest and most ruthless side wins. Its political effects will vary with the circumstances; unless the violent political organisations are very small or very troublesome, the effects are unlikely to be trivial. In any case, whatever its undeniable effectiveness, it is not an option for liberal democracies.

The only remaining lawful course open to reasonably democratic and reasonably liberal governments faced with large-scale violent politics is therefore to treat the paramilitaries as the belligerents they claim to be, and to adapt international humanitarian law, the Geneva Conventions, to internal conflict. In reality, violent politics is a form of internal war, not an extension of common crime. Armed paramilitaries are combatants even if they do not regard themselves, or are not regarded by others, as belligerents. They are, and should be, required to obey the laws and usages of armed conflict, just as states have to do; or pay the consequences.

There are four rules in such conflicts which democracies should not find difficult to write into domestic emergency legislation, since they are already part of international humanitarian law. Firstly, that combatants may lawfully be engaged when they are on active operations. Secondly, that they can be taken prisoner of war at any time. Thirdly, that neither the forces of the state nor the insurgents may deliberately attack civilians, kidnap anybody or take them hostage, assassinate people, try them in kangaroo courts, mutilate or torture them: if they do, they are committing war crimes. Fourthly, that their leaders, whether they themselves are armed or not, are answerable for crimes committed by the organisation they lead, or publicly support: the legal doctrine of *respondat superior* applies just as much to them as it does to heads of state, government ministers, and military commanders.

Prison camps would be much cheaper to run than prisons, and would offer opportunities for re-education, genuine rather than Gulag-type. Even if few were converted, all would be aware that others held different views, and why; they would not be left alone to reinforce their own creed. When the conflict ended, they would be released. No question of weakening the principles of criminal justice by releasing one set of criminals and retaining another. No question of the conflict having ended without surrender or safe custody of arms.

It could be argued, of course, that by recognising paramilitaries as belligerents the state would be legitimising attacks on its own forces. Indeed it would; but terrorists regard the forces of the state as legitimate targets anyway. They are certainly not deterred from attacking security forces just because they would be criminals if they were not belligerents. In any case, what is the difference between capturing a terrorist and making him a prisoner until the conflict ends, or convicting him of a crime, jailing him, and releasing him under an amnesty? Only that capture is much easier than conviction.

It would be open to states to try captured paramilitaries as war criminals if they had evidence that they had committed such crimes. Conviction would be no easier, of course, than in the case of a criminal charge, but it would be no more difficult either. Even those who supported the objectives of the paramilitaries could scarcely support the commission of war crimes by them.

What is important is that emergency legislation is effective – which means of course being effective in both modes: violence and politics. It is here that the greatest practical difficulty lies. The law must govern both sides in such internal wars. The government and its forces must obey the law in order to preserve the human rights of everyone affected

by the conflict; the violent politicians and their forces must be required
to do so too, for exactly the same reason – or pay the consequences:

> Therefore, even in its most severe crises, the liberal democracy must
> seek to remain true to itself, avoiding on the one hand the dangers
> of sliding into repression, and on the other the evil consequences of
> inaction, inertia and weakness, in upholding its constitutional
> authority and preserving law and order ... The government must
> show that its measures against terrorism are solely directed at
> quelling the terrorists and their collaborators and at defending
> society against terrorist attack.[1]

Here arises another paradox of violent politics: perhaps the one with
the most important practical consequences. Democratic states walk
along a knife-edge when countering violent politics. Their citizens may
be killed and maimed by terrorist attacks, livelihoods and lifestyles
wrecked and buildings destroyed, yet governments may find it difficult
to pass the legislation required to counter terrorism effectively.
Essential countermeasures may be difficult to sell to public opinion at
home and abroad, and may arguably conflict with international law,
which is not unambiguous. They may be too costly, too demanding on
the security forces, or simply too dangerous politically. The cure – or
the fear of it – can be worse than the disease. A certain level of violence
becomes tacitly accepted.

However, violence which is acceptable from far away may be wholly
unacceptable locally. Counter-gangs and vigilantes then arise, profiting,
just as the terrorists themselves do, from the inability of the state to
prevent them. Bank robberies, protection rackets, drugs and prostitution provide funds, and supportive (or terrorised) businesses launder
them. Terrorism and organised crime become one: a way of life.

Nevertheless, once *realpolitik* makes a state unable or unwilling to
prevent private armed forces murdering its citizens and dominating its
criminal underworld it has lost one essential component of sovereignty, its monopoly of force; one of its main reasons for existence, to
protect its citizens from harm; and an important part of its legitimacy.

In reality, the law can create opinion as well as reflect it. If a government takes no special action to counter acts of terrorism that would be
grave breaches of international humanitarian law, it is not surprising
that people come to regard such acts as ordinary, even 'legitimate'. The
human casualties of terrorism rate only a few lines on the inside pages
– but the real casualty is the rule of law itself. Violent politicians lay

claim to a no-man's land beyond the law: the justness of their ends justifies their means. There should however be no such zone, on either side, where the writ of law does not run.

If there are no effective rules which allow violent politics to be defeated and conventional politics restored, there are only two possible outcomes. One is that the insurgents fight a dirty war which they cannot win, and the state fights a clean war which it cannot win either; the conflict becomes endemic, and the initiative for ending it always lies with the insurgents. The other is that the conflict becomes a dirty war on both sides. It would therefore be wise for threatened countries to consider how they should adapt the international laws of armed conflict to internal wars on their conventional politics, and to plan how they might incorporate the principles of international humanitarian law into their emergency legislation, dormant or extant.

Britain has no body of legislation to do this. The continuation of the conflict in Northern Ireland, or the occurrence of another such, was specifically ruled out in the terms of reference for the 1996 Lloyd inquiry into emergency legislation against terrorism in the UK.[2]

Once a conflict cannot be dealt with effectively by treating terrorists as criminals, there are two powerful reasons for treating it as internal war, and incorporating elements of the international law of armed conflict into national emergency legislation: to prevent the conflict becoming a dirty war, and to make the rules of engagement clear to all sides. The rules change when paramilitaries are treated as belligerents, but there are no blind spots where any savagery goes.

The conflict in Northern Ireland may have ended, or it may not. What is certain is that others like it will arise. Dealing with any such conflict requires a 'two wars strategy': one to extend good government, the other to defeat the violence. The most significant indicator of the success of the war for good government in Northern Ireland was that the vast majority of the people in the province only briefly and sporadically resorted to violent politics on any scale. The most significant indicator of the failure of the war to defeat violence is that it lasted thirty years, cost nearly four thousand lives, ten times as many injuries, billions of pounds, had a huge impact on the family and economic life of the province, and had a negative impact on Britain's international reputation.

Yet the conflict was intellectually absurd. The warlords of one side saw themselves as the reincarnated heroes of a war of national liberation half a century earlier, and the once and future rulers of the promised land. Those of the other side saw themselves engaged in a holy war to prevent them, eye for eye, tooth for tooth; or worse. The army and the police were largely engaged in fighting the war for good government, protecting the communities from the paramilitaries as best they could, in much the same way as the police protect communities from crime as best they can. Although the security forces undoubtedly kept the conflict within bounds, it was in fact the paramilitaries who fought the war of violence. The paramilitaries on both sides had a deliberate policy of murdering civilians, assassinating politicians, judges and lawyers, destroying businesses, and trying and punishing their own side in kangaroo courts: of committing war crimes and gross violations of human rights as a matter of choice: waging a dirty war analogous to those in the Basque country, Chile, Argentina and Uruguay. The paramilitaries controlled each other. They determined the nature of the conflict.

It is interesting to speculate on what the course of the conflict would have been had there not been two sets of paramilitaries to fight the dirty war in Northern Ireland. It is chilling to speculate on what the course of the conflict could have been had Britain actually withdrawn its army and police, as one side wanted. Or what the course of events might be, if one day it did.

Northern Ireland is not unique. It is a salutary example of how easily violence trumps conventional politics; of how tiny amounts of people and resources were able to wreck the economic, social and political life of one and a half million people for more than a generation, in the service of an irredentist fantasy which, had the dream come true, could easily have unleashed a terrible civil war.

The mantra that there can only be a political solution to political violence is unidimensional and simplistic. Political ineptitude in Northern Ireland lit the fire in the province; political intransigence in the Republic fuelled it; political weakness in Britain failed to put it out. All counterinsurgency and counter-terrorism is multidimensional, and complex.

To return to principles it is impossible to produce a unifying theory of political violence. Nor is it possible to produce a universal doctrine or a single set of rules. Students of violent politics must therefore lower their sights. The most that can be expected from any study is to sensitise those who might be analysts or players in violent politics (on either side) to the problems they are likely to face, to the options open to them, and to the likely costs and benefits which may follow. Calibrating their imaginations, as it were, so that they are as sensitive as is humanly possible to the enormous complexity of such struggles in practice, however simple the political objectives may be. Giving people the right questions rather than the right answers.

In this respect at least, violent politics parallels war. In the words of von Clausewitz:

> Theory will have fulfilled its main task when it is used to analyse the constituent elements of war, to distinguish precisely what at first sight seems fused, to explain in full the properties of the means employed and to show their probable effects, to define clearly the nature of the ends in view, and to illuminate all phases of warfare in a thorough critical inquiry. Theory then becomes a guide to anyone who wants to learn about war from books; it will light his way, ease his progress, train his judgement and help him to avoid pitfalls.[3]

Appendix

Table A.1 Deaths by violence, Northern Ireland, England and Wales
(Three catholic civilians were killed by the UVF in 1966; there were no terrorist killings in 1967 and 1968.)

	1969	1970	1971	1972	1973	1974	1975	1976	1977	1978	1979
NORTHERN IRELAND											
Deaths from the troubles[1]	18	25	174	470	252	220	247	297	112	81	113
Murders known to the police[2]	5	14	123	376	200	205	238	282	116	82	128
Population (100,000s)[3]	15.14	15.27	15.4	15.39	15.3	15.27	15.24	15.24	15.23	15.23	15.3
Deaths from the troubles/100,000[3]	1.19	1.64	11.30	30.54	16.47	14.41	16.21	19.49	7.35	5.32	7.39
Murders/100,000	0.33	0.92	7.99	24.43	13.07	13.43	15.62	18.50	7.62	5.38	8.37
Murders reported cleared[2]	4	5	11	32	46	76	90	119	55	40	46
People found guilty of murder[4]	4	1	4	9	18	26	73	52	73	45	59
Attempted murders known to the police[2]	1	12	298	1210	914	1264	869	1007	838	387	338
ENGLAND & WALES[5]											
People indicted for murder	270	293	331	354	342	423	410	429	359	439	502
People indicted for manslaughter			77	77	99	86	93	94	84	87	
People indicted for infanticide				17	8	14	2	8	4	6	6
Total indicted for homicide	**270**	**293**	**331**	**448**	**427**	**536**	**498**	**530**	**457**	**529**	**595**
People convicted of murder	79	99	88	86	84	139	98	108	116	137	169
People convicted of manslaughter	138	147	183	235	229	282	279	280	240	279	299
People convicted of infanticide				18	9	15	5	6	6	8	7
Total convicted of homicide	217	246	271	339	322	436	382	394	362	424	475

Table A.1 Deaths by violence, Northern Ireland, England and Wales
(Three catholic civilians were killed by the UVF in 1966; there were no terrorist killings in 1967 and 1968.) (cont..)

	1969	1970	1971	1972	1973	1974	1975	1976	1977	1978	1979
People convicted of lesser offences	3	5	4	22	29	28	38	35	44	31	35
People unfit to plead/insane/not tried	10	4	8	11	8	8	9	9	4	3	7
People acquitted	40	38	48	76	68	64	69	92	47	71	78
Total dealt with for homicide	487	539	602	787	749	972	880	924	819	953	1070
Murders/conviction – NI	1.3	14.0	30.8	41.8	11.1	7.9	3.3	5.4	1.6	1.8	2.2
Murders/conviction – E&W	3.4	3.0	3.8	4.1	4.1	3.0	4.2	4.0	3.1	3.2	3.0
Homicide indictments/ conviction – E&W	1.2	1.2	1.2	1.3	1.3	1.2	1.3	1.3	1.3	1.2	1.3

Table A.1 Deaths by violence, Northern Ireland, England and Wales
(Three catholic civilians were killed by the UVF in 1966; there were no terrorist killings in 1967 and 1968.) (cont..)

	1980	1981	1982	1983	1984	1985	1986	1987	1988	1989	1990
NORTHERN IRELAND											
Deaths from the Troubles[1]	76	101	97	77	64	55	61	95	94	62	76
Murders known to the police[2]	85	95	99	86	63	59	85	100	111	67	71
Population (100,000s)[3]	15.33	15.38	15.38	15.43	15.5	15.58	15.67	15.75	15.78	15.83	15.89
Deaths from the Troubles/100,000	4.96	6.57	6.31	4.99	4.13	3.53	3.89	6.03	5.96	3.92	4.78
Murders/100,000	5.54	6.18	6.44	5.57	4.06	3.79	5.42	6.35	7.03	4.23	4.47
Murders reported cleared[2]	59	42	45	61	50	47	39	51	79	30	20
People found guilty of murder[4]	23	34	21	15	10	39	25	45	30	15	16
Attempted murders known to the police[2]	264	480	263	250	180	225	273	282	402	247	225
ENGLAND & WALES[5]											
People indicted for murder	428	454	441	417	462	480	551	569	555	543	553
People indicted for manslaughter	101	82	81	98	112	82	108	105	79	87	69
People indicted for infanticide	7	7	4	7	2	7	3	1	7	0	1
Total indicted for homicide	536	543	526	522	576	569	662	675	641	630	623
People convicted of murder	139	167	161	152	172	173	208	215	189	198	185
People convicted of manslaughter	274	274	275	254	275	268	295	298	295	257	252
People convicted of infanticide	9	7	6	10	2	8	3	1	8	1	4
Total convicted of homicide	422	448	442	416	449	449	506	514	492	456	441

Table A.1 Deaths by violence, Northern Ireland, England and Wales
(Three catholic civilians were killed by the UVF in 1966; there were no terrorist killings in 1967 and 1968.) (cont..)

	1980	1981	1982	1983	1984	1985	1986	1987	1988	1989	1990
People convicted of lesser offences	38	28	15	31	32	30	54	57	37	52	46
People unfit to plead/insane/not tried	8	3	4	6	5	2	4	2	0	7	1
People acquitted	68	64	65	59	90	88	98	102	112	115	135
Total dealt with for homicide	958	991	968	938	1025	1018	1168	1189	1133	1086	1064
Murders/conviction – NI	3.7	2.8	4.7	5.7	6.3	1.5	3.4	2.2	3.7	4.5	4.4
Murders/conviction – E&W	3.1	2.7	2.7	2.7	2.7	2.8	2.6	2.6	2.9	2.7	3.0
Homicide indictments/ conviction – E&W	1.3	1.2	1.2	1.3	1.3	1.3	1.3	1.3	1.3	1.4	1.4

Table A.1 Deaths by violence, Northern Ireland, England and Wales
(Three catholic civilians were killed by the UVF in 1966; there were no terrorist killings in 1967 and 1968.) *(cont..)*

NORTHERN IRELAND	1991	1992	1993	1994	1995	1996	1997	97/98	98/99	Total 1969—94
Deaths from the Troubles[1]	94	85	84	62	9	15	22	33	44	11 974
Murders known to the police[2]	114	108	101	82	22	35	40	47	71	2025
Population (100,000s)[3]	16.01	16.08	16.32	16.42	16.49	16.56	16.63	16.63	16.7	
Deaths from the Troubles/100,000	5.87	5.29	5.15	3.78	0.55	0.91	1.32	1.98	2.63	
Murders/100,000	7.12	6.72	6.19	4.99	1.33	2.11	2.41	2.83	4.25	
Murders reported cleared[2]	68	55	53	48	14	22	26	29	31	
People found guilty of murder[4]	11	14	18	17	19	13	3	..	..	117
Attempted murders known to the police[2]	360	311	416	225	35	71	116	113	85	
ENGLAND & WALES[5]										
People indicted for murder	622	625	579	543	349					
People indicted for manslaughter	79	71	94	80	49					
People indicted for infanticide	2	3	1	0	1					
Total indicted for homicide	**703**	**699**	**674**	**623**	**399**					14 116
People convicted of murder	197	211	222	220	146					4012
People convicted of manslaughter	299	282	269	253	161					6711
People convicted of infanticide	5	6	4	3	1					151
Total convicted of homicide	501	499	495	476	308					10 874

Table A.1 Deaths by violence, Northern Ireland, England and Wales
(Three catholic civilians were killed by the UVF in 1966; there were no terrorist killings in 1967 and 1968.) (cont..)

NORTHERN IRELAND	1991	1992	1993	1994	1995	1996	1997	97/98	98/99	Total 1969—94
People convicted of lesser offences	39	44	30	26	14					833
People unfit to plead/insane/not tried	2	5	2	6	0					138
People acquitted	161	151	147	115	77					2271
Total dealt with for homicide	1204	1198	1169	1099	707					24 990
Murders/conviction – NI	10.4	7.7	5.6	4.8	1.2					
Murders/conviction – E&W	3.2	3.0	2.6	2.5	2.4					
Homicide indictments/conviction – E&W	1.4	1.4	1.4	1.3	1.3					

Table A.1 Deaths by violence, Northern Ireland, England and Wales
(Three catholic civilians were killed by the UVF in 1966; there were no terrorist killings in 1967 and 1968.) *(cont..)*

Year	Annex	Table	Figs for
1971		1	69–71
1973		1	1972
1975		1	73–74
1979	2	2	75–79
1980	3	1	1980
1981	3	1	1981
1982	3	1	1982
1983	3	1	1983
1984	2	1	1984
1985	2	1	1985
1986	2	1	1986
1987	2	1	1987
1988	3	1	1988
1989	2	1	1989
1990	2	1	1990
1991	3	1	1991
1992	4	1	1992
1993	4	1	1993
1994	4	1	1994
1995	3	1	1995
1996	4		1996
97/98	6	1	1997
98/99	1	1	1998
97/98			98/99

Sources:
1. Royal Ulster Constabulary, *Chief Constable's Report 1997/98* (Belfast, RUC, 1998) Appendix 7, table 1, p. 99. RUC Chief Constable's Report 1998/99, Appendix 2, table 1 (for 97/98 and 98/99) 1969 figure: McKittrick *et al Lost Lives*, table 1 (RUC recording began August 1969)
2. RUC Chief Constable's Report

RUC Central Statistics Unit, personal communication

3. Office for National Statistics. *Annual Abstract of Statistics 1977* (London, Stationery Office, 1997) table 2.1 Figs after 1995 extrapolated.

19

Table A.1 Deaths by violence, Northern Ireland, England and Wales
(Three catholic civilians were killed by the UVF in 1966; there were no terrorist killings in 1967 and 1968.) *(cont..)*

4. Northern Ireland Office *Annual Abstract of Statistics* (Belfast, HMSO)

No	Year	Table	Figs for
1	1982	3.6	1969–1978
9	1990	4.6	1979–1984
14	1996	4.10	1985–1994
			1994–1997

NIO Statistics and Research branch – personal communication. Later figures not available November 99.

5. Home Office. *Criminal Statistics England and Wales.* (London, HMSO)

Cmnd	Year	Table	Figs for
5402	1972	31	1969–1971
6909	1976	8.10	1972–1976
233	1986	4.7	1977–1985
3421	1995	4.8	1986–1995

6. The RUC Chief Constable reported by calendar year up to and including 1996. The figures for 97/98 and 98/99 (financial years ending 31 March) are from the Chief Constable's reports for those years. The 1998/99 report includes figures back to 89/90 or 90/91 restated for financial years, and for new counting rules. The Home Office revised the counting rules with effect from 1 April 1998, particularly for offences against the person, criminal damage, fraud and forgery. The resulting incompatibilities in the figures do not affect the conclusions drawn in this book. The figures for calendar 1997 were provided by the RUC Statistics Branch for comparison. They have not been included in the total column. The total for 1968–1998 given in the final column includes calendar years up to and including 1996, FY 97/98 and FY 98/99, except for murder convictions where the 1997 figure has been included. The 1998 figure was not available by November 99.

Table A.2 Estimate of terrorist crime in Northern Ireland 1968–98   1995 = Const Seymour, died of wounds received in 1973; in coma since.

	1969	1970	1971	1972	1973	1974	1975	1976	1977	1978	1979	1980
Deaths: RUC	1	2	11	17	13	15	11	23	14	10	14	9
Deaths: Regular Army	0	0	43	105	58	30	14	14	15	14	38	8
Deaths: UDR/RIR	0	0	5	26	8	7	6	15	14	7	10	9
Deaths: civilians (including suspected terrorists)	17	23	115	322	173	168	216	245	69	50	51	50
Deaths: total	18	25	174	470	252	220	247	297	112	81	113	76
Injuries: RUC	711	191	315	485	291	235	263	303	183	302	165	194
Injuries: Regular Army	54	620	381	542	525	453	151	242	172	127	132	53
Injuries: UDR/RIR	0	0	9	36	23	30	16	22	15	8	21	24
Injuries: civilians	..	..	1887	3813	1812	1680	2044	2162	1017	548	557	530
Injuries: total	765	811	2592	4876	2651	2398	2474	2729	1387	985	875	801
Killed + injured	783	836	2766	5346	2903	2618	2721	3026	1499	1066	988	877
Shooting incidents	73	213	1756	10631	5019	3208	1803	1908	1081	755	728	642
Bomb explosions	9	153	1022	1382	978	685	399	766	366	455	422	280
Devices neutralised	1	17	493	471	542	428	236	426	169	178	142	120
Incendiaries ignited or defused						270	56	236	608	115	60	2
Firearms found	14	324	716	1259	1313	1236	820	736	563	393	300	203

Table A.2 Estimate of terrorist crime in Northern Ireland 1968–98   1995 = Const Seymour, died of wounds received in 1973; in coma since. *(cont..)*

	1969	1970	1971	1972	1973	1974	1975	1976	1977	1978	1979	1980
Explosives found (Kg)	102	305	1246	18819	17426	11848	4996	9849	1728	956	905	821
Armed robberies and attempts	..	..	489	1931	1317	1353	1325	889	676	493	504	467
Amount stolen (£K)	..	..	304	795	612	576	572	545	447	233	568	497
Rough total terrorist crime (3)	882	1549	7267	21396	12421	9765	7404	7948	4389	3359	3102	2605
People charged for terrorist crime (4)					1418	1374	1197	1276	1308	843	670	550
Crimes/charge	..	..	..	..	8.8	7.1	6.2	6.2	3.4	4.0	4.6	4.7
People killed in road traffic accidents	257	272	304	372	335	316	313	300	355	288	293	229

Table A.2 Estimate of terrorist crime in Northern Ireland 1968–98

1995 = Const Seymour, died of wounds received in 1973; in coma since. (cont..)

	1981	1982	1983	1984	1985	1986	1987	1988	1989	1990	1991
Deaths: RUC	21	12	18	9	23	12	16	6	9	12	6
Deaths: Regular Army	10	21	5	9	2	4	3	21	12	7	5
Deaths: UDR/RIR	13	7	10	10	4	8	8	12	2	8	8
Deaths: civilians (including suspected terrorists)	57	57	44	36	26	37	68	55	39	49	75
Deaths: total	**101**	**97**	**77**	**64**	**55**	**61**	**95**	**94**	**62**	**76**	**94**
Injuries: RUC	332	99	142	267	415	622	246	218	163	214	139
Injuries: Regular Army	112	80	66	64	20	45	92	211	175	190	197
Injuries: UDR/RIR	28	18	22	22	13	10	12	18	15	24	56
Injuries: civilians	878	328	280	513	468	773	780	600	606	478	570
Injuries: total	**1350**	**525**	**510**	**866**	**916**	**1450**	**1130**	**1047**	**959**	**906**	**962**
Killed + injured	**1451**	**622**	**587**	**930**	**971**	**1511**	**1225**	**1141**	**1021**	**982**	**1056**
Shooting incidents	1142	547	424	334	238	392	674	538	566	557	499
Bomb explosions	398	219	266	193	148	172	236	253	224	166	231
Devices neutralised	131	113	101	55	67	82	148	205	196	120	137
Incendiaries ignited or defused	49	36	43	10	36	21	9	8	7	33	237
Firearms found	357	288	166	187	173	174	206	489	246	179	164

Table A.2 Estimate of terrorist crime in Northern Ireland 1968–98

1995 = Const Seymour, died of wounds received in 1973; in coma since.   *(cont..)*

	1981	1982	1983	1984	1985	1986	1987	1988	1989	1990	1991
Explosives found (Kg)	3419	2298	1706	3871	3344	2443	5885	4728	1377	1969	4167
Armed robberies and attempts	689	693	718	710	542	839	955	742	604	492	607
Amount stolen (£K)	855	1392	830	702	656	1207	1900	1389	1079	1729	1673
Rough total terrorist crime (3)	4236	2528	2296	2486	2206	3219	3562	3463	2885	2535	2777
People charged for terrorist crime (4)	918	686	613	528	522	655	471	440	433	383	404
Crimes/charge	4.6	3.7	3.7	4.7	4.2	4.9	7.6	7.9	6.7	6.6	6.9
People killed in road traffic accidents	223	216	173	189	177	236	214	178	181	185	185

Table A.2 Estimate of terrorist crime in Northern Ireland 1968–98

1995 = Const Seymour, died of wounds received in 1973; in coma since. *(cont..)*

	1992	1993	1994	1995	1996	1997	1998	Total
Deaths: RUC	3	6	3	1	0	4	1	302
Deaths: Regular Army	4	6	1	0	1	1	1	452
Deaths: UDR/RIR	2	2	2	0	0	0	0	203
Deaths: civilians (including suspected terrorists)	76	70	56	8	14	17	53	2336
Deaths: total	**85**	**84**	**62**	**9**	**15**	**22**	**55**	**3293**
Injuries: RUC	148	147	170	370	459	357	384	8530
Injuries: Regular Army	302	146	120	8	53	136	69	5538
Injuries: UDR/RIR	18	27	6	5	2	14	17	531
Injuries: civilians	598	504	529	554	905	730	1094	27 238
Injuries: total	**1066**	**824**	**825**	**937**	**1419**	**1237**	**1564**	**41837**
Killed + injured	**1151**	**908**	**887**	**946**	**1434**	**1259**	**1619**	**45 130**
Shooting incidents	506	476	348	50	125	225	209	35 667
Bomb explosions	222	206	123	2	25	93	243	10 337
Devices neutralised	149	83	99	incl above	incl above	incl above	incl above	4909
Incendiaries ignited or defused	126	61	115	10	4	9	20	2181
Firearms found	194	196	178	118	98	105	88	11 483

Table A.2 Estimate of terrorist crime in Northern Ireland 1968–98

1995 = Const Seymour, died of wounds received in 1973; in coma since. (cont..)

	1992	1993	1994	1995	1996	1997	1998	Total
Explosives found (Kg)	2167	3944	1285	5	1677	1258	883	115 427
Armed robberies and attempts	739	643	555	620	655	621	632	21 500
Amount stolen (£K)	1666	1515	1709					23 451
Rough total terrorist crime (3)	3004	2591	2216	1736	2371	2328	2809	131 335
People charged for terrorist crime (4)	418	372	349	440	595	405	441	17 709
Crimes/charge	7.2	7.0	6.3	3.9	4.0	5.7	6.4	
People killed in road traffic accidents	150	143	157	144	142	144	160	6831

Sources:
1. Deaths and Injuries: Northern Ireland Annual Abstract of Statistics No 4 – 1996, table 4.3. Figures from 1995 to 1998: RUC Statistics Branch: www.ruc.police.uk/press/statistics/injury2.htm, 1 Nov 99. 1969 deaths: Mc Kittrick et al Lost Lives, table 1 (official records started only in Aug 1969).
2. other incidents: table 4.2. Figures for 1998: RUC Statistics Branch: figures are provisional.
3. deaths + injuries + shootings + bombs exploded and neutralised + firearms found + each 50kg of explosives found + armed robberies.
4. 'Number of persons charged with terrorist and serious public order offences 1972–95': Annual Report of the Chief Constable of the RUC, 1995, table 4.
5. Incendiaries 1974–1995 inc, and shootings, bombings, finds of explosives and arms 1995: Annual Report of the Chief Constable of the RUC, 1995, table 2

Table A.3 Comparative crime and conviction rates, UK, 1968–78

	1968	1969	1970	1971	1972	1973	1974	1975	1976	1977	1978
Indictable crime known to the police: E&W[1] (thousands)	1289	1498	1568	1666	1690	1658	1963	2106	2136	2636	2561
Indictable crime known to the police: Scotland[2] (thousands)	152	156	167	181	178	168	192	232	265	301	277
Indictable crime known to the police: NI[3]	16 294	20 303	24 810	30 828	35 884	32 057	33 314	37 239	37 779	45 335	45 335
Population (M): E&W[4]	48.7	48.7	48.9	49.2	49.3	49.5	49.5	49.5	49.5	49.4	49.4
Population (M): Scotland[5]	5.2	5.2	5.2	5.2	5.2	5.2	5.2	5.2	5.2	5.2	5.2
Population (M): NI[6]	1.5	1.5	1.5	1.5	1.5	1.5	1.5	1.5	1.5	1.5	1.5
Indictable crime/100,000 population: E&W	2647	3074	3207	3389	3426	3352	3968	4257	4319	5332	5180
Indictable crime/100,000 population: Scotland	2923	2995	3203	3457	3403	3210	3663	4434	5064	5760	5315
Indictable crime/100,000 population: NI	1079	1341	1625	2002	2332	2095	2182	2444	2479	2977	2977
Convictions for indictable crime E&W[7] (thousands)	257	304	323	322	340	337	375	402	415	429	424
Convictions for indictable crime: Scotland[8] (thousands)	31.2	33.3	36.6	32.5	30	27.5	30.4	32.8	34.6	36.3	37.7

Table A.3   Comparative crime and conviction rates, UK, 1968–78   (cont.)

	1979	1980	1981	1982	1983	1984	1985	1986	1987
Indictable crime known to the police: E&W (thousands)									
Indictable crime known to the police: Scotland[2] (thousands)									
Indictable crime known to the police: NI[3]	54 262	56 316	62 496	62 020	63 984	66 779	64 584	68 255	63 860
Population (M): E&W[4]	49.508	49.603	49.634	49.613	49.681	49.81	49.99	50.162	50.321
Population (M): Scotland[5]	5.204	5.194	5.18	5.167	5.153	5.146	5.137	5.123	5.113
Population (M): NI[6]	1.53	1.533	1.538	1.538	1.543	1.55	1.558	1.567	1.575
Indictable crime/100,000 population: E&W									
Indictable crime/100,000 population: Scotland									
Indictable crime/100,000 population: NI									
Convictions for indictable crime E&W[7] (thousands)									
Convictions for indictable crime: Scotland[8] (thousands)									

Table A.3 Comparative crime and conviction rates, UK, 1968–78   *(cont..)*

	1988	1989	1990	1991	1992	1993	1994	1995	1996
Indictable crime known to the police: E&W[1] (thousands)	55 890	55 147	57 198	63 492	67 532	66 228	67 886	68 808	
Indictable crime known to the police: Scotland[2] (thousands)									
Indictable crime known to the police: NI[3]									
Population (M): E&W[4]	50.487	50.678	50.869	51.1	51.277	51.439	51.621	51.82	51.979
Population (M): Scotland[5]	5.093	5.097	5.102	5.107	5.111	5.12	5.132	5.137	5.149
Population (M): NI[6]	1.578	1.583	1.589	1.601	1.608	1.632	1.642	1.649	1.654
Indictable crime/100,000 population: E&W									
Indictable crime/100,000 population: Scotland									
Indictable crime/100,000 population: NI									
Convictions for indictable crime E&W[7] (thousands)									
Convictions for indictable crime: Scotland[8] (thousands)									

Table A.3 Comparative crime and conviction rates, UK, 1968–78 *(cont..)*

	1968	1969	1970	1971	1972	1973	1974	1975	1976	1977	1978
Convictions for indictable crime: NI[9]	4592	4405	4195	4265	3182	3528	4524	4986	4857	5230	4803
Crimes per conviction: E&W[10]	5.0	4.9	4.9	5.2	5.0	4.9	5.2	5.2	5.1	6.1	6.0
Crimes per conviction: Scotland	4.9	4.7	4.6	5.6	5.9	6.1	6.3	7.1	7.7	8.3	7.3
Crimes per conviction: NI	3.5	4.6	5.9	7.2	11.3	9.1	7.4	7.5	7.8	8.7	9.4

Sources:

1.   Annual Abstract of Statistics 1972, table 81 to AAS 1980 table 4.2.
2.   AAS 1972, table 88 to AAS 1980 table 4.21. Data before 1972 not strictly comparable because of the Social Work (Scotland) Act, 1968.
3.   Ulster Year Book 1974, p. 37. 1977, table 1 p. 41; to 1980 table 33. See note 1 to UYB 1980, table 34 and note 1 to AAS 1980, table 4.32 for comparability caveats.

4, 5, 6.   AAS 1972, table 6; AAS 1980 table 2.12
7.   AAS 1971, table 75; AAS 1980 table 4.3. Data for 1968 not strictly comparable because of the Theft Act 1968.
8.   AAS 1971, table 81; AAS 1980, table 4.21. Data before 1972 not strictly comparable because of the Social Work (Scotland) Act 1968. Break in continuity in 1975 is due to a change in recording practice. The 1975 figure comparable to earlier years is 213.3.
9.   UYB 1972, p. 52; UYB 1974, p. 37; UYB 1975 p.39; UYB 1977 p.35; UYB 1980 table 34. Note to note 3 also applies. This appears to have made a difference of only about 100 convictions per year: compare UYB 1980 table 34 line 2 with UYB 1978/79 table 2 (p. 35) line 2.
10.   Until 1969 a table comparing the criminal statistics of England & Wales, Scotland and Northern Ireland was included each year in the Annual Abstract of Statistics. The comparison was always regarded as hazardous because of the differences in legal systems and methods of recording, and was made even more so by the introduction of the Theft Act 1968: (see AAS 1980, p.99). The effect, for the purposes of our broad comparison, is limited. AAS 1972 table 82 note 1 gives the adjustment to the 1969 figure of 304,000 convictions for indictable crime in England & Wales as 284,000, a difference of 20,000 or 7 percent.

Table A.4 Compensation expenditure in Northern Ireland

Fiscal Year (compensation)	68/69	69/70	70/71	71/72	72/73	73/74	74/75	75/76	76/77	77/78
Calendar year (casualties)	1968	1969	1970	1971	1972	1973	1974	1975	1976	1977
People killed and injured [1]	379	779	836	2766	5346	2903	2618	2721	3026	1499
Criminal injuries compensation (£K)[2]	2	132	443	724	2174	3886	6023	7938	6300	7492
Criminal damage compensation (£K)[2]	12	1977	2781	3967	26 592	27 901	40 209	45 845	49 975	37 218
TOTAL (£K)	14	2109	3224	4691	28 766	31 788	46 232	53 782	56 276	44 709
S63 compensation payments (£K)[3]						34	28	123	134	109

Table A.4 Compensation expenditure in Northern Ireland *(cont..)*

Fiscal Year (compensation)	78/79	79/80	80/81	81/82	82/83	83/84	84/85	85/86	86/87	87/88
Calendar year (casualties)	1978	1979	1980	1981	1982	1983	1984	1985	1986	1987
People killed and injured [1]	1066	988	877	1451	622	587	930	971	1511	1225
Criminal injuries compensation (£K)[2]	10613	8737	10 009	6251	7133	8377	9246	13 888	11 467	12 925
Criminal damage compensation (£K)[2]	39 099	39 526	44 627	36 524	31 058	19 473	19 872	17 218	15 266	19 004
TOTAL (£K)	49 711	48 263	54 637	42 775	38 191	27 850	29 118	31 106	26 732	31 929
S63 compensation payments (£K)[3]	83	149	157	115	144	174	235	379	318	579

Table A.4 Compensation expenditure in Northern Ireland (cont..)

Fiscal Year (compensation)	88/89	89/90	90/91	91/92	92/93	93/94	94/95	95/96	96/97	97/98	Totals
Calendar year (casualties) 1968–1998	1988	1989	1990	1991	1992	1993	1994	1995	1996	1997	
People killed and injured [1]	1141	1021	982	1056	1151	908	886	229	341	250	41 066
Criminal injuries compensation (£K) [2]	14 968	16 450	19 547	25 020	26 570	29 602	34 635	36 345	35 117	40 660	412 674
Criminal damage compensation (£K) [2]	20 606	22 124	22 711	33 096	75 928	67 871	53 812	32 102	23 330	25 418	895 141
TOTAL (£K)	35 575	38 574	42 259	58 116	102 498	97 472	88 447	68 447	58 446	66 078	1 307 816
S63 compensation payments (£K) [3]	1258	1149	1649	1884	2809	2601	1715	1353	1332	1535	20 044

Sources:

1. NI Annual Abstracts of Statistics: see table 4, then 1995 and 1996: RUC Chief Constable's Report, 1997. p. 39. 1998: RUC Chief Constable's Report 1997/98, pp 38–9.
2. Northern Ireland Compensation Agency, personal communication, 25 June 1997, updated to 1997/98 from NI Compensation Agency Corporate and Business Plan (NIO letter 16 February 99)
3. Compensation payments under section 63 of the NI (Emergency Provisions) Act 1991, and its predececessors, mostly for requisitioned property and damage caused during security forces searches and other operations. (1973/74 to 1992/93 incl) Northern Ireland Office Statistics and Research Bulletin 1/94 (Belfast, NIO, 1994), table 9.
(1993/94 to 1997/98) Northern Ireland Office Statistics on the Operation of the NI (Emergency Provisions) Act 1996: NIO, personal communication, 16 February 1999.

Notes

1 Violence and Politics

1 Or, to be exact, 185 members of the United Nations. www.un.org/ overview/unmembers.htm. February 1999.
2 PIOOM: the Dutch acronym for the Interdisciplinary Research Programme on Root Causes of Human Rights Violations. 1996 map in Darby, *Scorpions in a Bottle: conflicting cultures in Northern Ireland* (London, Minority Rights Group, 1997) p. 17.
3 Schmid and Jongman, 'Violent Conflicts and Human Rights Violations in the mid-1990s', *Terrorism and Political Violence*, vol. 9, no.4 (Winter 1997), pp. 166–192.
4 Stockholm Institute for Peace Research, *SIPRI Yearbook 1997: armaments, disarmament and international security* (Oxford, OUP and SIPRI, 1997) p. 17.
5 Lakos, A., *Terrorism 1980–1990: a bibliography* (Oxford, Westview Press, 1991)
6 Gordon, 'Terrorism on the Internet: Discovering the Unsought' in *Terrorism and Political Violence*, vol. 9, no. 4 (Winter, 1997) pp. 159–165.
7 Mickolus, and Simmons, *Terrorism 1992–1995: a chronology of events and a selective annotated bibliography* (Westport CT, Greenwood Press, 1997)
8 Hoffman and Claridge, 'The RAND-St Andrews Chronology of International Terrorism and Noteworthy Domestic Incidents, 1996' in *Terrorism and Political Violence*, vol. 10, no. 2 (Summer, 1998) p. 135.
9 Crenshaw and Pimlott, John (eds), *Encyclopaedia of World Terrorism* (Armonk, Sharpe Reference, 1997)
10 Definition recommended by the Lloyd Report; consistent with that used in the United States. Cm3420. *Inquiry into Legislation against Terrorism* (London, the Stationery Office, 1996) (The Lloyd Report) para. 5.23.
11 Davies, *Europe: a History* (London, Pimlico, 1997) Appendix III, p. 1328.
12 *(Ibid)*, p. 1329, after Roy Medvedev and Robert Conquest.
13 The Great War killed 1.8 million Germans, 1.7 million Russians, 1.6 million French (20 percent of the men of military age), 1.2 million Austro-Hungarians, 900 000 from the British Empire and 116 000 Americans. During the Second World War, the Soviet Union lost 8 or 9 million from the armed forces, and 16 to 19 million civilians; Poland lost over 12 million military and civilians. The Allies lost 10 of the 14 million from the services; Germans accounted for 3 1/2 million of the 4 million Axis deaths. The UK lost more than a quarter of a million military and nearly 100 000 civilians. The US lost about a third of a million military. As a rule of thumb, 10 people are wounded for every one killed. Such figures can never be more than estimates, but they indicate the scale of the casualties (Hobsbawm, *Age of Extremes: the short twentieth century, 1914–1991* (London, Michael Joseph, 1994) p. 26. Davies, *Europe: A History* (London, Pimlico, 1997) Appendix III, p. 1328.
14 Hobsbawm *(op. cit.)* p. 44.

15 Furet, François, 'Les crimes du communisme', in Courtois, Stéphane *et al.*, *Le livre noir du communisme: crimes, terreur, répression* (Paris, Robert Laffont, 1997) p. 14.

16 Furet, François, *op. cit.*, p. 16.

17 Darby, *Scorpions in a Bottle: conflicting cultures in Northern Ireland* (London, Minority Rights Group, 1997) p. 27.

18 Flackes and Elliott, *Northern Ireland: a political directory 1968–1993* (Belfast, The Blackstaff Press, 1994) p. 1.

19 On 23 October 1983, suicide drivers bombed the American and French barracks of the US/French/British/Italian multinational force in Lebanon, killing 241 US marines and 58 French soldiers. President Reagan repeatedly insisted that the marines would remain, but withdrew them suddenly in January 1984. Britain and Italy followed; the French left an observer force, which was withdrawn in April 1986 after repeated attacks.

20 In 1993, the American-led UN expeditionary force sent to protect famine relief in Somalia and restore order became embroiled in battles with the Somali warlords; the US Rangers attacked General Aidid's headquarters by helicopter; two were shot down, 18 Rangers were killed and one captured. President Clinton withdrew US troops six months later; 30 US servicemen had been killed and 175 wounded.

21 Successor governments often claimed that they had themselves defeated the might of the colonial power: an indispensable nation-building myth, not often consistent with reality.

22 The Popular Front for the Liberation of Palestine attacked an El Al aircraft in Athens in December 1968, killing one Israeli; Israel launched a commando raid on Beirut airport, destroying 13 airliners. The Palestine Liberation Organisation attacked a bus in March 1978, killing 34 Israelis; Israel invaded South Lebanon, killing some 2000 Palestinians and Lebanese. When the Israeli Ambassador in London was attacked by Abu Nidal in June 1982, they invaded Lebanon again.

23 Festinger *et al.*, *When Prophecy Fails* (Minneapolis, University of Minnesota Press, 1956). Mackay, *Memoirs of Extraordinary Popular Delusions and the Madness of Crowds* (New York, Random House, 1980): originally published in London, 1841.

24 Showalter, *Hystories: hysterical epidemics and modern culture* (London, Picador, 1997). Furedi, *Culture of Fear: risk-taking and the morality of low expectation* (London, Cassell, 1997). Sokal, and Bricmont, *Intellectual Impostures: postmodern philosophers' abuse of science* (London, Profile Books, 1998). And of course: Garner, *Politically Correct Bedtime Stories, Politically Correct Holiday Stories*, and *Once Upon a More Enlightened Time* (New York, Macmillan, 1995).

25 Showalter, 'Diary' in *London Review of Books*, 2 April 1998, p. 29. Some, like the woman who claimed she had caught Gulf War Syndrome at a party and given it to her dog, were amusingly bizarre; others thought Showalter akin to a revisionist denying the Holocaust, and threatened her life.

26 Dahrendorf, *The Modern Social Conflict: an essay on the politics of liberty* (London, Weidenfeld & Nicolson, 1988) p. 17.

27 Professor Jeffrey Hadden of the Department of Sociology at the University of Virginia lists more than 130 new religious movements, mostly in the United States: www.relfreedom.org.

28 For interesting surveys of religious terrorists, including the radical right in
    the US, see Juergensmeyer, 'Terror Mandated by God' in *Terrorism and
    Political Violence*, vol. 9, no. 2 (Summer, 1997) pp. 16–23, and Gallagher,
    'God and Country: Religion as a Religious Imperative on the Radical
    Right' in *Terrorism and Political Violence*, vol. 9, no. 3 (Autumn, 1997)
    pp. 63–79.

29 Eamonn Collins, IRA activist and defector, murdered in Newry in January
    1999. Collins, *Killing Rage* (London, Granta Books, 1997) pp. 36–37.

30 Weaver, 'Violence as Memory and Desire: Neo-Nazism in Contemporary
    Germany', in Apter (ed.), *The Legitimization of Violence* (Basingstoke,
    Macmillan, 1997) pp. 148–151.

31 *NS-Kampfruf* (March/April 1998) quoted in Weaver, *op. cit.*, p.138.

32 *NS-Kampfruf* (Summer 1986 and July/August 1987) quoted in Weaver, *op.
    cit.*, p.145.

33 Animal Liberation Front defector, quoted in *The Sunday Telegraph*, 16 August
    1998, p. 12. In October 1999 the maker of a documentary on the organisation
    was kidnapped, and its initials burned into his back. *The Times*, 8 November
    1999, p. 4. The Lloyd Report estimated that animal rights groups had exploded
    100 incendiaries in Britain during 1995, causing four million pounds worth of
    damage. Cm3420. *Inquiry into Legislation against Terrorism* (London, the
    Stationery Office, 1996) p. 4.

34 Jacon Kenison, 19, serving 16 months in prison for arson and weapons-
    possession. Allan Hall, *The Scotsman*, 3 September 1998, p. 12.

35 Stephen Farrell, *The Times*, 5 September 1998, p. 17.

36 For example the four women who caused £1.5 million damage to a British
    Aerospace Hawk fighter in 1996, claiming that Indonesia was going to use it
    against nationalists in East Timor; they were acquitted by the jury.

37 Walker, *The Times*, 30 September 1998, p. 1. On atrocities committed by the
    Serb forces in Kosovo.

38 Picard, 'The Lebanese Shi'a and Political Violence in Lebanon' in Apter, *op.
    cit.*, p. 213.

39 Gott, Richard, *Rural Guerrillas in Latin America* (Harmondsworth, Penguin,
    1973) p. 273.

40 A.J.P Taylor, cited by Adam Roberts, *Oxford Magazine*, vol. 141 p. 11.

41 6 February 1996. Two people were killed, and many buildings severely
    damaged. The IRA blamed British demands and unionist intransigence, as if
    bombs were a natural disaster. Four days after the opening of the Northern
    Irish Forum in May 1996 a huge bomb in the centre of Manchester injured
    more than 200 people, and destroyed many businesses. It was the sixth IRA
    bomb in Britain since the IRA had ended its ceasefire in February, and the
    largest ever exploded on the mainland. In October, just before the opening
    of the Conservative Party Conference, a bomb inside the Army barracks in
    Lisburn, Northern Ireland, injured many; a second bomb detonated as the
    injured were being tended to, killing a soldier.

42 In August 1998, a few months after the signature of the Good Friday peace
    agreement in Belfast, a group calling itself the Real IRA bombed the town
    centre of Omagh injuring 220 people and killing 28, including a pregnant
    woman, her mother and daughter, a Spanish boy and his teacher, and visit-
    ing children from the Republic: the worst single atrocity in the whole of the

troubles. The leaders of the Real IRA's political wing, including the sister of Bobby Sands, the first Maze hunger striker to die, had to flee from their homes in the Republic. *The Economist*, 22 August 1998, p. 21.

43 Hoffman, 'The Confluence of International and Domestic Trends in Terrorism' in *Terrorism and Political Violence*. vol. 9, no. 2 (Summer, 1997), pp. 1–15.

44 Apter, *op. cit.*, p. 5.

45 Fianna Fail descends from the politicians and paramilitaries, the original IRA, who were opposed to the signature of the 1921 treaty which partitioned Ireland into a Free State and the UK province of Northern Ireland. The other main party in the Republic, Fine Gael, descends from those who signed the treaty.

46 A bizarre example of this was when a drunken group of IRA men fired shots in a Manchester restaurant because they were unhappy with the service. Their arrest led directly to that of Brendan Dowd, the commander of the IRA in England. Sean, O'Callaghan, *The Informer* (London, Bantam Press, 1998) p. 77.

47 See the stinging attack by Ed Vulliamy on the western reluctance to use force in Bosnia: 'Bosnia: the crime of appeasement', *International Affairs*, 74:1 (1998), pp. 73–91.

48 Gray, 'Global utopias and clashing civilisations: misunderstanding the present', *International Affairs*, 74:1 (1998), p. 161.

49 Strobel, *Late-breaking Foreign Policy: the news media's influence on peace operations* (Washington DC, US Institute of Peace, 1997)

50 Taylor, *Global Communications, International Affairs and the Media since 1945* (London, Routledge, 1997)

51 Cook, *Governing with the News: the news media as a political institution* (Chicago, University of Chicago Press, 1998)

52 Urban, Book review in *International Affairs*, vol. 74:3 (1998), p. 656.

53 See the excellent review article by Crelinstein, 'Television and Terrorism: Implications for Crisis Management and Policy Making' in *Terrorism and Political Violence*, vol. 9, no. 4 (Winter, 1997), pp. 8–32.

54 Wilkinson, 'The Media and Terrorism: a Reassessment', in *Terrorism and Political Violence*, vol. 9, no. 2 (Summer, 1997), pp. 51–64.

55 Ignatieff, *The Warrior's Honor: ethnic war and the modern conscience* (London, Chatto & Windus, 1998) p. 25.

56 Wilkinson's Law: 'He who wants the biggest headlines has to spill the most blood.' Cm3420. *Inquiry into Legislation against Terrorism* (London, the Stationery Office, 1996) (The Lloyd Report) vol. 2, p. 27.

57 For discussions of the 'propaganda war' in Northern Ireland see Curtis, *Ireland: the propaganda war: the British media and the 'battle for hearts and minds'* (London, Pluto, 1984); Miller, *Don't mention the war: Northern Ireland, propaganda and the media* (London, Pluto, 1994).

58 Leyne, 'The CNN Factor: the Role of the Media in the New World Order'. Oxford University Strategic Studies Group, 20 May 1997.

2   The Search for Theory

1 Brogan, *World Conflicts, 3rd edn* (London, Bloomsbury, 1998) Appendixes I, II, III.

2 Hoffman, *Inside Terrorism* (London, Victor Gollancz, 1998) Chapters 6, 7. For a survey of the likely impact of the internet see *Studies in Conflict and Terrorism* vol. 22, no. 3, July–September 1999, *Special Issue: netwar across the spectrum of conflict.*

3 Ember and Ember, 'Cross-cultural Studies of War and Peace: recent achievements and future possibilities' in Reyna and Downs (eds), *Studying War: anthropological perspectives* (Langhorn, Pennsylvania, Gordon & Breach, 1993), p. 186.

4 von Lipsey, *Breaking the Cycle: a framework for conflict intervention* (Basingstoke, Macmillan, 1997)

5 James Gow, Book review in *International Affairs,* vol. 74, no. 3, July 1998, p. 641.

6 Leiden and Schmitt, *The Politics of Violence: revolution in the modern world* (Englewood Cliffs, NJ, Prentice Hall, 1968) p. 214.

7 Fukuyama, *The End of History and the Last Man* (New York, Free Press, 1992).

8 Bloor, *Knowledge and Social Imagery, second edition* (Chicago, University of Chicago Press, 1991) p. 5. Quoted in Sokal, Alan and Bricmont, Jean, *Intellectual Impostures: postmodern philosophers' abuse of science* (London, Profile Books, 1998) p. 81.

9 Barnes and Bloor, 'Relativism, rationalism and the sociology of knowledge'. In Hollis, M. and Lukes, S., *Rationality and Relativism* (Oxford, Blackwell, 1981) p. 27. Quoted in Sokal and Bricmont, *Intellectual Impostures: postmodern philosophers' abuse of science* (London, Profile Books, 1998) p. 82.

10 'The Seville Statement on Violence', *American Psychologist*, vol. 45 (1990) pp. 1167–8, quoted in Pinker, *How the Mind Works* (London, Allen Lane the Penguin Press, 1997) p. 46.

11 Pinker, *How the Mind Works* (London, Allen Lane the Penguin Press, 1997) p. 42.

12 *Ibid.* , p.58.

13 Horowitz, *The Rise and Fall of Project Camelot: Studies in the Relationship between Social Science and Practical Politics* (Cambridge, Mass. and London, MIT Press, 1967) p. 4.

14 *Ibid.,* p. 67.

15 Gurr, *Why Men Rebel* (Princeton, Center for International Studies, 1970) p. 352 *et seq.* The theory of relative deprivation and other hypothetical causes of political violence are discussed in Wilkinson, *Terrorism and the Liberal State* (London, Macmillan, 1977) pp. 34–8, p. 93.

16 Dahrendorf, *After 1989: Morals, Revolution and Civil Society* (London, Macmillan, 1997) p. 86.

17 Though Locke argues that it is a universal law, even in a state of nature, 'that no-one ought to harm another in his life, health, liberty or possessions', and that anyone 'may bring such evil on anyone who hath transgressed that law, as may make him repent the doing of it, and thereby deter him, and by his example, others from doing the like mischief.' Locke, *Of Civil Government* Book 2, Chapter II, s. 6, s. 8 (London, Dent, Everyman Edition, 1924 [first published 1690]), pp. 119, 121.

18 Brown, *Human Universals* (New York, McGraw Hill, 1991)

19 Polti, *The Thirty-six Dramatic Situations* (Boston, The Writer Inc, 1977): originally published 1921.

20 Pinker, *How the Mind Works* (London, Allen Lane The Penguin Press, 1998) p. 427.

21   Dahrendorf, *op. cit.* p. 28.
22   *Janatha Vimuthki Peramuna*: People's Liberation Front. Sri Lanka, an island about the same size as the island of Ireland, 75 per cent Buddhist Sinhalese and 20 per cent Hindu Tamil, with its Tamil north 20 miles from the Tamil south of India, has been plagued by both Tamil separatism and the Maoist JVP. Nearly half a million Tamils live abroad and contribute funds to the Tamil cause, just as funding from the Irish, Cypriot and Kurdish diasporas flows into the conflicts in their homelands.
23   Kapferer, 'Remythologizing Discourses: State and Insurrectionary Violence in Sri Lanka', in Apter, *op. cit.,* p. 166.
24   *Ibid.* p. 163.
25   US State Department estimate, quoted in Brogan, *World Conflicts*, Third edition (London, Bloomsbury, 1998) p. 257.
26   Kapferer, *op. cit.,* p. 184, note 2.
27   See, for example, Walt, *Revolution and War* (Ithaca, NY, Cornell University Press, 1996); Holsti, *The State, War, and the State of War* (Cambridge, CUP, 1996).
28   Or rather they can be, but without success, or with laughable results: see, for example, Sokal, and Bricmont, *Intellectual Impostures: postmodern philosophers' abuse of science* (London, Profile Books, 1998).
29   Thompson, *Defeating Communist Insurgency; experiences from Malaya and Vietnam* (London, Chatto & Windus, 1966) pp. 50–7.
30   The figures for indictable offences and 'outrages' (raids, casualties and property damage) given in graph 1 (p. 123) and Appendices IV and V (pp. 213, 214) of Townshend, *The British Campaign in Ireland, 1919–1921* (Oxford, OUP, 1975) are of the same order, *mutatis mutandis*, as those during the early years of the Northern Ireland troubles of 1968–98. Even so, during the 1919–1921 campaign the IRA prevented the legislature and the courts from operating, paralysed the police as a community force, and compelled its conversion into an armed gendarmerie with the bulk of its recruits drawn from non-Irishmen (see Townshend, Appendix I); a force which allowed itself to be provoked into reprisals of the kind typical of violent politics outside the law, which will be examined later.
31   Lenin, *What Is To Be Done? Burning Questions of our Movement* (Peking, Foreign Languages Press, 1975): first published 1902. Chapter V: The 'Plan' for an All-Russian Political Newspaper.
32   Martinez-Allier, 'The Peasantry and the Cuban Revolution from the Spring of 1959 to the End of 1960', in Carr, Raymond (ed.), *St Antony's Papers No. 22: Latin American Affairs* (Oxford, Oxford University Press, 1970), p. 137.
33   Thomas, *Cuba, or the Pursuit of Freedom* (London, Eyre & Spottiswode, 1971) p. 1955.
34   Taber, *The War of the Flea: Guerilla Warfare in Theory and Practice* (St Albans, Paladin, 1970) p. 11, p. 13. The publishers claim that the first edition was entirely bought out by the US armed forces.

3   The Search for Strategy

1   Kolakowsi, *Main Currents of Marxism: its rise, growth and dissolution* (Oxford, OUP, 1978) vol. 3, p. 526.

2 Degregori, 'The Maturation of a Cosmocrat and the Building of a Discourse Community: the Case of the Shining Path' in Apter (ed.), *The Legitimization of Violence* (Basingstoke, Macmillan, 1997) pp. 33–82.

3 Sendero documents, quoted by Degregori, *op. cit.*, pp. 56, 66, 67, 69.

4 Balbi, cited in Degregori, *op. cit.*, p. 77, footnote 4.

5 Dahrendorf, *The Modern Social Conflict: an essay on the politics of liberty* (London, Weidenfeld & Nicolson, 1988) p. 8.

6 Lenin, *What Is To Be Done?* [1902] in *Collected Works* (Moscow, Novosti Press Agency, 1966) vol. xxxi, p. 85.

7 In August 1918 the Allies broke through on the Western Front. Shortly afterwards, Bulgaria and Austro-Hungary collapsed, and Germany began to sue for peace. At the end of October the Naval Command ordered the High Seas Fleet to seek battle, in an attempt to show that Germany could still fight, and secure better peace terms. The sailors mutinied, seized Kiel, and started a revolution which swept through Germany in a few days, ended the War, and deposed the Kaiser. A civil war raged between January and May 1919, between revolutionary workers and soldiers on one side and the Socialist government they had brought to power on the other (the Socialist Party of Germany, SPD), aided by party armies, *freikorps*, recruited from the selfsame soldiers.

8 Bane and Lutz, *The Blockade of Germany after the Armistice, 1918–1919* (Stanford CA, Stanford University Press, 1942); Coper, *Failure of a Revolution: Germany 1918–1919* (Cambridge, CUP, 1955); Haffner, *Failure of a Revolution: Germany 1918–1919* (London, Deutsch, 1973): originally published as *Die Verratene Revolution* (Berne, Scherz Verlag, 1969); Lutz, *The German Revolution 1918–1919* (Stanford CA, Stanford University Press, 1922); Lutz (ed.), *Fall of the German Empire 1914–1918: documents of the German revolution* (Stanford CA, Stanford University Press, 1932); Waite, *Vanguard of Nazism: the free corps movement in postwar Germany 1918–1923* (Cambridge Mass, Harvard University Press, 1952). Wheeler-Bennett, *The Nemesis of Power: the German army in politics 1918–1945* (London, Macmillan, 1973).

9 Bracher, *The German Dictatorship: the origins, structure and effects of National Socialism* (London, Weidenfeld & Nicolson, 1970): originally published in German, 1969; Bullock, *Hitler: a study in tyranny* (London, Odhams, 1955): first published 1952; Fest, *Hitler* (Harmondsworth, Penguin, 1977): first published in German, 1973; Heiden, *A History of National Socialism* (London, Methuen, 1934): first published in German, 1932; Göring, *Germany Reborn* (London, Elkin Mathews and Marrot, 1934). Hitler, *Mein Kampf* (New York, Reynal & Hitchcock, 1939): first published in German, 1925; Manvell and Fränkel, *The Hundred Days to Hitler* (London, Dent, 1974); Micklem, Nathaniel, *National Socialism and the Roman Catholic Church* (Oxford, OUP for Chatham House, 1939); von Papen, *Memoirs* (London, Deutsch, 1952).

10 Moore, *Social Origins of Dictatorship and Democracy: lord and peasant in the making of the modern world* (Harmondsworth, Peregrine, 1977): originally published 1966. p. 445.

11 Merkl, *The Making of a Stormtrooper* (Princeton NJ, Princeton University Press, 1980) p. 241. This, and Merkl's earlier work, *Political Violence Under The Swastika: 581 early Nazis* (Princeton NJ, Princeton University Press, 1975) analyse the background, actions and motivation of a sample of Nazis,

many of whom had earlier been attracted by the similar appeal of the Communists.

12 See, for example, Allen, *The Nazi Seizure of Power* (London, Eyre & Spottiswoode, 1966) for an account of the rise of Nazism in a small German town, documenting the efforts made by the embryo party to organise entertainment and activities for the young, and help for the old, infirm and unemployed. He concludes that: 'Hardly anyone in Thalburg in those days [1930–35] grasped what was happening. There was no real comprehension of what the town would experience if Hitler came to power, no real understanding of what Nazism was ... The problem of Nazism was primarily a problem of perception. In this respect Thalburg's difficulties and Thalburg's fate are likely to be shared by other men in other towns under similar circumstances. The remedy will not easily be found' (p. 281). Exactly the same could be said of Bolshevism and its variants, *mutatis mutandis*.

13 Though Rawls argues that they could be. Even if this were true in theory, no state has yet approached such an ideal in practice. See Rawls, *A Theory of Justice* (Oxford, OUP, 1972), particularly the chapter on 'The Justification of Civil Disobedience', whose arguments are predicated on a hypothetical nearly-equal society.

14 'Neuberg, A', *Armed Insurrection* (London, New Left Books, 1970). *Armed Insurrection* was originally published illegally in Germany in 1928 as a revision of Alfred Langer's *The Road to Victory: the art of armed insurrection,* which had been published earlier in the same year. Both 'Langer' and 'Neuberg' are *noms de plume (de guerre?)* for a group of Soviet-trained specialists in insurrection, including Marshal Tukhachevsky, who was to be executed during Stalin's purges, and Ho Chi Minh.

15 Albania, Bulgaria, Czechoslovakia (where the Communist Party came to power via a coup), East Germany, Hungary, Poland, Rumania, San Marino, Yugoslavia. The same is true of the areas of the Baltic, the Balkans, Central Asia and the Far East which were incorporated into the USSR.

16 Afghanistan, Cambodia, China, Laos, North Korea, North and South Vietnam. Mongolia's communist government was established in the 1920s.

17 Although during the 1950s and 1960s the received idea of both guerrillas and counter-guerrillas was that People's War was a new and powerful technique, by the 1970s their beliefs were being widely challenged. See for example Johnson, *Autopsy on People's War* (Berkeley, Los Angeles and London, University of California Press, 1973). Johnson had been a contributor to the typology of revolution which he later rejected: see his *Revolutionary Change* (London, University of London Press, 1968). For other examples, see Laqueur, *The Guerrilla Reader: a historical anthology* (London, Wildwood House, 1978), p. 6, and Dunn, *Modern Revolutions: an introduction to the analysis of a political phenomenon* (Cambridge, Cambridge University Press, 1972) p. 233.

18 See, for example: Mao Tse Tung, *Strategy in China's Revolutionary War;* (Lectures to the Red Army College, 1936) in *Selected Works of Mao Tse Tung* (Peking, Foreign Languages Press, 1967) vol. 1, p.189.

19 That is, Mao's stages of 'mobile war, guerrilla war and regular war' (*Selected Works,* vol. 2, p. 183); Vo Ngyuen Giap's 'contention, equilibrium and counter-offensive phases' (*People's War, People's Army,* p. 79); the British

Army's 'pre-revolutionary, insurgency and limited war phases' (Land Operations, vol. 3 – *Counter-Revolutionary Operations* (London, Ministry of Defence, 1977), part 1, p. 12; and the US Army's 'latent and incipient phase, guerrilla warfare and war of movement' (US Field Manual 100–20: *Field Service Regulations – Internal Defense and Development.*)

20 See, for example, Trinquier, *Modern Warfare* (London and New York, Praeger, 1964): first published 1961 as *La Guerre Moderne*; p. 6; Paret, Peter, *French Revolutionary Warfare from Indochina to Algeria; the analysis of a political and military doctrine* (London, Pall Mall Press for Princeton University Center for International Studies, 1964) p. 4.

21 Haber, 'From Protest to Radicalism: an appraisal of the student movement 1960', in Cohen and Hale (eds), *The New Student Left* (Boston, Mass, Beacon Press 1966) p. 40. Haber was the president of Students for a Democratic Society, one of the principal movements of the New Left in the United States.

22 Quoted in Pendle, *A History of Latin America* (Harmondsworth, Penguin, 1978) p. 109.

23 Thomas, *Cuba or The Pursuit of Freedom* (London, Eyre and Spottiswode, 1971) pp. 1037, 1038. Thomas estimates that the total casualties in the revolution (the vast majority suffered in the towns) amounted to between 1500 and 2000, (footnote 21, p. 1044), though greater figures are claimed, especially by the guerrillas, whose total strength was in the hundreds until the last two months, when it climbed to about 3000 (p. 1042). See also Goldenberg, *The Cuban Revolution and Latin America* (London, Allen and Unwin, 1965) p. 144, for a discussion of the probable casualty figures.

24 Debray, *Revolution in the Revolution? Armed struggle and political struggle in Latin America* (New York and London, Monthly Review Press, 1976) p. 116. (Translated by Ortiz, Bobbye. First published in France by Librairie François Maspero, 1967.) Interestingly, and perhaps alarmingly had he known it, Debray's title echoed the very phrase Hitler used to describe the revolution that brought him to power: 'for the National Socialist revolution was itself a revolution in the revolutionary tradition'. (Hitler, Adolf, Speech to the Reichstag on 30 January 1937 in Norman H. Baynes (ed.), *The Speeches of Adolf Hitler April 1922–August 1939* (Oxford, OUP for Chatham House, 1942) vol. 1, p. 214.

25 Letter from Althusser to Debray, 1 March 1967, reproduced as Appendix 2 in Debray, *A Critique of Arms* (Harmondsworth, Peregrine/Pelican, 1977): first published 1974. vol. 1, p. 260.

26 Debray, *Che's Guerrilla War* (Harmondsworth, Penguin, 1975): first published in Paris by Editions de Seuil, 1974.

27 James (ed), *The Complete Bolivian Diaries of Che Guevara and other Captured Documents* (London, Allen & Unwin, 1968) p. 286. 'Mario' was the pseudonym of Estanislao, the Secretary of the Bolivian Communist Party, who acted as the link between Guevara and Castro.

28 The small boat in which Castro and his handful of men returned to Cuba in 1956, after having been exiled by Batista.

29 Guevara, *Guerrilla Warfare* (Harmondsworth, Penguin, 1969): originally published 1961. p. 13.

30 Debray, *Revolution in the Revolution?; armed struggle and political struggle in Latin America* (New York and London, Monthly Review Press, 1976) p. 35.

31 Neuberg, A. (pseud), *Armed Insurrection* (1928) (London, New Left Books, 1970) p. 192.
32 Leiden and Schmitt, *The Politics of Violence: revolution in the modern world* (Englewood Cliffs NJ, Prentice Hall, 1968) p. 25.
33 See the classic study by Finer, *The Man on Horseback: the role of the military in politics* (London, Pall Mall, 1962).
34 The 'assets-to-liabilities shift': Wilkinson (ed.), *British Perspectives on Terrorism* (London, Allen & Unwin, 1981) pp. 2, 17.
35 The IRA training manual *The Green Book*; O'Brien, *The Long War: the IRA and Sinn Féin from 1985 to today* (Dublin, O'Brien Press, 1993) p. 23.

4 Politics: Northern Ireland

1 Mallie and McKittrick, *The Fight for Peace; the secret story behind the Irish peace process* (London, Mandarin, 1997) is a thorough and detailed account, up to and including Canary Wharf. For a chronology see Bew and Gillespie, *The Northern Ireland Peace Process 1993–1996: a chronology* (London, Serif, 1996).
2 Conventionally traced back as far as the Battle of the Boyne in 1690, when the Catholic James II, attempting to regain the throne from which he had been deposed two years earlier, was defeated by William of Orange, his Protestant successor as king. The precursors included the invasion of Ireland in 1169 by Henry II, who had been granted its overlordship by Pope Adrian IV in order to force the Irish Catholic Church into obedience to Rome; resistance in Ulster, crushed by Elizabeth I in 1607 and settled by immigrants from England and Scotland; risings during the English Civil War, crushed by Cromwell in 1642–51; the Revocation of the Edict of Nantes in 1685, leading to the flight of the protestant Huguenots from France; the overthrow of James II three years later, and the Battle of the Boyne two years after that. Many Huguenots settled in Ulster. The tit-for-tat has continued ever since, and the injustices to one side or another are often slammed down on the debating table or the pub counter in a sort of Green versus Orange game of snap. The stories do not lose in the telling.
3 See, for example, Bew, Patterson, *The British State and the Ulster Crisis* (London, Verso, 1985); Bew, Gibbon, and Patterson, *Northern Ireland 1921–94: political forces and social classes* (London, Serif, 1996); Boyle, and Hadden, *Northern Ireland: the choice* (London, Penguin, 1994). Dudley Edwards, *The Faithful Tribe: an intimate portrait of the loyal institutions* (London, Harper Collins 1999); Foster, Roy, *Modern Ireland 1600–1972*, (London, Penguin, 1989); Foster, and Crozier, *Cultural Traditions in Northern Ireland: varieties of Irishness* (Belfast, Institute of Irish Studies, Queen's University, 1989); Guelke, *Northern Ireland – the International Perspective* (Dublin: Gill & Macmillan, 1989); Lyons, FSL, *Ireland Since the Famine* (New York and London, Scribner, 1971); Lyons and Hawkins (eds), *Ireland under the Union* (Oxford, Clarendon Press, 1980); Ruane and Todd, *The dynamics of conflict in Northern Ireland: power, conflict and emancipation* (Cambridge, Cambridge University Press, 1996); Whyte, *Interpreting Northern Ireland* (Oxford, Clarendon Press, 1990).
4 1991 censuses.

5 In the 1969 Stormont general election, for example, the unionists had 39 seats out of 52; in the 1970 Westminster general election 8 out of 12, and in the 1973 elections for the Northern Ireland Assembly 50 of 78. Flackes and Elliott, *Northern Ireland: a political directory 1968–1993* (Belfast, The Blackstaff Press, 1994) pp. 359–72.

6 Robbins, 'Britain and Europe: devolution and foreign policy', *International Affairs*, vol. 74:1 (1988), p. 109.

7 The republican and loyalist paramilitary organisations metamorphosed over the years, splitting, changing leaders, feuding. The Provisional IRA, committed to ending British rule in Northern Ireland, and thus arguably the true inheritor of the name, split from the Marxist Official IRA. The 'Provisional' adjective, which reflected the anti-treaty 'Provisional Government' of the Free State after partition, was gradually dropped as it became the principal republican paramilitary organisation, responsible for over 90 per cent of republican killings. Republican paramilitaries were responsible for nearly 60 per cent of all deaths. Loyalist paramilitaries, who also had their feuds and power struggles, were responsible for nearly 30 per cent of all deaths, and the security forces for 10 per cent: McKittrick, Kelters, Feeney, and Thornton, *Lost Lives: the stories of the men, women and children who died as a result of the Northern Ireland troubles* (Edinburgh and London, Mainstream Publishing, 1999) p. 1483. For our purposes it is not necessary to follow the shifts in power and nomenclature: the IRA has been used as shorthand for the principal republican paramilitary organisation, its dissident factions and breakaway groups, regardless of adjective. Similarly, all protestant paramilitaries have been considered as one group, and the security forces – military, police and other services – as another. Sinn Fein metamorphosed similarly; the party split in 1970 over whether it should change its policy of not recognising the legitimacy of the Dublin and Westminster governments. Those who wanted to maintain non-recognition split, and formed Provisional Sinn Fein. The remainder became Official Sinn Fein, then, reflecting its Marxism, Sinn Fein The Workers' Party, and finally just The Workers' Party. The 'Provisional' adjective gradually dropped from Sinn Fein, as it did from the IRA.

8 The results of the 1983, 1987 and 1992 general elections for the UK parliament were: Official Unionist Party (OUP): 34, 38 and 35 per cent respectively; Democratic Unionist Party (DUP): 20, 12 and 13 per cent Social Democratic and Labour Party (SDLP): 18, 21 and 24 per cent;Sinn Fein (SF): 13, 11 and 10 percent Alliance: 8, 10 and 9 percent. The result of the 2001 General Election which the Alliance party did not contest were Ulster Unionist Party (UUP) 26.8 per cent; Sinn Fein (SF) 21.7 per cent; Social Democratic and Labour Party (DUP), 22.5 per cent

The OUP and the SDLP are generally characterised as moderate unionist and nationalist parties, the DUP and SF as extreme loyalist and republican parties, and Alliance as a moderate centrist party.

9 Summarised from many public statements. See also extracts from the IRA training manual, *The Green Book* in O'Brien, *The Long War: the IRA and Sinn Féin, 1985 to today* (Dublin, The O'Brien Press, 1993) p. 23.

10 McGuinness, 'We will never be slaves again', *An Phoblacht/Republican News*, 28 June 1984. Adams, *The Politics of Irish Freedom* (Dingle, Brandon Books,

1986) p. 64. In 1992 the creed was changed to read: *armed force is a last resort, but there is an onus on those who proclaim that the armed struggle is counterproductive to advance a credible alternative.* Sinn Fein, *Towards a lasting peace in Ireland* (Dublin, 1992), reproduced in O'Brien, appendix 3, p. 296.

11 IRA *Green Book*, quoted in Coogan, *The Troubles: Ireland's ordeal 1966–1996 and the search for peace* (London, Arrow, 1996) p. 246.

12 Government of Ireland Act, 1920: explanatory memorandum; quoted in Northern Ireland Office, *The Future of Northern Ireland: a paper for discussion.* (London, HMSO, 1972) annex 1.

13 Constitution of Eire (Dublin Government Stationery Office, 1937) articles 2 and 3. *Saorstat Eireann* is the Irish Free State.

14 1972: Northern Ireland Office, *The Future of Northern Ireland: a paper for discussion* (London, HMSO, 1972) para. 79(a), p. 35.

15 Sunningdale Agreement, December 1973, between the UK and Irish governments, with the parties involved in the Northern Ireland Executive (Unionists, SDLP and Alliance). The Agreement set up a power-sharing executive, provided for a Council of Ireland, and envisaged reciprocal law enforcement. The formal declaration of the status of Northern Ireland was never signed, and the power-sharing executive collapsed in 1974 in the face of a loyalist Ulster Workers' Council strike. Flackes and Elliott, *Northern Ireland: a political directory 1968–1993* (Belfast, The Blackstaff Press, 1994) p. 316.

16 Article 1 of the Anglo-Irish Agreement signed by Prime Minister Thatcher and Taoiseach FitzGerald, November 1985 (London, HMSO, 1985). The agreement also accepted that the Irish government could put forward policy or legislative proposals on behalf of the republican community in Northern Ireland, and have a say in appointments to public bodies. It made provision for cross-border co-operation in security, economic and social matters. Interestingly, two members of the Ulster Unionist Party challenged the legality of the Anglo-Irish Agreement in the Irish courts. The Supreme Court ruled in March 1990 that it could not overturn the Agreement, and, surprisingly, added that Articles 2 and 3 of the Irish Constitution were claims of legal right to govern the whole of the island, and were constitutional imperatives rather than aspirations (Flackes and Elliott, *op. cit.*, pp. 84–5).

17 Articles 4 and 5 of the Downing Street Declaration signed by Prime Minister Major and Taoiseach Reynolds, December 1993 (London, HMSO, 1993). Flackes and Elliott, *op. cit.*, p. 84.

18 The 1998 Good Friday Agreement: Agreement between the Government of the United Kingdom of Great Britain and Northern Ireland and the Government of Ireland, signed in Belfast on 10 April 1998 by Prime Minister Blair and Taoiseach Ahern. UK Government Information Service: http://www.open.gov.uk.

19 Four IRA men convicted in the 1970s for 50 bombings and shootings in Britain which killed 16; imprisoned in England, transferred to prison in Ireland shortly after the Good Friday agreement, and temporarily released for the conference.

20 *The Times*, 11 May 1998, p. 1.

21 *Sunday Times*, 24 May 1998, p. 1. In 1971, twenty-seven years earlier, Cardinal Conway, the Catholic Primate of Ireland, was reported to have told the then Home Secretary, Reginald Maudling, that 'the secret of securing a

political settlement was for the government to take an initiative when the
Catholics knew the IRA was beaten, but before the Protestants realised this'.
Cole, *As It Seemed to Me: political memoirs* (London, Phoenix, 1996). p. 136.

22 *The Economist*, 11 July 1998, p. 27; 18 July 1998, p. 25. Dudley Edwards,
Ruth, *The Faithful Tribe: an intimate portrait of the loyal institutions* (London,
HarperCollins, 1999) pp. 422–30. See Chapters 13–19 for a detailed discussion of the Drumcree confrontations between 1995 and 1998, and their
background.

23 *The Economist*, 22 August 1998, p. 21.

24 For a thorough analysis of the problems of geographical proximity and
political separateness see Sloan, *The Geopolitics of Anglo-Irish Relations in the
Twentieth Century* (London, Leicester University Press, 1997).

25 Speech by the Secretary of State for Northern Ireland (Peter Brooke) in
London on 9 November 1990. Reiterated in the Downing Street Declaration
by John Major and Albert Reynolds, 15 December 1993, para 4.

26 Sinn Fein, *Strategy for Peace*, 1988.

27 Garret FitzGerald, who was Minister for Foreign Affairs of the Republic, and
later Taoiseach, attributes the lack of documentation on the Second World
War in the Irish archives to their having been burned in case they fell into
the hands of German invaders, because they would have revealed the
extent of secret co-operation with the United Kingdom. FitzGerald, 'When
Ireland Became Divided' in *London Review of Books*, 21 January 1999, p. 17.
David Stafford reinforces this: 'To most intents and purposes Ireland had
become an integral part of the United Kingdom security system.' Stafford,
Churchill and Secret Service (London, Abacus, 1997) pp. 187–90.

28 See, for example, Hussey, *Ireland Today: anatomy of a changing state*
(London, Viking, 1993): first published in Ireland by Town House and
Country House, 1993. Chapter 8.

29 Sinn Fein, *Towards a lasting peace in Ireland* (Dublin, 1992), reproduced in
O'Brien, *The Long War: the IRA and Sinn Féin, 1985 to today* (Dublin, The
O'Brien Press, 1993) appendix 3, p. 297.

30 Adams has only once admitted being a member of the IRA: *Republican News*,
8 May 1976, quoted in Taylor, *Provos: the IRA and Sinn Fein* (London,
Bloomsbury, 1997) p. 201. IRA member and Special Branch agent
McGartland reports him as quartermaster, then commander of the IRA in
the Ballymurphy district of Belfast when 52 people were killed, then commander of the Belfast 'brigade'; and a member of the seven-man IRA Army
Council while he was President of Sinn Fein: McGartland, *Fifty Dead Men
Walking* (London, Blake, 1997) pp. 215–16. O'Callaghan reports the same
progress through the ranks of the IRA, and that Twomey and Adams were
responsible for Bloody Friday in July 1972, when 19 bombs in Belfast killed
nine and injured 130: O'Callaghan, *The Informer* (London, Bantam Press,
1998) pp. 40–1. Coogan reports that Adams took over from McGuinness as
chief of staff of the IRA in 1976: Coogan, *The Troubles: Ireland's ordeal
1966–1996 and the search for peace* (London, Arrow, 1996) p. 254.
McGuinness admitted being the commander of the Derry 'brigade' of the
IRA for two years, and was imprisoned twice in the Republic for IRA mem-
bership; he was later head of the IRA's Northern Command, and a member
of the IRA Army Council while chief negotiator for Sinn Fein: McGartland,

op. cit., p. 217. Adams and McGuinness are identified as members of the Army Council until late 1995 in Holland and Phoenix, *Phoenix: policing the shadows* (London, Hodder & Stoughton, 1997) p. 303, and in 1984 in O'Callaghan, *op. cit.,* p. 188.

5 Violence: Northern Ireland

1 342 men were arrested on 9 August 1971, of whom 105 were released and 237 detained under the Civil Authorities (Special Powers) Act (Northern Ireland) 1922. By November nearly 1000 had been arrested, 300 interned, 100 detained and 500 released. Flackes and Elliott, *op.cit.,* pp. 458–61.

2 UK Home Office, Cmnd 4823, *Report of the enquiry into allegations against the security forces of physical brutality in Northern Ireland arising out of events on the 9th August, 1971* (London, HMSO, November 1971).(The Compton Report)

3 The British used internment without trial during the 1919–21 troubles because the legal system had become paralysed. No-one had been convicted for any outrage; witnesses would not come forward and juries would not convict. In July 1920 all the circuit judges, even in the areas of greatest violence, were presented with the white gloves indicating that there were no cases to be tried. Townshend, *Britain's Civil Wars: counterinsurgency in the twentieth century* (London, Faber and Faber, 1986) p. 56. The IRA began a bombing campaign in Britain at the start of the 1939–1945 war; de Valera interned IRA members to preserve Irish neutrality.

4 Bew and Patterson, *The British State and the Ulster Crisis* (London, Verso, 1985) p. 2.

5 O'Callaghan, *op. cit.,* p.17.

6 Collins, *Killing Rage* (London, Granta Books, 1997) pp. 59–60.

7 *Ibid.,* p. 101.

8 *Ibid.,* p. 23.

9 *Ibid.,* p. 98.

10 Peter Brooke, quoted in Mallie and McKittrick, *The Fight for Peace: the secret story behind the Irish peace process* (London, Mandarin, 1997) p. 100.

11 Martin McGuinness, quoted in Mallie and McKittrick, *op.cit.,* p. 101.

12 These figures are taken from the statistical annex to McKittrick, *et al., Lost Lives: the stories of the men, women and children who died as a result of the Northern Ireland troubles* (Edinburgh and London, Mainstream Publishing, 1999) pp. 1473–84. *Lost Lives,* which was published in late 1999, is by far the most comprehensive, detailed and self-evidently reliable record of the deaths during the troubles of 1968 onwards, since it gives details of all the victims and the circumstances in which each died. The principal reference for the figures in this book is Sutton, *An Index of Deaths from the Conflict in Ireland 1969–93* (Belfast, Beyond the Pale Publications, 1994). Sutton's figures (and *Lost Lives*) include those killed outside Northern Ireland; the RUC's figures do not. Another useful reference, which also appeared after the bulk of the analysis in this book had been done, is Fay, *Northern Ireland's Troubles: the human costs.* (London and Sterling, VA, Pluto Press, 1999). It contains a detailed analysis of the statistics of the violence, related to the economic and social background of the community.

13 Collins, *op. cit.*, p. 4.

14 A 1978 assessment by Brigadier James Glover of the British Defence Intelligence Staff, which somehow reached the IRA and public view, estimated that the IRA had about 300 paid volunteers. Coogan, *op.cit.*, p. 252. Taylor, *op.cit.*, pp. 214–217. Other estimates ranged from 500 to 2000: Fay, *et al.*, p. 13. O'Callaghan gives the figures for Southern Command, the part of the IRA in the Republic, when he became its chief in 1983, as a headquarters of some twelve people controlling about 25 full timers and 500 part-time volunteers or sympathisers in seven geographical areas. O'Callaghan, *op. cit.*, p. 176.

15 O'Callaghan, *op. cit.*, pp. 167, 168. Collins (see footnote 180) and O'Callaghan say how little IRA volunteers were paid: £10–£50 a week. The IRA tried laundering counterfeit money, kidnapped Shergar, a Derby winner retired to stud in the Republic, for ransom (unsuccessfully, though they killed the horse); attempted to kidnap the Canadian millionaire Galen Weston from his house in the Republic, and later abducted one of his executives, Don Tidey, for ransom; an Irish soldier and a Garda were killed in his rescue.

16 For the wooing of the diaspora see the collection of articles written by Adams for the Irish–American paper *The Irish Voice* between 1993 and 1997: Adams, *An Irish Voice: the quest for peace* (Niwot, CO, Roberts Rinehart, 1997). The narrative is that the IRA is engaged in a just war; the British in a dirty war, aided by the loyalists. All initiatives for peace come from Sinn Fein, which is totally separate from the IRA; the UK government refuses to negotiate, and the Irish government cannot even hold the British to the commitments they have already given.

17 IRA man Martin Meehan, quoted in Taylor, *Provos: the IRA and Sinn Fein* (London, Bloomsbury, 1997) p. 62. The Dublin government was also reported to have supplied funds covertly: p. 61.

18 *Ibid.*, p. 1.

19 The *Claudia* contained 250 rifles, 240 other small arms, anti-tank mines and explosives: and the IRA's Joe Cahill. Taylor, *op. cit.*, p. 156.

20 The *Eksund* contained 150 tons of armaments. Searches in the Republic later found five underground bunkers, one 55 feet long, 11 feet wide and 9 feet high. Mallie and McKittrick, *The Fight for Peace; the secret story behind the Irish peace process* (London, Mandarin, 1997) p. 62.

21 *Ibid.*, p. 60. Taylor, *Provos: the IRA and Sinn Fein* (London, Bloomsbury, 1997) p. 277. A kilo of Semtex is enough for a lethal booby trap, aircraft bomb or mortar round.

22 Royal Ulster Constabulary, *Chief Constable's Report, 1992* (RUC, Belfast, 1993) p. 12.

23 McGartland, *op. cit.*, p. 226. He also describes the IRA's logistic system (pp. 222–8). Collins describes IRA training and explosives manufacture: Collins, *op. cit.*, Chapter 4.

24 Even a very poor group in a poor country such as the Revolutionary United Front in Sierra Leone managed to mount a major campaign against the incumbent government, which was assisted by forces from the Economic Community of West African States. It built itself up by kidnapping, looting, stealing and trading diamonds, palm oil and cacao. It also obtained some

arms, men and shelter from Liberia across the border. De Torrenté, 'Rebels Bounce Back', *The World Today*, vol. 55, no. 2 (February 1999) p. 8.

25   Sutton, *An Index of Deaths from the Conflict in Ireland 1969–1993* (Belfast, Beyond the Pale Publications, 1994) p. 206.

26   Loyalist and republican combined. Royal Ulster Constabulary, *Chief Constable's Report, 1997/98*. (RUC, Belfast, September 1998) Appendix 7, table 2, p. 100.

27   Mallie and McKittrick, *op.cit.*, p. 53.

28   The threat of betrayal was obviously important to the IRA, which killed at least twenty alleged informers between 1986 and 1994; after one such murder, Gerry Adams was reported as saying 'I think that Mr McIlmurray, like anyone else in West Belfast, knows that the consequence for informing is death'. Mallie and McKittrick, *op.cit.*, p. 52. It also killed at least eight former members, 25 non-members and a handful of others, all accused of passing on information or being British agents. Many were blown up by their own bombs; all told, the IRA killed 149 of its own people, and 198 catholic civilians: McKittrick, *et al.*, *Lost Lives: the stories of the men, women and children who died as a result of the Northern Ireland troubles* (Edinburgh and London, Mainstream Publishing, 1999) p. 1479, table 20, p 1484.

29   Collins, *op. cit.*, Chapter 5: The Recruiting Sergeant.

30   O'Callaghan, *op. cit.*, p. 82.

31   *Ibid.*, p. 89.

32   Attributed by O'Callaghan to a £2M reward from the GRU (Soviet military intelligence) via Syria. O'Callaghan, *op.cit.*, p. 103.

33   The measures used in the Republic included internment and military courts.

34   Statement by the Taoiseach, Mr Jack Lynch, 13 August 1994: Government of Northern Ireland Cmd 566, *Violence and Civil Disturbances in Northern Ireland in 1969* (Belfast, HMSO, 1972) (The Scarman Report) pp. 43–44. The Irish government also set up field hospitals across the border for those who did not wish to be treated in the province. The Bogside lies below the city walls of Londonderry, from which the protestant Apprentice Boys (commemorating the defence of the city from the Catholic King James in the seventeenth century) threw coins to show their contempt. The Bogside flats in turn dominate the ground below, and thus the RUC or any other intruder. The area was also the scene for Bloody Sunday: see note 197.

35   See, for example, the analysis by O'Doherty, *The Trouble with Guns: republican strategy and the Provisional IRA* (Belfast, Blackstaff Press, 1998) Chapters 2 and 3.

36   3 February 1971. Coogan, *op. cit.*, p. 133. The chapter is entitled 'Letting slip the dogs of war'.

37   6 February 1971. Coogan, *op. cit.*, p. 133. Malachi O'Doherty cites *Republican News*, 30 October 1971: O'Doherty, *op.cit.*, p. 66.

38   7 February 1971. Taylor, *Provos: the IRA and Sinn Fein* (London, Bloomsbury, 1997) p. 99.

39   Figures 5.1 to 5.3, and 5.10, show deaths in Northern Ireland only. Figures 5.4 to 5.9 include killings outside Northern Ireland. During the 30 years, 3370 people were killed in Northern Ireland and 260 elsewhere: McKittrick, *op.cit.*, table 14, p. 1481.

40   By October 1971 the Bogside, a catholic area about a quarter of a mile (400m) square beneath the western city wall of Londonderry had become a

no-go area, fortified and controlled by the IRA. The walled city, itself only about 400 metres by 300, was protestant. In the six months between Internment and Bloody Sunday over 2500 shots had been fired at the security forces, 450 bombs had been thrown, and 225 explosions had caused £6m in damage. The security forces had fired 840 live rounds in return. In the last two weeks of January 1972, 319 shots were fired at the security forces and 84 nail bombs thrown; two soldiers were killed and two wounded. Up to the end of 1970, 39 people had been killed, including two from the RUC. In 1971, 174 were killed, including 43 soldiers (most shot by snipers) and 11 policemen. By the time of Bloody Sunday, well over 200 people had been killed in the Troubles. An Ulster Volunteer Force bomb attack on McGurk's Bar in Belfast had killed 15 Catholic civilians in December. On 30 January 1972 troops were deployed to contain a protest march from 'Free Derry'. They were attacked by missiles, and replied with water cannon and rubber bullets. As the march was ending, a company of the first battalion of the Parachute Regiment was ordered to arrest hooligans. Shooting began; the company fired 108 rounds: 13 civilians were killed and another 13 injured; no soldiers were hit; no weapons were found on any of the victims. The Widgery Tribunal blamed confusion rather than conspiracy or lack of discipline. *Report of the Tribunal appointed to inquire into the events on Sunday, 30 January 1972, which led to loss of life in connection with the procession in Londonderry on that day* (London, HMSO, 1972) (H.L.101, H.C. 220) (The Widgery Report) Others blamed the policy of the Army and the aggressiveness and lack of control of 1 Para. For a balanced account, see Taylor, *op. cit.*, Chapter 9. For a recent assessment see Wilkinson, 'Reflections on Bloody Sunday' , in *Terrorism and Political Violence*, vol. 9 no. 2 (Summer, 1997) pp. 132–4.

41 On 'Bloody Sunday', 21 November 1920, an IRA squad led by Michael Collins assassinated twelve British officers in their homes in Dublin. The Auxiliary Division of the Royal Irish Constabulary, recruited from former army officers (and though distinct from the Black and Tans often given the same label), killed several spectators in a shoot-out in Croke Park football stadium later the same day.

42 The other IRA representatives were O'Connaill, Bell and Twomey. O'Brien, *The Long War: the IRA and Sinn Féin from 1985 to today* (Dublin, O'Brien Press, 1993) p. 169. O'Callaghan, *op. cit.*, p. 40.

43 Pakenham, Frank (Lord Longford), *Peace by Ordeal: the negotiation of the Anglo-Irish treaty, 1921* (London, Pimlico, 1992): originally published in London by Jonathan Cape, 1935.

44 O'Brien, *op.cit.*, p. 169. Coogan, *op. cit.*, pp. 174–7. Adams, *Before the Dawn: an autobiography* (London, Mandarin, 1997) pp. 203–6.

45 The meeting is said to have been organised by an MI6 officer in Northern Ireland, Frank Steele, who was 'appalled at their naivety and lack of understanding of political realities', told them they were wasting their time shooting and bombing, and that they should instead persuade the protestants that they would have a good life if the North were linked with the South. His message took twenty years to sink in. Taylor, *Loyalists* (London, Bloomsbury, 1999) p. 105.

46 Sutton, *An Index of Deaths from the Conflict in Ireland 1969–1993* (Belfast, Beyond the Pale Publications, 1994) pp. 24–28.

47 David Ervine of the UVF: Taylor, *Loyalists* (London, Bloomsbury, 1999) p. 126.
48 Taylor, *Loyalists*, p. 106. Taylor goes on to describe why Bloody Friday, and other atrocities such as the killing of six Protestant pensioners on an outing to Coleraine a year later, both increased recruitment for the loyalist paramilitaries and legitimised (in their eyes) their deliberate campaign of murdering Catholic civilians chosen at random.
49 RUC, *The Chief Constable's Reports* (Belfast, RUC, published annually)
50 Northern Ireland Office, *The Future of Northern Ireland: a paper for discussion* (London, HMSO, 1972)
51 The Detention of Terrorists Order replaced internment under the Special Powers Act in November 1972, and was itself replaced by the Emergency Provisions Act in August 1973. The last 75 detainees were released in December 1975. Flackes and Elliott, *Northern Ireland: a political directory 1968–1993* (Belfast, The Blackstaff Press, 1994) pp. 458–61.
52 Coogan, *op. cit.*, p. 211.
53 See, too, McPhilemy, *The Committee: political assassination in Northern Ireland* (Boulder, Colorado, Roberts Rinehart Publishers, 1999). When the book was published, Mr McPhilemy (p. vi) was suing the *Sunday Times*, which had accused him of bribery and deception, for libel, and was himself being sued in the United States by two people he accused of conspiracy to murder. Both cases were heard: a British court found in favour of McPhilemy in March 2000, a judgment which was upheld on appeal in June 2001. In the USA, however, McPhilemy and his publishers agreed to pay in order to settle the libel suit before it went to trial.
54 It often seems from the media that marches in Northern Ireland are simply riots set to music. However, there was disorder during only 15 of the 3161 marches in 1996, for example, only 6 of the 3322 in 1997 and only 25 of the 3472 in 1998/99. Marching is a national pastime: there are about 2500 unionist parades each year and 250 nationalist ones; boys' and girls' brigades, Remembrance Day, the Lord Mayor's and similar non-tribal parades account for some 500 marches. All the disorders in 1997 occurred at unionist parades claiming 'traditional rights' to march through republican areas. In 1998 disorders occurred at 19 loyalist parades and 6 nationalist ones. RUC, *Chief Constable's Report 1997/98* (Belfast, RUC, 1998) p. 35, and *1998/1998*, p. 32.
55 The modus operandi of 14 Intelligence Company, for long a closely-guarded secret, is described in Rennie, *The Operators: on the streets with 14 Company* (London, Century, 1996). A personal story of one policeman's part in RUC and Army covert operations is given in Holland and Phoenix, *Phoenix: policing the shadows* (London, Hodder & Stoughton, 1997); and that of a Special Branch agent in McGartland, *op. cit.* A journalistic account of the SAS in Northern Ireland is given by Urban, *Big Boys' Rules: the SAS and the secret struggle against the IRA* (London, Faber & Faber, 1992).
56 Paradoxically, although intercepts can be authorised under section 2 of the Interception of Communications Act 1985, section 9 of the same act prohibits their being produced as evidence. The Lloyd report recommended the removal of this anomaly. Cm3420. *Inquiry into Legislation against Terrorism* (London, the Stationery Office, 1996) para. 7.25. There were of course IRA penetration attempts too. McGartland, *op. cit.*, p. 220.

57 Glimpses of agent-running and interrogation techniques, and of the disillusionment that led to the defection of IRA members, are given in Collins, *Killing Rage* and O'Callaghan, *The Informer*.

58 Special category status was introduced by the UK government in June 1972 after a hunger strike in Belfast prison. Prisoners could wear their own clothes, were housed in compounds rather than cells, and were not required to work. The paramilitary organisations ran a POW-style organisation within the compounds which led to loss of control, and special category status was phased out from 1976. New prisoners were put in cells in eight newly-built H-blocks at the Maze prison. From the beginning, Republican prisoners refused to wear prison clothing ('went on the blanket'), because they did not regard themselves as criminals. In 1978 they fouled their cells (the dirty protest) and in 1980 went on a three-month hunger strike. Both reflected Republican history: republicans had always regarded themselves as 'political prisoners' and claimed the right to wear their own clothes instead of the uniform of common criminals; in the 1919–21 campaign, the Mayor of Cork, Terence McSwiney, fasted to death, saying that it was not those who could inflict the most but those who could suffer the most who would conquer. In January 1981 Bobby Sands started another fast and died two months later, having been elected to the UK parliament in April; his election agent was elected in his place at the by-election which followed. Nine others died before the strike petered out under pressure from relatives on the remaining six strikers, and concessions about clothing and remission. Special category status for those originally granted it ended in 1991. Flackes and Elliott, *Northern Ireland: a political directory 1968–1993. op. cit.*, p. 176.

59 By 30 492 votes to the unionist candidate's 29 046; the SDLP did not contest the seat, for which it was much criticised at the time.

60 'The British Government makes a contribution of over £3000 million a year to maintain social services at the level of those in Great Britain, to meet the cost of security measures, and to compensate for the natural disadvantages of geography and lack of resources.' (Central Office of Information, *Britain 1997: an official handbook*. (London, the Stationery Office, 1996) p. 16. It is not clear whether this includes the cost of the Army, the RUC, judiciary and prison service, compensation payments and so on. Even so, it amounts to £2000 per man, woman and child in Northern Ireland, and takes no account of the costs that fall directly on them.

61 O'Doherty, *op. cit.*, p. 112. Adams had been interned in 1973, and later sentenced for attempting to escape.

62 O'Callaghan, *op. cit.*, p. 178.

63 Hoffman, *Inside Terrorism* (London, Victor Gollancz, 1998) p. 170. Rapoport estimates that the life expectancy of at least 90 per cent of terrorist organisations is less than a year, and half of the remainder do not last a decade: cited on the same page.

64 Sinn Fein won only 2 per cent of the votes in the election of February 1989 in the Republic; a typical figure. See Chapter 4, note 28..

65 O'Callaghan, *op. cit.*, p. 253.

66 See Cox, 'Bringing in the "international": the IRA ceasefire and the end of the Cold War', *International Affairs*, vol. 73:4 (1997) p. 671.

67 Adams, interview in *An Phoblacht/Republican News*, 8 June 1995, quoted in Cox, *op. cit.*, p. 678.

68 Adams, *Selected writings* (Dingle, Brandon, 1997) p. 274, quoted in Cox, *op. cit.*, p. 678. Another similarity was of course that both Nelson Mandela and Gerry Adams had been imprisoned.
69 Guelke, book review in *Terrorism and Political Violence*, vol. 8 no. 21 (Spring, 1996) p. 189.
70 Many of the 36 jurors were unwilling to serve, citing personal knowledge, personal inconvenience, or the fact that they were Basque and the law required Spanish jurors. *The Times*, 18 March 1997, p. 43.
71 Parallels have often been drawn with Sinn Fein because of political, demographical and methodological similarities; they are frequently reported to have close contact.
72 *The Economist*, 6 December 1997, p. 55.
73 Cited in Taylor, *Provos: the IRA and Sinn Fein*, p. 302.
74 Mallie and McKittrick, *op. cit.*, p. 75. Taylor, *op. cit.*, p. 302. Flackes and Elliott, *op. cit.*, p. 286.
75 Mallie and McKittrick, *op. cit.*, p. 145.
76 Taylor, *op. cit.*, p. 323.
77 Albeit through tactical voting by the unionists.
78 Mallie and McKittrick, *op. cit.*, p. 147.
79 Full text in Mallie and McKittrick, *op. cit.*, Appendix 3, pp. 421–4.
80 Quickly nicknamed the 'Tactical Use of Armed Struggle'.
81 Malachi O'Doherty sees these as analogous to the beatings traditionally handed out by the Christian Brothers who educated many republicans; but the loyalists did them too. There had been on average 50 punishment attacks per year from 1982, when records started, until 1993, when there were 40. They multiplied fivefold in 1994 to 192 (106 republican and 86 loyalist; 70 beatings and 122 shootings), and rose again to 220 in 1995, though shootings dropped to three, all loyalist. Loyalist beatings (141) overtook republican ones (76): RUC, *Report of the Chief Constable of the RUC, 1995* (Belfast, RUC, 1996) p. 32. For an insider's view of the IRA's relationships with the republican community see O'Doherty, *The Trouble with Guns: republican strategy and the Provisional IRA* (Belfast, Blackstaff Press, 1998) Chapter 7.
82 The Mitchell committee was set up by the British and Irish governments in November 1995 to make an independent assessment of the problem of decommissioning paramilitary arms. Its members were Senator George Mitchell from the USA, General John de Chastelain, former Canadian Chief of Defence Staff and Ambassador to the United States, and Harri Holkeri, former Prime Minister of Finland. It reported on 24 January 1996, setting out six principles which it invited the parties to the peace process to sign: to renounce the threat or use of force to influence the negotiations; to abide by the agreement reached through the peace process; to use only democratic and peaceful means of resolving political issues; to agree to total and verifiable disarmament of all paramilitary organisations. *Report of the International Body on Arms Decommissioning*. www.nio.gov.uk/mitchrpt.htm.
83 Taylor, *op. cit.*, *Provos: the IRA and Sinn Fein*. p. 352.
84 IRA statement on their bombing of Canary Wharf: Adams, *An Irish Voice: the quest for peace* (Niwot, CO, Roberts Rinehart, 1997) p. 201.
85 Adams, *The Independent*, 17 February 1999, p. 8.

86 See O'Brien, *The Long War: the IRA and Sinn Féin from 1985 to today* (Dublin, O'Brien Press, 1993) pp. 278–80 for an assessment of the arms remaining from the Libyan shipments at the end of 1992.
87 or even in the Odeon.
88 Like the other phases of the Troubles, the peace process has been written about extensively and well. See, for example: Mallie and McKittrick, *op. cit.*; O'Doherty, *op. cit.*; Taylor, *Provos: the IRA and Sinn Fein. op. cit.* and *Loyalists. op. cit.*; Bew and Gillespie, *op. cit.*; and Adams, *Before the Dawn: an autobiography* (London, Mandarin, 1997); Adams, *An Irish Voice op. cit.*; Coogan, *op.cit.*

6   Crime: Northern Ireland

1 American Declaration of Independence, 4 July 1776.
2 Finer, *Five Constitutions; contrasts and comparisons* (Harmondsworth, Penguin, 1979) p. 269.
3 Article 20 (Basic Principles of the Constitution – Right to Resist). Finer, *op. cit.*, p. 205.
4 Violent crime fell by 39 per cent in Harlem and 45 per cent in the Bronx between 1993 and 1997. In 1994, 31 per cent of Americans told pollsters that crime was the most important challenge to the country; in 1997 only 14 per cent thought so. *The Economist*, 3rd October 1998, p. 79. The putative reasons are drawn from the same article.
5 For maps of where people were killed by republican groups from 1980 to June 1993 see O'Brien, *The Long War: the IRA and Sinn Féin, 1985 to today, op. cit.*, p. 167. The distribution of killings is also discussed in McKittrick, et al. *Lost Lives: the stories of the men, women and children who died as a result of the Northern Ireland troubles* (Edinburgh and London, Mainstream Publishing, 1999) pp.1481–2.
6 See Table A.1. Between 1969 and 1994 there were 3095 murders in Northern Ireland's population of 1.6 million and 14 116 in England and Wales from a population of 49 million. See also Cmnd 7670 *Criminal Statistics England and Wales, 1978* (London, HMSO, 1979) table 9.1; and later issues in the series.
7 Colombia (38), Mexico (34): Radzinowicz and King, *The Growth of Crime* (London, Hamish Hamilton, 1977) p. 10. United States Federal Bureau of Investigation, *Crime in the United States 1979, Uniform Crime Reports.* (Washington DC, US Govt Printing Office for Department of Justice, 1980). Table 1 (p. 40) shows the US average of 9.7 murders and non-negligent manslaughters per hundred thousand inhabitants. Table 3 shows the rates by area, ranging from 1.4 in Vermont to 17.5 in Nevada. Table 5 shows the rates in major cities: the 15–22 range includes Albany GA, Albuquerque NM, Dallas-Fort Worth TX, Los Angeles CA, Miami FL, Mobile and Montgomery AL, New York City NY, and fifteen others. Five cities had murder rates above 22/100,000; the highest, at 30, was Houston TX. Table 2 (p. 41) shows the change of murder rate in the US as a whole from 6.9/100,000 in 1968 to 9.7 in 1979.
8 (November 1979–May 1980) Andrew Mango, 'Managing the Turkish Crisis', *The World Today*, vol. 36 (July 1980) p. 262.

9 *The Economist,* 27 September 1980, p. 56.
10 *The Economist,* 8 November 1980, p. 36.
11 *The Guardian,* 7 November 1980.
12 *The Economist,* 20 February 1999, p. 50. There are about 15 million Kurds among the 60 million people in Turkey.
13 Wilkinson, *Terrorism and the Liberal State* (London, Macmillan, 1977) pp. 88–92.
14 In the UK, a crime is reported as cleared when the police have identified the perpetrators, even though they cannot be charged because the evidence is not good enough, or they are under the age of criminal responsibility. In the US, there must be both arrest and charge before a crime is reported cleared.
15 'Murders known to the police' and 'reported cleared': Chief Constable of the RUC *Annual Report, 1971* (Belfast, HMSO, 1972) Appendix 2, table 1. 'Persons found guilty of murder': *Ulster Year Book 1970* (Belfast, HMSO, 1970) p. 49.
16 Home Office, Cmnd 7289 *Annual Criminal Statistics, England and Wales, 1977* (London, HMSO, 1978) tables 9.3 and 9.11. See also Table 1. Comparisons of murder rates and convictions are fraught with difficulty. Murder is one of the categories of homicide, which also includes manslaughter and infanticide. A crime recorded as murder may result in a conviction for murder, manslaughter or infanticide; or a lesser offence; or not be dealt with because the suspects are unfit to plead or below the age of criminal responsibility. In England and Wales, most homicides result in indictments: in 1974, for example, there were 600 homicides and 536 indictments (89 per cent); in 1980, 620 and 536 (86 per cent); in 1990, 676 and 623 (92 per cent). Not many of those indicted are acquitted: 64 of the 536 in 1974 (12 per cent); 68 of 536 in 1980 (13 per cent), and 135 of 623 in 1990 (22 per cent). Those convicted (or acquitted) in one year may of course have been indicted in previous years and indeed have committed their crimes in years before they were indicted, so fine distinctions between the figures are not reliable. To confuse things still further, the definitions of offences and the categories in which the statistics are reported may also change over the years. Nevertheless, the broad conclusions of this chapter are robust enough not to be affected by these factors.
17 Cmd 532. *Disturbances in Northern Ireland* Report of the Commission appointed by the Governor of Northern Ireland, September 1969 (Belfast, HMSO, 1969) (The Cameron Report)
18 Table A.1. Assessing the total of one person convicted by the courts for every 4.6 murders is made difficult by the figures including multiple murders committed by professional gunmen, and by multiple responsibility for most, if not all, of the killings. It would be impossible to reconcile these without going through police and terrorist records (if the latter exist) case by case, but some indications are provided by the fact that the four IRA men arrested after the Balcombe Street Siege in London in December 1975 were tied to 66 terrorist incidents, including nine murders. IRA active service units (ASUs) in Britain normally contain eight to ten people, all of whom would in law be guilty of a murder committed by any of the unit, as would the individuals issuing orders to the ASU. It seems likely therefore, that the factors of multiple murders by multiple people more or less cancel

each other out – or at least that the multiplier is small. It is also relevant (and interesting) that for the first eight years deaths from the troubles exceeded murders, and that for the next fourteen years the murder figure, though larger, was within ten of the terrorist figure, implying that most, if not all, murders were terrorist-related. From 1991 until 1997, however, there were about twenty more murders each year than there were deaths from the troubles. In 1997/98 there were 71 murders and 44 deaths from the troubles, a difference of nearly thirty: 38 per cent of the murders were not attributed to the troubles. As time went on therefore, the number of non-terrorist murders rose.

19 Source: Appendix, Table A.1.
20 Appendix, Table A.1. Murders known to the police divided by convictions for murder in the same year. The ratio for England and Wales runs at about three murders per conviction for murder, only because many people charged with murder are found guilty of manslaughter. The ratio of convictions for homicide to indictments for homicide is around 1.3. Most homicides in Northern Ireland are murders, and although it is not possible to be sure without going through individual cases, it looks as if murders either attract a conviction for murder or no conviction, rather than one for manslaughter, as would be expected from the different nature of the crimes in the two countries.
21 Appendix, Table A.1. The ratio is not very significant, because some murders will have gone to trial later. Nevertheless, had this happened to a significant extent there would have been some years with more convictions than murders. That did not happen.
22 1969–72: 518 murders, 52 cleared. 1973–6: 925 murders, 331 cleared. 1977–94: 1652 murders, 888 cleared. Appendix, Table A.1.
23 RUC Central Statistics Unit, personal communication. The Force Statistician points out that interpreting such figures is not straightforward: some deaths, for example those of terrorists killed by the security forces, are not murders; in some incidents which are murders, the terrorists also kill themselves and are obviously not charged; in some incidents where there is more than one murder, it may be that charges are brought in respect of only one representative victim.
24 RUC Chief Constable's *Annual Reports*, passim.
25 Appendix, Table A.3.
26 RUC Chief Constable's *Annual Report, 1972*. p. 32.
27 Flackes and Elliott, *op. cit.*, p. 53.
28 Or £2000 for every person in Northern Ireland. Central Office of Information, *Britain 1997: an official handbook* (London, Stationery Office, 1996) p. 16.
29 Total net costs in the year ended 31 March 1998: Northern Ireland Prison Service *Annual Report 1996/97*. Prison numbers in 1997 from Northern Ireland Office, *A Commentary on Northern Ireland Crime Statistics 1997*.
30 Total expenditure for FY 97/98. RUC, *Chief Constable's Report 1997/98* (Belfast, RUC, 1998) p. 76.
31 Phasing differences stemming from payment being made long after the event do not entirely explain the inverse relationship between casualties and compensation. The 1990s rise in compensation for criminal damage may be due to terrorists targeting property rather than people.

32 Appendix, Table A.4.
33 About three-quarters of female victims of homicide in England and Wales and two-thirds of male victims were related to, or knew, their attacker. Central Statistical Office, *Social Trends 22, 1992* (London, HMSO, 1992) p. 203, chart 12.10.
34 *Ulster Year Books:* 1974, p. 37; 1977, table 1; 1980, table 33. The rise was actually higher, because from 1968 to 1974 hybrid offences (indictable if tried on indictment, non-indictable if tried summarily) were included under indictable offences. For later years they are included under non-indictable offences.
35 Appendix, Table A.2. There is a summary of 'persons charged with terrorist offences' between 1988 and 1993 in the RUC Chief Constable's *Annual Report, 1993,* p. 45. The offences include murder, attempted murder, firearms, explosives, armed robbery and 'other'.
36 Details: Appendix, Table A.2.
37 Cmd 566. *Violence and Civil Disturbances in Northern Ireland in 1969* (London, HMSO, 1972) (The Scarman Report) vol. 1 p. 247, table 4.
38 Chief Constable of the Royal Ulster Constabulary, *Annual Report, 1977* (Belfast, HMSO for the RUC, 1978). Appendix 2, table 6.
39 Cmd 566. *Violence and Civil Disturbances in Northern Ireland in 1969* (London, HMSO, 1972) (The Scarman Report) vol. 1, p. 248 (para 31.23, table 5).
40 Cmd 566, *op. cit.,* vol. 1, p. 248 (para 31.25).
41 In three per cent of cases the offence was taken into consideration; another three per cent were cautioned, and six per cent were not proceeded with. RUC Chief Constable's *Annual Reports, 1971–1995.* Data before 1975 and for 1976 and 1983 are not given in the reports for those years. Figure 6.8 is derived from the average of the 19 years between 1975 and 1997 for which data is reported.
42 Home Office, *British Crime Survey, 1994* (London, Stationery Office, 1995) and Office for National Statistics, *Social Trends 26, 1996* (London, HMSO, 1996) table 9.2. Data for England and Wales, 1993.
43 Northern Ireland Department of Finance, *Social and Economic Trends in Northern Ireland, No 3* (Belfast, HMSO, 1977) p. 43.

7 Countermeasures: Criminal Law

1 Gray, 'Global utopias and clashing civilisations: misunderstanding the present', *International Affairs,* vol. 74, no. 1 (1998) p. 150.
2 In 1986 only 17 per cent of the arrests under the Emergency Provisions Act led to charges. However, most arrests which did lead to a charge ended in a conviction. 596 defendants appeared before Diplock (judge-only) courts; 567 were convicted. Eighty-nine per cent of the defendants had pleaded guilty. Of the eleven per cent who had pleaded not guilty, 43per cent (28 people)were acquitted. Flackes and Elliott, *op.cit.,* p. 455. It is not publicly known how many of the 3500 arrested were known to have committed a crime but could not be prosecuted. The figure of 33 per cent of all offences being cleared, in that the people responsible were known, applies to all offences, not just to terrorist ones, and to offences rather than to offenders (Figure 6.8).

3   Quoted in Cmnd 4823: *Report of the enquiry into allegations against the secu-
     rity forces of physical brutality in Northern Ireland arising out of events on the 9th
     August 1971* (The Compton Report) (London, HMSO, 1971) p. 18.
4   See the typology in Wilkinson,*Terrorism and the Liberal State* (London,
     Macmillan, 1977) p. 32.
5   Cmd 566.*Violence and Civil Disturbances in Northern Ireland in 1969* (London,
     HMSO, 1972) (The Scarman Report) vol. 1 p. 17.
6   A study in Oxfordshire showed that only a small proportion of those sus-
     pected of crimes were identified by police investigations. More than four-
     fifths of the crimes were first reported by the public, and more than
     three-quarters of the suspects were caught in the act or were known. Royal
     Commission on Criminal Procedure, *Uncovering Crime, the Police Role.
     Research Study No 7* (London, HMSO, 1980).
7   Walker, *Crimes, Courts and Figures; an introduction to criminal statistics*
     (Harmondsworth, Penguin, 1971) pp. 18–21.
8   'over the years, the IRA leadership has learned that our army has one
     weakness: the interrogation of our members by the RUC. We have many
     details of IRA members who have broken under strong police questioning.'
     IRA trainer, quoted in McGartland, *Fifty Dead Men Walking, op. cit.,* p.137.
     For a description of an RUC interrogation see Collins, *Killing Rage, op. cit.,*
     pp. 259–88.
9   A study of crown courts in Birmingham and London showed that only a
     quarter of the defendants on serious charges reached their trials without
     having earlier made damaging admissions to the police. Fewer than one in
     forty defendants in Birmingham and one in twenty in London who had
     made a written confession were acquitted: most pleaded guilty. One-fifth of
     all cases depended on confession – had there not been one, the trial would
     not have gone ahead, or the chance of acquittal would have been high. See:
     Royal Commission on Criminal Procedure, *Confessions in Crown Court
     Trials. Research Study No. 5* (London, HMSO, 1980).
10   For a description of this training see McGartland, *op. cit.,* pp. 135–42.
11   The search for the 'Yorkshire Ripper' between 1975 and 1981 cost several
     million pounds. Two hundred police were employed full time on the search
     for this one man – whose voice, handwriting, blood-group, height, foot size
     and car type were known, but who eluded capture for five years (*Sunday
     Times,* 23 November 1980, p. 13).
12   Paradoxically, the Irgun Zvai Leumi (National Military Organisation) had
     been modelled by Begin (later Prime Minister of Israel) and Jabotinsky on
     the IRA of 1919–21. Bengali terrorist groups had also done so. Cm3420.
     Inquiry into Legislation against Terrorism (London, the Stationery Office,
     1996) (The Lloyd Report) Volume 2 – Survey by Professor Paul Wilkinson,
     p. 15.
13   Charles Dickens to Macvey Napier, July 28, 1845, Dickens and Hogarth,
     (eds), *The Letters of Charles Dickens, vol. III* (London, Chapman & Hall Ltd,
     1882) pp. 79–80. Quoted in Tuttle, *The Crusade Against Capital Punishment
     in Great Britain* (London and Chicago, Stevens, Quadrangle, 1961) p. 14.
14   For examples see Scott, *The History of Capital Punishment* (London,
     Torchstream, 1950) There were plenty of executions, since by the beginning
     of the nineteenth century there were some 220 capital offences in England:

shooting a rabbit, forging a birth certificate, stealing handkerchiefs, adopting disguise, damaging a public building ... At one assize alone 13 people were sentenced to death for associating with gypsies, and in 1814 a man was hanged at Chelmsford for cutting down a cherry tree (p. 40).

15 Footman, *Red Prelude: a life of A. I. Zhelyabov* (London, Barrie & Rockliff, 1968) p. 225. The occasion was the execution of the assassins of Tsar Alexander in 1881.

8 Countermeasures: Political Crime

1 *Treason Act, 1351*: 'when a man doth compass or imagine the death of our Lord the King, or of our lady his Queen, or of their eldest son and heir; or if a man do violate the King's companion [wife] or the King's eldest daughter unmarried, or the wife [of] the King's eldest son and heir; or if a man do levy war against our lord the King in his realm, or be adherent to the King's enemies in his realm, giving them aid and comfort in the realm, or elsewhere ...' 25 Edward III Statute 5: *The Statutes Revised* (London, Eyre & Spottiswode, 1870) vol. 1 p.185.

2 East, *A Treatise of the Pleas of the Crown* (London, Butterworth & Cook, 1803) p. 72.

3 The Treason Felony Act 1848: (11 & 12 Vict c12, s3. S6) includes a caveat: 'Provided always, that nothing herein contained shall lessen the force of or in any manner affect any thing enacted by the Treason Act 1351.'

4 Smith, and Hogan, *Criminal Law (Fourth Edition)* (London, Butterworth, 1978) p. 803.

5 Incorporated into British domestic law by the Extradition Act, 1870, s 3 (i). Article 13 of the 1977 European Convention on the Suppression of Terrorism permits a state to 'declare that it reserves the right to refuse extradition in respect of any offence ... which it considers to be a political offence, an offence connected with a political offence or an offence inspired by political motives'.

6 (1891) 1QB 149.

7 Wortley, 'Political Crime in English Law and in International Law', *British Year Book of International Law,* vol. 45 (1971) p. 219.

8 Grotius' doctrine of extradite or try – *aut dedere aut judicare* – is gaining currency in the discussions of international law and transnational terrorism, but has so far rarely been applied. It is the basis of the Council of Europe Convention on the Suppression of Terrorism which was signed in January 1977 by 17 of the 19 members of the Council (Malta and Ireland were the exceptions). Britain ratified the Convention in 1978. It has had no practical effect. Ireland regards it as incompatible with its constitution. Prior to the Irish Extradition Act 1965, Ireland and the UK simply exchanged 'fugitive offenders' – no issue of an international frontier arose.

9 *The Economist,* 15 January 1977, p. 43.

9 Countermeasures: Internal War

1 Jaures, *Législative.* quoted by Sorel, in *Reflections on Violence* (1906) Tr Hulme and Roth (London, Collier Macmillan, 1970) p. 170.

2 For a discussion of this, and references, see Bellamy,*The Tudor Law of Treason – an introduction.* (London, Buffalo & Toronto, Routledge and Kegan Paul, University of Toronto Press, 1979) Appendix: Martial Law.

3 *Ibid.*, p. 235.

4 *Notes on Imperial Policing, 1934* (London, The War Office, 1934) p. 5.

5 *Imperial Policing and Duties in Aid of the Civil Power 1949* (London, The War Office, 1949) pp. 25–26.

6 *Orders for Guidance of the Troops in Affording Aid to the Civil Power in Ireland* (Dublin, HMSO 1910) p. 12. Interestingly, these orders, unlike their modern equivalent, bear no warnings against publication or disclosure of their contents. The civil power could call upon the army directly to control riots, but government approval had to be sought for military assistance to collect rates or execute civil decrees (p. 40).

7 *The Queen's Regulations for the Army, 1975* (London, HMSO, 1975) p. 11–1 (para. J11–002).

8 *Notes on Imperial Policing, 1934* (London, The War Office, 1934) p. 33.

9 *Ibid.*, p 35.

10 Gwynn, *Imperial Policing* (London, Macmillan, 1934) p. 250.

11 Allen, *Law and Orders: An Enquiry into the Nature and Scope of Delegated Legislation and Emergency Powers in English Law* (London, Stevens & Sons, 1965) p. 65.

12 *Imperial Policing and Duties in Aid of Civil Power* (London, The War Office, 1949) p. 22.

13 *Keeping the Peace (Duties in Support of the Civil Power)* (London, The War Office, 1957) p. 11.

14 *Keeping the Peace. Part 1 – Doctrine* (London, The War Office, 1963) p. 17.

15 *Land Operations, Volume III – Counter Revolutionary Operations. Part I – General Principles* (London, Ministry of Defence, 1977) p. 6.

16 *Record of the Rebellion in Ireland in 1920–21, and of the Part Played by the Army in Dealing With It.* London, General Staff, The War Office, March 1922) vol. 1, p. 55 (para. 7). See also Townshend, *The British Campaign in Ireland 1919–1921: the development of political and military policies* (Oxford, OUP, 1975) Chapter V: Martial Law.

17 Humphrey, *Some Reflections on the Malayan Emergency.* Seminar, St. Antony's College, Oxford, 22 May 1979.

18 For examples of the Emergency Regulations, many of them as draconian as any martial law regulation (though the author appears to be unaware of this), see: Walter, *A study of the Emergency Regulations in Malaya, 1948–1960* (Stanford, CA, Stanford Research Institute Technical Note OAD-TN4923–19.)

19 Cm3420. *Inquiry into Legislation against Terrorism* (London, the Stationery Office, 1996) (The Lloyd Report) para 1. Volume Two of the report contains an excellent survey of the British experience of terrorism and counter-terrorism at home and abroad by Professor Paul Wilkinson.

20 *Ibid.*, Annex E. In 1999, however, two long trials of former prime minister Giulio Andreotti decided that there was too little evidence to convict him of protecting the Mafia, and of killing a journalist. *The Economist* judged that the acquittals had probably put paid to the use of *pentiti*, supergrasses, to gain convictions. *The Economist*, 30 October 1999, p. 20.

21 *Ibid.,* Chapter 18.
22 Text in Roberts and Guelff, *Documents on the Laws of War* (Oxford, OUP, 1982) p. 172.
23 Annex to 1907 Hague Convention IV Respecting the Laws and Customs of War on Land, Article 1. Text in Roberts and Guelff, *op.cit.,* p. 48.
24 *Manual of Military Law Part III – The Law of War on Land* (London, HMSO for the War Office, 1958) p. 6.
25 *Ibid.* note 1 to p. 178. For detailed discussion of *respondat superior* see Roling, 'Aspects of the Criminal Responsibility for Violations of the Laws of War', in Cassese, *The New Humanitarian Law of Armed Conflict* (Naples, Editoriale Scientifica, 1979) pp. 214–220.
26 Protocol Additional to the Geneva Conventions of 12 August 1949, and Relating to the Protection of Victims of International Armed Conflicts (Protocol I). For text and discussion see Roberts and Guelff, *Documents on the Laws of War* (Oxford, OUP, 1982) p. 387. For a discussion of the historical background of the just war see Dugard, 'International Terrorism and the Just War' in *Stanford Journal of International Studies,* vol. 12 (Spring, 1977) p. 21.
27 *'armed conflicts in which peoples are fighting against colonial domination and alien occupation and against racist regimes in the exercise of their right of self-determination, as enshrined in the Charter of the United Nations and the Declaration on Principles of International Law concerning Friendly Relations and Co-operation among States in accordance with the Charter of the United Nations.'* Protocol I, Article 1 (4).
28 For discussion and criticism, see Draper, 'Wars of National Liberation and War Criminality', in Howard, *Restraints on War: studies in the limitation of armed conflict* (Oxford, OUP, 1979) p. 157.
29 Best, *Humanity in Warfare: the modern history of the international law of armed conflicts* (London, Weidenfield & Nicolson, 1980) p. 315.
30 For text and discussion see Roberts and Guelff, *op.cit.,* p. 447. For a detailed discussion of the emasculation of Protocol II, and its remaining shortcomings and advantages, see Eide, 'The New Humanitarian Law in Non-International Armed Conflict', in Cassese, *op. cit.,* p. 227 *et seq.*
31 Roberts and Guelff, *op. cit.,* p. 455.
32 'In order to promote the protection of the civilian population from the effects of hostilities, combatants are obliged to distinguish themselves from the civilian population while they are engaged in an attack or in a military operation preparatory to an attack. Recognizing, however, that there are situations in armed conflicts where, owing to the nature of the hostilities an armed combatant cannot so distinguish himself, he shall retain his status as a combatant, provided that, in such situations, he carries his arms openly: (a) During each military engagement, and (b) During such time as he is visible to the adversary while he is engaged in a military deployment preceding the launching of an attack in which he is to participate.' Protocol I, article 44 (3).
33 Protocol I, article 57 (2)(a)(iii).
34 Cassese, *op. cit.,* p. 195, footnote 105.
35 Roberts and Guelff argue that 'In view of the large number of states parties to the 1949 Geneva Conventions and the status which the Conventions have acquired in the international community it is reasonable to assume

that the Conventions are (at least in large part) declaratory of customary international law.' Roberts and Guelff, *op. cit.,* p. 170.

36 Professor Draper argued that 'penal processes against perpetrators of "grave breaches" of the Geneva Conventions of 1949 are virtually unenforceable' Draper, *op. cit.,* p. 53.

37 Montesquieu, *Notes sur l'Angleterre: Oeuvres Complètes* (Paris, Editions du Seuil, 1964) p. 331.

38 By February 1999, 60 individuals had been publicly indicted and 28 apprehended; two had been tried and sentenced to imprisonment; another three trials were in progress: www.un.org/rights/HRToday/hrconfl.htm. p. 5.

39 Between half a million and one million of the Tutsi minority were killed by Hutu militiamen between April and July 1994. By mid-July, more than two million refugees were living in camps in Burundi, Tanzania and Zaire. The international criminal tribunal issued its first indictment in November 1995. By August 1998 35 indicted individuals were in custody. In May 1998 a former Prime Minister, Jean Cambanda, pleaded guilty to genocide and was sentenced to life imprisonment. He was the first person ever to have been convicted of genocide. In September 1998 a former mayor was also convicted, and sentenced to life: www.un.org/rights/HRToday/hrconfl.htm. p.6.

40 Seventy-five states signed the Rome Statute setting up the ICC. It enters into force after it has been ratified by 60 states. Ratification status: www.un.org/law/icc/statute/status.htm.
   Overview: www.un.org/law/icc/general/overview.htm. Text: UN. document A/CONF.183.9 dated 17 July 1998: www.un.org/law/icc/general.

41 Though states can arraign states before the European Court of Human Rights, as the Irish Republic did in 1978 by charging the UK government with the ill-treatment of detainees during 'interrogation in depth'. The court ruled that some detainees had been subjected to 'inhuman and degrading treatment', but not to torture. The UK derogated from part of the Convention when the Court ruled in 1988 that detention for seven days breached the requirement to bring suspects to court promptly. It reversed its decision in 1993. It has also ruled that the treatment of the H Block hunger strikers was not a breach of the convention; nor was the use of plastic bullets in riots. Its aim is to enforce (or rather to shame states into enforcing, since it has no powers of its own) the 1950 European Convention for the Protection of Human Rights and Fundamental Freedoms signed by 40 members of the Council of Europe, including those from the former Soviet Union and Eastern Europe, which reflected the 1948 UN Declaration of Universal Human Rights. The rights include life, liberty and security; fair trials; freedom of thought, conscience, religion, expression, assembly, association and movement; and non-discrimination. By 1997 the number of files opened each year had risen to over 12,000. The Court was reformed to cope with this flow, and replaced the former court in November 1998. www.dhcour.coe.fr.

42 Statute of the International Criminal Court, Article 7.

43 Statute of the International Criminal Court, Article 8, para 1.

44 Statute of the International Criminal Court, Article 8, para 2.

45 Statute of the International Criminal Court, Article 8, para 2.

46 Statute of the International Criminal Court, Article 26, para 3.

47 Draft International Convention for the Suppression of Terrorist Bombings, to supplement the Declaration on Measures to Eliminate International Terrorism (Resolution 49/60 of 9 December 1994). Article 5. www.un.org/law/.

10 Countermeasures outside the law

1 Browne, 'A small elite rebel band harasses Uruguayan regime', *New York Times*, 23 January 1969, quoted in Gott, *Guerrilla Movements in Latin America* (London, Nelson, 1970) p. 358.
2 Gott, Richard, in September 1972. Introduction to Labrousse, *The Tupamaros: urban guerrillas in Uruguay* (Harmondsworth, Penguin, 1973), p. 13. (Originally published by Editions du Seuil 1970.)
3 Gillespie, 'Peronism and Left Militarism', *School of Latin American Studies Bulletin,* Summer 1979, p. 73.
4 Cox, 'Argentina – Political Terror, Human Rights and the Return of Democracy' Lecture at Chatham House, 14 January 1980.
5 The reports were later confirmed during the trials of Admiral Massena and General Videla for their activities during the 'dirty war' of 1976 to 1980, in which between 15 000 and 30 000 people are believed to have 'disappeared'. Both were pardoned by President Menem in 1989, but re-arraigned in 1998 on charges of kidnapping children. *The Economist*, 5 December 1998.
6 Best,*War and Law Since 1945* (Oxford, OUP, 1997) p. 388.
7 *The Economist*, 6 November 1999.
8 Ray, *The Economist*, 7 November 1988. p. 6.
9 Netherclift, *The Economist*, 7 November 1988. p. 6.
10 Campos, *The Economist*, 7 November 1988, p. 6.
11 de Brito, 'Recording the Past: the "Never Again" Reports on Human Rights Violations' *Oxford International Review,* Summer 1992, p. 16. *Human Rights and Democratization in Latin America: Uruguay and Chile* (Oxford, OUP, 1997).
12 Tutu, *Report of the Truth and Reconciliation Commission* October 1998.
13 Garton Ash, 'Bad Memories', *Prospect.* August–September 1997. pp. 20–23. *The File: a personal history* (London, Random House, 1997).

11 Conclusions and Consequences

1 Wilkinson, in Cm3420. *Inquiry into Legislation against Terrorism* (London, the Stationery Office, 1996) (The Lloyd Report) vol. 2, p. 59.
2 *Ibid.*, para. 1 (p. v); paras 12–13 (p. vii).
3 von Clausewitz, *On War.* Edited and translated by Michael Howard and Peter Paret (Princeton, Princeton University Press, 1976) p. 141.

References

Adams, G. (1997) *An Irish Voice: the quest for peace* (Niwot, CO: Roberts Rinehart).

Adams, G. (1997) *Before the Dawn: an autobiography* (London: Mandarin).

Adams, G. (1986) *The politics of Irish Freedom* (Dingle: Brandon Books).

Allen, Sir C.K. (1965) *Law and Orders: An Enquiry into the Nature and Scope of Delegated Legislation and Emergency Powers in English Law* (London: Stevens & Sons).

Allen, W.S. (1966) *The Nazi Seizure of Power* (London: Eyre and Spottiswoode).

Apter, D.E. (ed) (1997) *The Legitimization of Violence* (Basingstoke: Macmillan).

Bane, S.L. and Lutz, R.H. (1942) *The Blockade of Germany after the Armistice, 1918–1919* (Stanford, CA: Stanford University Press).

Baynes, N.H. (ed.) (1942) *The Speeches of Adolf Hitler April 1922–August 1939* (Oxford: OUP for Chatham House).

Bellamy, J.G. *The Tudor Law of Treason – an introduction* (London, Buffalo and Toronto: Routledge & Kegan Paul, University of Toronto Press, 1979).

Best, G. *Humanity in Warfare: the modern history of the international law of armed conflicts* (London: Weidenfield & Nicolson, 1980).

Best, G. *War and Law Since 1945* (Oxford: OUP, 1997).

Bew, P. and Gillespie, G. *The Northern Ireland Peace Process 1993–1996: a chronology* (London: Serif, 1996). Bew, P. and Patterson, H. *The British State and the Ulster Crisis* (London, Verso, 1985).

Bew, P., Gibbon, P. and Patterson, H. *Northern Ireland 1921–94: political forces and social classes* (London: Serif, 1996)

Bloor, D *Knowledge and Social Imaginary,* Second Edition (Chicago: University of Chicago Press, 1991).

Boyle, K. and Hadden, T. *Northern Ireland: the choice* (London: Penguin, 1994).

Bracher, K.D. *The German Dictatorship: the origins, structure and effects of National Socialism* (London: Weidenfeld & Nicolson, 1970).

Brogan, P. *World Conflicts, Third Edition* (London: Bloomsbury, 1998).

Brown, D.E. *Human Universals* (New York: McGraw Hill, 1991).

Bullock, A. *Hitler: a study in tyranny* (London: Odhams, 1955).

Cassese, A. (ed) *The New Humanitarian Law of Armed Conflict* (Naples: Editoriale Scientifica, 1979).

Central Office of Information. *Britain 1997: an official handbook* (London: Stationery Office, 1996).

Central Statistical Office. *Social Trends 26, 1996* (London: HMSO, 1996).

Central Statistical Office. *Social Trends 22, 1992* (London: HMSO, 1992).

Cohen, M. and Hale, D. (eds) (1966) The New Student Left (Boston MA, Beacon Press)

Cole, J. *As it Seemed to Me: political memoirs* (London: Phoenix, 1996).

Collins, E. *Killing Rage* (London: Granta Books, 1997). Coogan, T.P. *The troubles: Ireland's ordeal 1966–1996 and the search for peace* (London: Arrow, 1996).

Cook, T.E. *Governing with the News: the news media as a political institution* (Chicago: University of Chicago Press, 1998).

Coper, R. *Failure of a Revolution: Germany 1918–1919* (Cambridge: CUP, 1955).
Cox, M. 'Bringing in the "international": the IRA ceasefire and the end of the Cold War', *International Affairs*, vol. 73:4 (1997).
Crelinstein, R.D. 'Television and Terrorism: Implications for Crisis Management and Policy Making', *Terrorism and Political Violence*, vol. 9, no. 4 (winter, 1997).
Crenshaw, M. and Pimlott, J. (eds) *Encyclopaedia of World Terrorism* (Armonk: Sharpe Reference, 1997).
Curtis, L. *Ireland: the propaganda war: the British media and the 'battle for hearts and minds'* (London: Pluto, 1984).
Dahrendorf, R. *After 1989: Morals, Revolution and Civil Society* (London: Macmillan,1997).
Dahrendorf, R. *The Modern Social Conflict: an essay on the politics of liberty* (London: Weidenfeld & Nicolson, 1988).
Darby, J. *Scorpions in a Bottle: conflicting cultures in Northern Ireland* (London: Minority Rights Group, 1997). Davies, N. *Europe: A History* (London: Pimlico, 1997).
de Brito, A.B. 'Recording the Past: the 'Never Again' Reports on Human Rights Violations', *Oxford International Review* (Summer 1992).
De Torrenté, N. 'Rebels Bounce Back' *The World Today*, vol. 55, no. 2 (February 1999).
Debray, R. *A Critique of Arms* (Harmondsworth: Peregrine/Penguin, 1977).
Debray, R. *Che's Guerilla War* (Harmondsworth: Penguin, 1975).
Debray, R. *Revolution in the Revolution? Armed struggle and political struggle in Latin America* (New York and London: Monthly Review Press, 1976).
Draper, G.I.A.D. 'Implementation of International Law in Armed Conflicts' *International Affairs*, vol 48 (January, 1972).
Dudley Edwards, R. *The Faithful Tribe: an intimate portrait of the loyal institutions* (London: HarperCollins Publishers, 1999).
Dugard, J. 'International Terrorism and the Just War' *Stanford Journal of International Studies*, vol. 12 (Spring, 1977).
Dunn, J. *Modern Revolutions: an introduction to the analysis of a political phenomenon* (Cambridge: Cambridge University Press, 1972).
East, E.H. *A Treatise of the Pleas of the Crown* (London: Butterworth & Cook, 1803).
Fay, M.T., Morrisey, M. and Smyth, M. *Northern Ireland's Troubles: the human costs* (London and Sterling,VA: Pluto Press, 1999).
Fest, J. *Hitler* (Harmondsworth: Penguin,1977).
Festinger, L. Reilken, H.W., Schachter, S. *When Prophecy Fails* (Minneapolis: University of Minneapolis Press, 1956).
Finer, S. *Five Constitutions; constrasts and comparisons* (Harmondsworth: Penguin, 1979).
Finer, S.E. *The Man on Horseback: the role of the military in politics* (London: Pall Mall, 1962).
Flackes, W.D and Elliott, S. *Northern Ireland: a political directory 1968–1993.* (Belfast: The Blackstaff Press, 1994).
Footman, D.J. *Red Prelude: a life of A I Zhelyabov* (London: Barrie & Rockliff, 1968).
Foster, R. and Crozier, M. *Cultural Traditions in Northern Ireland: varieties of Irishness* (Belfast: Institute of Irish Studies, Queen's University, 1989).
Foster, R. *Modern Ireland 1600–1972* (London: Penguin, 1989).
Fukuyama, F. *The End of History and the Last Man* (New York: Free Press, 1992).
Furedi, F. *Culture of Fear: risk-taking and the morality of low expectation* (London: Cassell, 1997).

Furet, F. *Le livre noir du communisme: crimes, terreur, répression.* (Paris: Robert Laffont, 1997).

Gallagher, E.V. 'God and Country: Religion as a Religious Imperative on the Radical Right', *Terrorism and Political Violence*,vol. 9, no. 3 (Autumn 1997).

Garner, J.F. *Politically Correct Bedtime Stories, Politically Correct Holiday Stories* and *Once Upon a More Enlightened Time* (New York: Macmillan, 1995).

Garton Ash, T. 'Bad Memories' *Prospect* (August–September 1997).

Gillespie, R. ' Peronism and Left Militarism', *School of Latin American Studies Bulletin* (Summer, 1979).

Goldenberg, B. *The Cuban Revolution and Latin America* (London: Allen & Unwin, 1965).

Gordon, A. 'Terrorism on the Internet: Discovering the Unsought', *Terrorism and Political Violence*, vol. 9, no. 4 (Winter, 1997).

Göring, H. *Germany Reborn* (London: Elkin Mathews & Marrot, 1934).

Gott, R. *Guerrilla Movements in Latin America* (London: Nelson, 1970).

Gott, R. *Rural Guerillas in Latin America* (Harmondsworth: Penguin, 1973).

Gray, J. 'Global utopias and clashing civilisations: misunderstanding the present', *International Affairs*, vol. 74, no. 1 (1998).

Guelke, A. *Northern Ireland – The International Perspective* (Dublin: Gill & Macmillan, 1989).

Guevara, C.E. *Guerilla Warfare* (Harmondsworth: Penguin, 1969).

Gurr, TR. *Why Men Rebel* (Princeton: Center for International Studies, 1970).

Gwynn, Major-General Sir C. *Imperial Policing* (London: Macmillan, 1934).

Haffner, S. *Failure of a Revolution: Germany 1918–1919* (London: Deutsch, 1973).

Heiden, K. *A History of National Socialism* (London: Methuen, 1934).

Hitler, A. *Mein Kampf* (New York: Reynal & Hitchcock, 1939 [first published in Germany 1925]).

Hobsbawm, E. *Age of Extremes: the short twentieth century, 1914–1991* (London: Michael Joseph, 1994).

Hoffman, B 'The Confluence of International and Domestic Trends in Terrorism', *Terrorism and Political Violence*, vol 9, no. 2 (Summer, 1997).

Hoffman, B. and Claridge, D. 'The RAND-St Andrews Chronology of International Terrorism and Noteworthy Domestic Incidents, 1996', *Terrorism and Political Violence*, vol. 10, no. 2 (Summer,1998).

Hoffman, B. *Inside Terrorism* (London: Victor Gollancz, 1998).

Holland, J. and Phoenix, S. *Phoenix: policing the shadows* (London: Hodder & Stoughton, 1997).

Hollis, M and Lukes, S. *Rationality and Relativism* (Oxford: Blackwell, 1981).

Holsti, KJ. *The State, War, and the State of War* (Cambridge: CUP, 1996).

Home Office. *British Crime Survey 1994* (London: Stationery Office, 1995).

Horowitz, I.L. *The Rise and Fall of Project Camelot: Studies in the Relationship between Social Science and Practical Politics* (Cambridge, Mass and London: MIT Press, 1967).

Howard, M. (ed) *Restraints on War: studies in the limitation of armed conflict* (Oxford: OUP, 1979)

Hussey, G. *Ireland Today: anatomy of a changing state* (London: Viking, 1993).

Ignatieff, M. *The Warrior's Honor : ethnic war and the modern conscience* (London: Chatto & Windus, 1998).

James, D. (ed.) *The Complete Bolivian Diaries of Che Guevara and other Captured Documents* (London: Allen & Unwin), 1968).

Johnson, C. *Autopsy on People's War* (Berkeley, Los Angeles, London: University of California Press, 1973).

Johnson, C. *Revolutionary Change* (London: University of London Press, 1968).

Juergensmeyer, M. 'Terror Mandated by God', *Terrorism and Political Violence*, vol. 9, no. 2 (Summer, 1997).

Kolakowsi, L. *Main Currents of Marxism: its rise, growth and dissolution* (Oxford: OUP, 1978).

Labrousse, A. *The Tupamaros: urban guerrillas in Uruguay* (Harmondsworth: Penguin, 1973).

Lakos, A.*Terrorism 1980–1990: a bibliography* (Oxford: Westview Press, 1991).

Laqueur, W. *The Guerilla Reader: a historical anthology* (London: Wildwood House, 1978).

Leiden, C. and Schmitt, K.M. *The Politics of Violence: revolution in the modern world* (Eaglewood Cliffs, NJ: Prentice Hall, 1968).

Lenin, V.I. *What is To Be Done? Burning Questions of our Movement* (Peking: Foreign Languages Press, 1975, [first published 1902]).

Locke, J. *Of Civil Government. Book 2* (London: Dent, Everyman Edition 1924 [first published 1690]).

Lutz, R.H. (ed) *Fall of the German Empire 1914–1918: documents of the German revolution* (Stanford, CA: Stanford University Press,1932).

Lyons, F.S.L. *Ireland Since the Famine* (New York and London: Scribner, 1971).

Lyons, F.S.L and Hawkins, R.A.J. (eds) *Ireland under the Union* (Oxford: Clarendon Press, 1980).

Mackay, C. *Memoirs of Extraordinary Popular Delusions and the Madness of Crowds* (New York: Random House, 1980).

Mallie, E. and McKittrick, D., *The Fight for Peace; the secret story behind the Irish peace process* (London: Mandarin, 1997).

Mango, A. 'Managing the Turkish Crisis', *The World Today*, vol. 36 (July, 1980).

Manvell, R. and Fränkel, H. *The Hundred Days to Hitler* (London: Dent 1974).

Mao Tse Tung. *Selected Works of Mao Tse Tung* (Peking: Foreign Languages Press, 1967).

Martinez-Allier, J. 'The Peasantry and the Cuban Revolution from the Spring of 1959 to the End of 1960' *St Antony's Papers No. 22: Latin American Affairs* (Oxford: OUP, 1970).1997).

McKittrick, D. Kelters, S. Feeney, B. and Thornton, C. *Lost Lives: the stories of the men, women and children who died as a result of the Northern Ireland troubles* (Edinburgh and London: Mainstream Publishing, 1999).

Merkl, P.H. *Political Violence Under the Swastika: 581 early Nazis* (Princeton, NJ: Princeton University Press, 1975)

Merkl, P.H. *The Making of a Stormtrooper* (Princeton NJ: Princeton University Press, 1980).

Micklem, N. *National Socialism and the Roman Catholic Church* (Oxford: OUP for Chatham House, 1939).

Mickolus, E.F. and Simmons, S.L. *Terrorism 1992–1995: a chronology of events and a selective annotated bibliography* (Westport, CT: Greenwood Press, 1997).

Miller, D. *Don't mention the war: Northern Ireland, propaganda and the media* (London: Pluto, 1994).

Montesquieu, C. *Notes sur l'Angleterre* (Paris: Editions du Seuil, 1964).

Moore, B. *Social Origins of Dictatorship and Democracy: lord and peasant in the making of the modern world* (Harmondsworth: Peregrine, 1977).

Neuberg, A. (pseud) *Armed Insurrection* (London: New Left Books, 1970).

Northern Ireland Department of Finance. *Social and Economic Trends in Northern Ireland, No. 3* (Belfast: HMSO, 1977).

Northern Ireland Office *The Future of Northern Ireland: a paper for discussion* (London: HMSO, 1972).

O'Brien, B. *The Long War: the IRA and Sinn Féin from 1985 to today* (Dublin: O'Brien Press, 1993).

O'Callaghan, S. *The Informer* (London: Bantam Press, 1998). O'Doherty, M. *The Trouble with Guns: republican strategy and the Provisional IRA* (Belfast: Blackstaff Press, 1998).

Pakenham, F. (Lord Longford) *Peace by Ordeal: the negotiation of the Anglo-Irish Treaty, 1921* (London: Pimlico 1992).

Paret, P. *French Revolutionary Warfare from Indochina to Algeria; the analysis of a political and military doctrine* (London: Pall Mall Press, 1964)

Pendel, G. *A History of Latin America* (Harmondsworth: Penguin, 1978).

Pinker, S. *How the Mind Works* (London: Allen Lane the Penguin Press, 1997).

Polti, G. *The Thirty-six Dramatic Situations* (Boston: The Writer Inc, 1977 [originally published 1921]).

Radzinowicz, L. and King, J. *The Growth of Crime* (London: Hamish Hamilton, 1977).

Rawls, J. *A Theory of Justice* (Oxford: OUP, 1972).

Rennie, J. *The Operators: on the streets with 14 Company* (London: Century, 1996).

Reyna, S.P. and Downs, R.E. (eds) *Studying War: anthropological perspectives* (Langhorn, Pennsylvania: Gordon & Breach, 1993)

Robbins, K. 'Britain and Europe: devolution and foreign policy' *International Affairs,* vol. 74, no. 1 (1988).

Roberts, A. and Guelff, R. *Documents on the Laws of War* (Oxford: OUP, 1982)

Royal Ulster Constabulary *Chief Constable's Report 1995* (Belfast: RUC, 1996).

Royal Ulster Constabulary *Chief Constable's Report 1992* (Belfast: RUC, 1993).

Royal Ulster Constabulary *Chief Constable's Report 1997/98* (Belfast: RUC, 1998).

Ruane, J. and Todd, J. *The Dynamics of conflict in Northern Ireland: power, conflict and emancipation* (Cambridge: Cambridge University Press, 1996).

Schmid, A.P. and Jongman, A.J. 'Violent Conflicts and Human Rights Violations in the mid-1990s' *Terrorism and Political Violence,* vol. 9, no. 4 (Winter, 1997).

Scott, G.R. *The History of Capital Punishment* (London: Torchstream, 1950).

Showalter, E. *Hystories: hysterical epidemics and modern culture* (London: Picador, 1997).

Sloan, G.R. *The Geopolitics of Anglo-Irish Relations in the Twentieth Century* (London: Leicester University Press, 1997).

Smith, J.C. and Hogan, B. *Criminal Law (fourth edition)* (London: Butterworth, 1978).

Sokal, A. and Bricmont, J. *Intellectual Impostures: postmodern philosophers' abuse of science* (London: Profile Books, 1998).

Sorel, G. *Reflections on Violence* (London: Collier Macmillan, 1970).

Stafford David (1997) *Churchill and Secret Service* (London: Avacus) Stockholm Institute for Peace Research, *SIPRI Yearbook 1997: armaments, disarmament and international security* (Oxford: OUP and SIPRI, 1997).

Strobel, W.P. *Late-breaking Foreign Policy: the news media's influence on peace operations* (Washington DC: US Institute of Peace, 1997).

Sutton, M. *An Index of Deaths from the Conflict in Ireland 1969–1993* (Belfast: Beyond the Pale Publications, 1994).

Taber, R. *The War of the Flea: Guerilla Warfare in Theory and Practice* (St Albans: Paladin, 1970).

Taylor, P.M. *Global Communications, International Affairs and the Media since 1945* (London, Routledge, 1997).

Thomas, H. *Cuba, or the Pursuit of Freedom* (London, Eyre & Spottiswoode, 1971).

Thompson, R. *Defeating Communist Insurgency: experiences from Malaya and Vietnam* (London: Chatto & Windus, 1966).

Townshend, C. *The British Campaign in Ireland 1919–1921: the development of political and military policies* (Oxford: OUP, 1975).

Townshend, C. *Britain's Civil Wars: counterinsurgency in the twentieth century* (London: Faber & Faber, 1986).

Townshend, C. *The British Campaign in Ireland, 1919–1921* (Oxford: OUP, 1975).

Trinquier, R. *Modern Warfare* (London and New York: Praeger, 1964).

Tuttle, E.O. *The Crusade Against Capital Punishment in Great Britain* (London and Chicago: Stevens, Quadrangle, 1961).

Urban, M. *Big Boys' Rules: the SAS and the secret struggle against the IRA* (London: Faber & Faber, 1992).

von Clausewitz, C. *On War* (Princeton: Princeton University Press, 1976).

von Lipsey, R.K. *Breaking the Cycle: a framework for conflict intervention* (Basingstoke: Macmillan, 1997).

von Papen, F. *Memoirs* (London: Deutsch, 1952).

Waite, R.G.L. *Vanguard of Nazism: the free corps movement in postwar Germany 1918–1923* (Cambridge Mass: Harvard University Press, 1952).

Walker, N. *Crimes, Courts and Figures; an introduction to criminal statistics* (Harmondsworth: Penguin, 1971).

Walt, S.M. *Revolution and War* (Ithaca, NY: Cornell University Press, 1996).

Walter, P.G.B. *A study of the Emergency Regulations in Malaya, 1948–1960* (Stanford, CA: Stanford Research Institute Technical Note OAD-TN4923–19).

Weaver, O. (1997) 'Violence as Memory and Desire': Neo-Nazism in Contemporary Germany' in D. Apter (ed.), *The Legimization of Violence*
Wheeler-Bennett, Sir J. *The Nemesis of Power: the German army in politics 1918–1945* (London: Macmillan, 1973).

Whyte, J. *Interpreting Northern Ireland* (Oxford: Clarendon Press, 1990).

Wilkinson, P. *Terrorism and the Liberal State* (London: Macmillan, 1977).

Wilkinson, P. *Inquiry into Legislation against Terrorism* (London: The Stationery Office, 1996).

Wilkinson, P. 'Reflections on Bloody Sunday' *Terrorism and Political Violence*, vol. 9, no. 2 (Summer, 1997).

Wilkinson, P. 'The Media and Terrorism: a Reassessment', *Terrorism and Political Violence* vol. 9, no. 2 (Summer, 1997).

Wilkinson, P. (ed.), *British Perspectives on Terrorism* (London: Allen & Unwin, 1981).

Wortley, B.A. 'Political Crime in English Law and in International Law', *British Year Book of International Law* vol. 45 (1971).

Index